THE BEAUTY AND LORE OF COINS

THE BEAUTY AND LORE OF

COINS

CURRENCY AND MEDALS

**Elvira and Vladimir
Clain - Stefanelli**
*Curators of Numismatics
Smithsonian Institution*

Photography by **Lee Boltin**

DAVID & CHARLES : NEWTON ABBOT

Some of the color illustrations by Lee Boltin appeared previously in the *Smithsonian Magazine*.

First published in the United Kingdom in 1975 by
David & Charles (Holdings) Ltd.
South Devon House
Newton Abbot - Devon

ISBN 0 7153 6691 2

Conceived by Lee Boltin

PROJECT STAFF

Managing Editor: Gerald Stearn
Editor: John Purcell
Designer and Picture Editor: Ray Ripper
Editorial Assistants: Ruth Tyler, Dorothy M. Stearn, Ann O'Connor,
　　　　　　　　　　Elizabeth Ames Nelson.

Printed and Bound in the United States of America
by R. R. Donnelley and Sons Company.
Type set in Melior by Typographic Art, Incorporated, Hamden, Connecticut.
Color Separated by Offset Separations Corporation, New York.

CONTENTS

INTRODUCTION

INTRODUCTION

"Money makes the world go around . . ." (Popular lyric)

NOTE TO THE READER: Actual sizes of all coins, currencies, and medals reproduced in this book are noted in millimeters (mm). One inch equals approximately 25 millimeters.

We are lifelong students of numismatics, the science of coins. Unfortunately, "science" often implies impersonal measurements or dry categories. But our world of numismatics embraces many exciting, "living things." They include the indestructible coins and medals struck for civilizations and heroes long reduced to ashes; the peculiar metal and cardboard objects which survived centuries of war and desolation; the many-colored paper currencies which have passed through millions of hands — indeed, all negotiable relics which "speak" to the present about the artistic trends, elements of trade, and historic events of the past — all the indispensable aspects of human society through the ages.

What is money? What are its uses? Money is a medium of exchange. It is a store of value. It is a status symbol. Money has religious, ceremonial, and political functions. Money has countless other, varied and abstract defini-

2. English "touch coins": a half groat of Richard II (1377-1399) and a "touch piece" of King James II (1685-1688) showing the Archangel Michael killing the dragon. 20 & 19 mm.

3. Cromwell crown with die-break leading to edge inscription. 40 mm.

tions. Finally, money is one of man's oldest, if not always most faithful, companions. Where man thinks, money lives.

Money also has about it an aura of mystery and intrigue. Countless legends tell of monsters guarding hoards of wealth set deep in the folds of the earth. Rumors of lethal curses evolve from tales of lost or illusive treasures. However, no folklore or legend, no rumor or curse, rivals the priceless reality of authentic coin discoveries. Treasures of limitless wealth and exquisite beauty, yielding immense value to historians, are found continually, enriching our numismatic world.

Coins have had a special place in man's life. The key to riches and the enjoyment of life, coins often influenced the fate of rulers and nations, assured victories, and fortified the power of kings. Some coins were considered inventions and tools of the devil who armed them with special occult powers. Indeed, since antiquity, many customs and superstitions relate to an almost magical symbolism attached to some coins.

Innumerable hoards found in places of pilgrimage or sanctuaries reveal the use of coins as tokens of sacrifice. The custom of throwing coins into fountains derives from a habit of the ancient Greeks of depositing a coin in a

health-bringing mineral source or placing riches in the sacred waters or realm of a forest divinity, as a protective offering. Placing a coin in the cornerstone of a new building is a reminder of the ancient belief that a sacrifice is required to insure the durability of any structure. One small ancient Greek silver coin, *Charon's obol,* when placed in the mouth of the dead, was believed to serve as fare paid to Charon for ferrying the departed over the mythical River Styx into the underworld.

For centuries, gold coins were considered to have supernatural powers. Even today many people carry "good luck" pieces believing them to have special talismanic powers shielding the bearer from bad luck. The Kremnitz coin, showing St. George killing the dragon on one side and Jesus in a boat on a stormy sea on the reverse, was highly regarded as having the power to protect the bearer in battle and on the high seas. Such coins had an added spiritual value out of proportion to their purchasing power in the market place. Instruments of trade were thus transformed into symbolic wealth, enabling the possessor to "buy" other worldly "goods."

No other custom better illustrates the supernatural powers vested in coins

than their use in healing. For example, gold shavings from *ducats* of King

Matthias of Hungary (1457-1485) were given to children as protection against cramps. "Jesus pennies" were used in northern Germany to ward off epilepsy. So-called "touch coins" were used in France and England in the Middle Ages. Kings of England (15th-17th centuries) used "angel" coins to make the sign of the cross over afflicted parts of the body, supposedly bringing miraculous cures. The Maoris of New Zealand believe that the cause of a disease may be transferred to a coin which is then burned and thrown into the sea. If recovered later, the finder suffers bad luck.

Coins were also given prophetic powers. Oliver Cromwell's crown, struck in 1658, the same year he died, developed a flaw on its obverse after a few strikings. A crease ran across his neck to the rim of the coin where it stopped at the Latin word *"NEMO"* which spelled *"OMEN"* when read backwards. It was believed that this foretold imminent doom: that the Lord Protector would soon lose his head. Later that year Cromwell died of natural causes. His body was exhumed by royalists three years afterwards and his head severed from the trunk, fulfilling the prophecy of the imperfect coin.

As the symbolic representation of wealth, coins were often regarded as odious, impure examples of man's base instincts. Paintings depict the wickedness of misers, Judas's betrayal, and the dissipation of gamblers. But coins were also used as decorative ornaments on rings, necklaces, bracelets, and clothing, showing pride in their aesthetic beauty.

*   *   *   *   *   *   *

With the artistic photography of Lee Boltin, we have attempted to show the beauty and lore of money throughout recorded history up to the present. We cannot, of course, cover the entire massive and complex subject. Rather, we have tried to highlight the human experience in all its versatile, intriguing, and fascinating ways as reflected in coins, currency, and medals.

Quod potui feci,
faciant meliora potentes.

Elvira E. Clain-Stefanelli

V. Clain Stefanelli.

Washington, D.C.
1972-1974

10

4. "A Miser's Dream". Flemish painting of the 17th century.

I | PRIMITIVE MONEY

I: PRIMITIVE MONEY: EARLY MEANS OF EXCHANGE

The shield of Pallas Athene was described as having "a hundred tassels . . . all gold, each one [worth] a hundred oxen's price."

Money and value are states of mind. Many of the earliest forms of money defy the economists' definition of a proper currency: that it be easily transportable, homogeneous, indestructible, divisible, and stable in worth. Trade in early civilizations took a form which is common to underdeveloped cultures of modern times in that surplus was traded off for necessary goods. The means of exchange met one central requirement: that man invested it with confidence as to its worth to him, be it cattle, metals, or shells.

Barter, the direct exchange of goods, is the oldest form of trade; it existed long before the first civilizations of ancient times arose. It has continued throughout human history or reappeared again and again whenever more advanced exchange systems collapsed due to war, famine, or political upheavals. In early agricultural and pastoral societies, cattle or sheep were the most commonly bartered goods. For example, the ox served among the Greeks of Homer's time. The shield of the great goddess Pallas Athene is described as having "a hundred tassels . . . all gold, each one [worth] a hundred oxen's price." Again, Priam's son was ransomed for 300 oxen, whereas slave girls could be bought for 20 oxen each.

6. Cowries, described by Marco Polo as "white porcelain found in the sea," among the earliest forms of currency in China and other parts of the world, used since the second millenium B.C. String 130 mm.

The modern banker's term "pecuniary" has its origin in the Latin words *pecunia* and *pecus* ("cattle"). Among the early forms of Roman currency, the *aes signatum* (c. 269 B.C.), a large bronze tablet, carried the image of an ox; and Germanic and Gallic tribes during the Roman period used cows as one of their main units of exchange. Even in India the coin denomination *rupee* takes its name from the old Sanscrit word *rupa*, ("cattle").

That cattle appear to have been the most popular of all barter substitutes for currency is evidenced by several words in various European languages. The English "fee" is derived from the Germanic word *Vieh* ("cattle") after passing through the intermediate Anglo-Saxon form, *feoh*. In Russian the oldest name for money is *skot*, meaning "cattle." The Gothic word *skatts* ("cattle") passed into the German language as *Schatz*, meaning "treasure" or "wealth."

Farm produce, such as wheat and barley, was also widely used as currency in the past. In Babylon barley determined the basic unit of weight, the *shekel;* it was equal to 180 grains of barley. Grain was also a form of currency in India, and in China during the first century A.D. grain actually took the place of a metallic currency that had become debased. Ancient Egypt had government grain banks where grain was stored, exchanged, and transferred; in brief, the commodity was manipulated much as money is today.

Salt left a permanent record. Salary, from the Latin *salarium* indicating the allowance in salt given to military personnel, is proof of its use as a commodity currency within the Roman Empire, as it was also in China. The Irish *kumal* should be regarded as a highly unusual standard of value designating a slave girl or bondsmaid. And there are frequent references in Irish historical literature to fines in *kumal*. In 15th century Ireland a poet was paid two cows for a poem. Among the Mongols cattle, sheep, and camels were the main currencies; a Kirghiz could buy a bride with 100 sheep. Indian corn was widely traded in Canada and in the American colonies during the 17th century, but rice out-

ranked it by far. In South Carolina rice was accepted in payment for taxes during the early 1700s. Japan used rice as a unit of account for centuries, and in many rural areas during World War II rice provided the basic currency substitute.

7. Egyptian fresco from Thebes, depicting a barter scene, c. 1500 B.C.

Other unusual staple goods accepted as currency included tea, almonds, sugar, butter, salt, and rum. This list actually makes one wonder how much restraint people exercised in order not to literally eat or drink up their entire fortune. The Chinese, for example, used tea and salt as main currencies. Marco Polo tells how salt was pressed into cakes which were stamped by the government and circulated at a value of 40 salt bars to one gold bar. Mongols would accept skins for tax payments. Bear and moose skins in Canada, the reindeer skins in Lapland, and especially marten and squirrel skins in Norway and Poland were important trading items and were often cited as units of value. The beaver pelts in the American colonies were in great demand since they provided a very desirable export item. But furs and skins reached the highest degree of importance in the national economy of Russia. There an intensive trade in furs since the Middle Ages led to accepting them as a unit of value and account. Squirrel and marten skins in bundles were used even in the international trade, based on a unit, the *grivna kun,* consisting of a determined number of pelts. Peter the Great, through a ukase in 1700, put an end to fur money which had circulated for centuries, even along with metallic currency.

In the Solomon Islands ten strings of shells and 1,000 porpoise teeth could buy a wife or a girl of high standing, but with inflation setting in, the initial fee was raised to thirty and up to fifty strings. In some islands shell money was used combined with teeth money. Five hundred porpoise teeth would buy 16

8. *Hollow-handle spade-money — pu — from China, c. 400 B.C. 50 x 95 mm.*

9. *Gold ring "money" used in ancient Britain (first century B.C.), as well as in Abyssinia. Front left: 20 mm.*

10. *Early Russian silver bars (14th century) from Novgorod. Dividing lines on some indicated the place where the bar could be cut into fractions. Longest: 160 mm.*

a wife "of good quality" in the Solomons, and lovers would mention porpoise teeth in their poetry. Porpoises yield up to 150 teeth per animal; therefore in order to keep the supply down, the hunting of porpoises was declared a religious ceremony and could be performed only on special dates. This system of checking the inflation shows that often primitive societies were quite clever in acknowledging the dangers of inflation, and used practical means to stop it.

Dog teeth were quite valuable since only the two upper teeth, the canines, were used. One hundred such teeth could buy a woman or could be exchanged in New Guinea for boar tusks, which were "big money" used only in large transactions. One of the best known currencies in the Pacific area is the stone money of Yap. These millstone-like slabs of aragonite, of various sizes from a few inches in diameter up to ten feet and more, impressed the world not only through their size and weight but, also, through the myth and poetry which surrounds them. Accepted in all kinds of payments, stone money became in Yap above all a symbol of wealth and prestige. As if these currencies were not strange enough, the list of commodity-currencies of the Pacific area includes also rats, flying foxes, and feather money.

A well known form of African currency primarily used on the Gold Coast were *manillas* in copper, brass, or iron, in the form of open bracelets. Imported by the Portuguese, they were often used in the slave trade, eight to ten *manillas* being the price for one slave.

People in Malaya extensively used tin after casting it in the shape of animals, such as crocodiles, elephants, or frogs, each animal corresponding to a certain weight or size, or in the form of a square hat, as the so-called "hat money."

Perhaps the most famous currency used among Indian tribes, even before the arrival of the white man and later in their trading relations with the colonists, was money made from purple and white clam shells, called *wampum* in the Indian language. *Wampum* or *wampumpeag* fulfilled a great role in the life of the Indian; it served as an ornament, a means of making peace, sealing alliances and friendship, transmitting messages, and recording tribal history. Columbus and other travelers to Central America came across one of the most diffused currencies of those parts: cocoa beans. In earlier periods Mexicans also used quills filled with gold dust, and the Aztecs are said to have used copper hatchets in trade.

Shells and Metals as Money

People found more convenient forms of money. One such form was the cowrie shell. Accounts indicate that in India in the third century B.C. cowries sufficed to pay the daily expenses of one man. In 16th century India rich landowners had large storage houses full of cowries; in Bengal, for example, the shells were traded in baskets holding 12,000 shells each. Cowries were also among the earliest forms of currency in China, going back to the second millennium B.C. During his stay in China some 3,000 years later, Marco Polo was intrigued by the use of this "white porcelain found in the sea" as a currency. Another early development, metal, had the advantage of being compact, stable, and divisible into units of equal weight or size. Among the metals most frequently used in the first days of money were copper (deemed a particularly valuable

11. Purple and white wampum (center) of North American Indians circulated at a fixed rate of exchange. Alaska also used blue-colored glass beads. Long, red string: 300 mm.

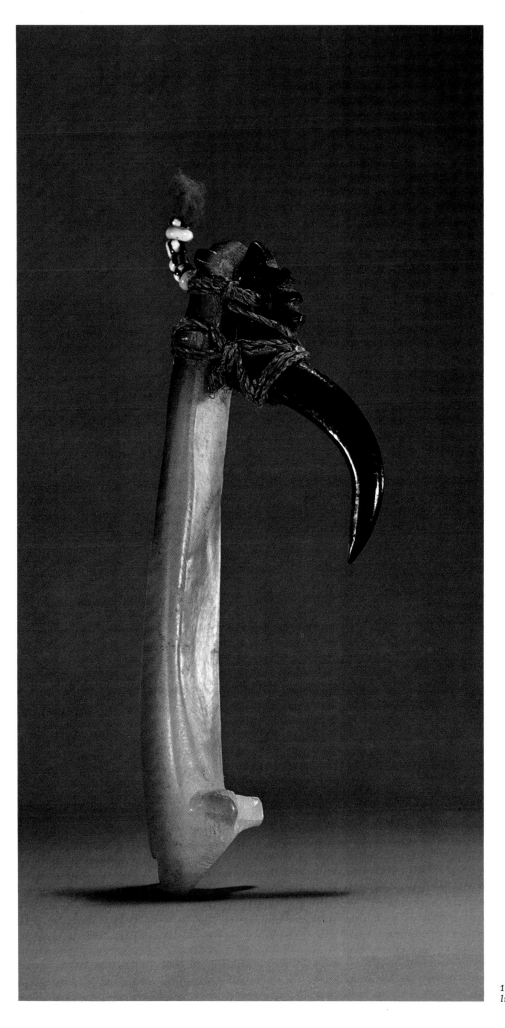

12. Fish-hook "money" from Vella Lavella Island in the Solomons. 68 mm.

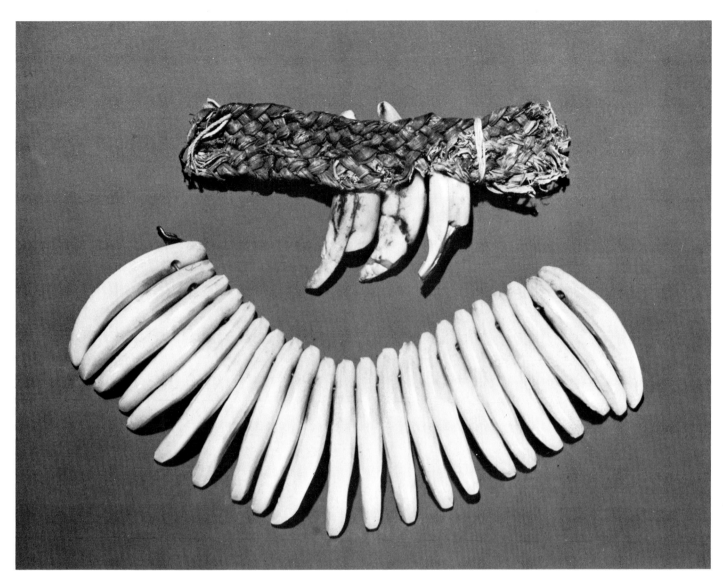

13. *Dogs' teeth, considered quite valuable in the Solomons, were therefore counterfeited in porcelain in Germany, 1890s.*

metal by the Egyptians), lead, gold, and especially silver. Silver was mentioned in Moses' Table of Laws to indicate the value of houses, cattle, and fields. Many mural paintings in Egypt show prisoners of war presenting the Pharaoh with large metallic ingots; other scenes depict the weighing of fairly large rings. The ring or bracelet form, resulting from a simple process of bending metallic bars or wires into a circle which permitted easier transportation, was used by many civilizations.

In another part of the world, in the British Isles, the use of metal in rings and ingots continued throughout the Middle Ages. For example, an Anglo-Saxon poem of A.D. 937 praises the generosity of King Athelstan as a "ring-giver." In adjacent Ireland during the late Middle Ages, rings were of standard weight.

Since metallic utensils, like axes, hoes, and arrows, were extensively traded objects, less refinished pieces were in time cast with the sole purpose of serving as units of value in trade. Similar rudimentary utensils, including cauldrons and tripods, were found in large quantities in archeological excavations.

14. Manilla *in form of an open bracelet used in West Africa. 60 mm.*

15. Malayan *"hat money" in four different denominations. Largest: 70 x 70 mm.*

The Roman *aes rude* was a shapeless lump of raw copper or bronze; it varied in size and weight and circulated extensively before metal was given more formal preparation for use as currency. Heinrich Schliemann, who excavated ancient Troy, found tongue-shaped silver bars, probably used as currency during the 14th century B.C.; and his excavations at Mycenae yielded round metal discs, a more advanced and coinlike form of currency.

In China ever since the second millennium B.C., miniature metal tools, such as hoes, spades, and sickles, comprised a kind of currency that was valued according to its weight. One similar form of currency, a series of bronze knives that were never meant to cut, was issued by Chinese merchants' guilds beginning in the seventh century B.C.

The custom of valuing metals such as gold and silver by weight persisted in most of Europe even after the time when formal coinages came into circulation. Many coins were accepted and valued only according to their weight, a logical action because both wear and tear and illicit "clipping" diminished

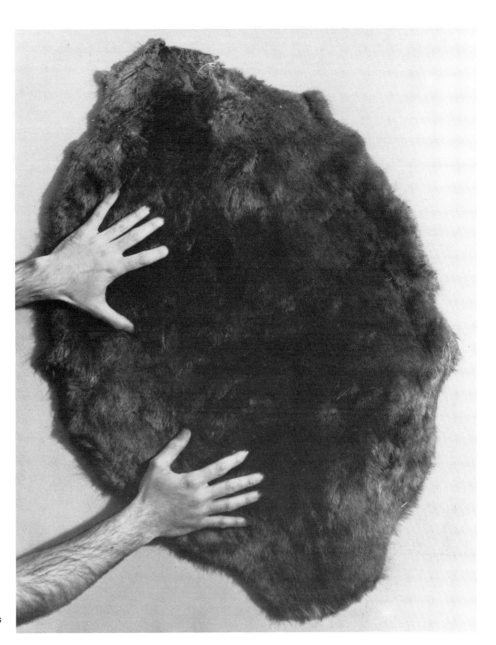

16. Beaver skins were the main trade-goods along the east coast of North America.

the intrinsic value of many coins. The Scandanavian countries used metals in large quantities — in raw lumps or in the form of rings valued according to weight. In Sweden up to the 13th century A.D. gold wire spirals, gold bars, and gold plates were accepted as currency. In Russia, at Kiev and Novgorod, silver bars, either plain or marked for subdivision, were in frequent use during medieval times. Indeed the Russian word "ruble" is said to have its roots in a verb, *rubit,* meaning to "chop" or "cut;" it is indicative of the custom of cutting sections from silver bars according to need. Gold dust carried in bags, or "pokes," (customary during gold-rush days in California, for example) was a form of currency familiar in Japan in medieval times when bags or small packets of gold dust were exchanged by merchants before the introduction of gold bars. All the elements of modern economic operations are found, in primitive or rudimentary form, in these early means of exchange. These and other even more exotic forms of currency have continued in use up to the present day in many parts of the world.   □

23

II | GREEK COINS

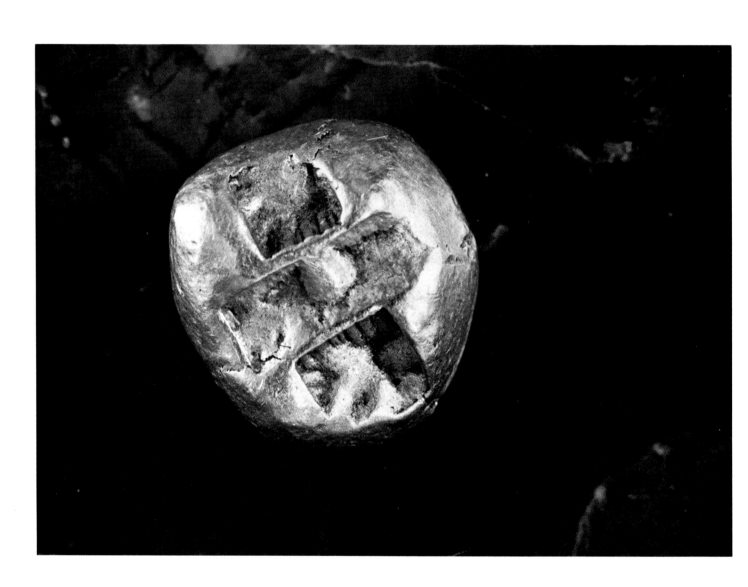

II: GREEK COINS: MIRROR OF AN ANCIENT WORLD

To Greeks, a coin was a work of love.

Historians tell us that the Greek coin mirrors that ancient world, indicates the progress of its art, perpetuates the fame of noble generations, and keeps alive the memory of great men. Greek art and life were united in a spiritual harmony. Beauty was the common denominator of existence. And coinage was created not only to provide money but to make permanent the aesthetic ambitions of this civilization, the understanding of which is so essential to the understanding of our own.

Greek coins reveal a dynamic civilization. Statues long destroyed survive as images on recovered coins. Their ancient heroic literature is better understood as the enormous wealth of mythological figures is made available by merely examining coins and their inscriptions. Outlines of illusive history, from the rise of Macedonia, the emergence of Alexander the Great, and the fall of Athens, may be traced with near chronological precision. To Greeks, a coin was a work of love, combining art and necessity, and by these unique talents, casting a permanent archive for use by posterity. The Greeks told a pretty tale to account for the great wealth in gold enjoyed by the kingdom of Lydia in Asia Minor (today a district in Turkey), one of whose early rulers, Midas, has left his name as a synonym for spontaneous wealth. King Midas had rescued the old drunkard Silenos and returned him to the youthful god of wine, Dionysus. In return the deity promised Midas that he would grant any favor the king should wish. Midas thereupon wished that whatever he might touch would turn into gold. Dionysus granted him the wish, but soon enough Midas returned to the god in despair; he could neither eat nor drink because every morsel of meat and sip of wine was turned into gold by his touch. Dionysus directed the king to purify himself in the waters of the nearby River Pactolus, and ever since that day the sands of the river have been rich in gold.

Whatever may have been the true cause of the river's richness in gold-bearing sands, tradition tells us that it was in the realm of the kings of Lydia that mankind's first coins were struck. Early kings (7th Century B.C.) minted coins made of pale gold from the Pactolus and displaying the head of a lion as the king's blazon, a visible guarantee of the weight and fineness of his coinage. Actually it may be that these kings were only following a practice already established in the neighboring Greek colony of Ionia. A few bean-shaped pieces of pale native gold seem to have been in circulation in the Ionian cities of Asia Minor even before the time of Lydian kings. Some of these gold beans, marked on one side only with striations, showed a set of four square indentations on the opposite side. Other coins bore representations of animals, possibly the blazons of the cities that had issued them.

In any event, one of their successors, King Croesus (560-546 B.C.) — a Lydian monarch of almost legendary wealth — improved the kingdom's coinage even further. The coins of Croesus, called *staters*, were issued both in silver and in gold; one gold *stater* was equal in value to 20 silver *staters*. This was the world's first bimetallic currency. The coins of Croesus displayed a lion facing a horned bull, perhaps intended as symbols of power and life. In time the

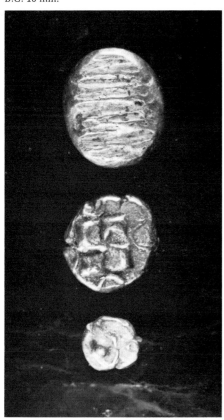

◁ 18. Earliest form of coinage. An electrum stater from Asia Minor, late seventh century B.C. 16 mm.

19. Early Greek coins from Ionia, in Asia Minor, struck in electrum or "pale gold" (7th to 6th century B.C.), adorned only with a striated surface, primitive designs of a swastika, or a frontal view of an eye. Largest: 9 mm.

27

20. Some of the earliest coins from the kingdom of Lydia. Lion facing a bull, symbols of
power and life, used on gold and silver coins
of King Croesus (561-546 B.C.). First left: 13
mm.

21. A gold daric and a silver siglos of the Persian empire, 4th century B.C. 14 x 15 mm.

kings of Persia adopted a bimetallic system which attained world-wide
circulation.

The practice of minting coins, although originating in Asia Minor, soon spread
to Europe. The first people to adopt this practice were those inhabiting the
Greek island of Aegina. Mainland cities such as Athens and Corinth began to
issue coins; the first of them dates back almost to Croesus's day. After almost
half a century of issuing silver coins marked with a miscellany of symbols
such as vases, wheels, or horses, Athens revised its designs and introduced
the largest silver coin known up to that time, a four-*drachm* piece that weighed
twice as much as, and was twice the size of, the earlier coins.

The new Athenian coinage was unique in another respect: it was the first to
bear a full design on both sides of the coin. The helmeted head of the city's
patron-goddess, Athene, graced one face; and the other showed Athene's
sacred bird, the owl. The head of Athene was always shown in profile, wearing 28

22. Two "turtles" (Greek: chelonai) from Aegina. The sea-turtle with its plain shell was used on coins of the 6th and early 5th centuries. Later the land tortoise, with a quartered shell, adorned the coins. 21 mm.

the helmet of an Athenian soldier. Despite her warlike attire, Athene did not appear extremely stern and severe; on some coins her lips bore the famous archaic smile, imparting a youthful charm to her face. The eye was unusually large, shown, as was the archaic convention, not in profile but full face.

Athens controlled the rich silver mines of Laurium, and such a supply of silver allowed the city to issue its coinage in large quantities. Because they were hastily minted, many of the coins are inferior in execution and design, but their reputation as a currency of good weight and undebased silver content soon carried them to the far corners of the Greek world and helped Athens prosper as a trading state. Archeological findings in recent years reveal the magnitude of Athens's monetary expansion. Her silver *tetradrachms* have been unearthed as far away as Syria in the Near East, and in Egypt, in 1946, almost 10,000 pieces of Athenian silver were uncovered. Westward, the silver of Athens reached Sicily and even Spain. The saying "to bring owls to Athens"

23. The goddess Athena, with helmet, depicted on a tetradrachm of Athens (5th century B.C.) and on a vase fragment. 24 mm.

24. Changing designs of the owl on Athenian tetradrachms struck between the 6th and the late 4th century B.C. 21-23 mm.

may have originated during this period, perhaps because Athenian traders overseas insisted on being paid in their own coinage.

Corinth was another mainland city well known in the ancient world as a trading center and a colonizing power. The Corinthians, as did other Greeks, wanted their coinage to be under divine aegis. They chose Pegasus, the winged horse tamed by the hero Bellerophon, as their symbol. In their early coins Pegasus is represented with curled wings on one side of the coin while a swastika pattern appears on the other. This design was replaced toward the end of the sixth century B.C. with a more "modern-looking" Pegasus with pointed wings. The reverse side of the coin bears a graceful profile of Athene, seen wearing a simple, unadorned Corinthian helmet. These silver coins, weighing about eight grams, were called *staters*, and two were reckoned to be equivalent to one *tetradrachm*.

The Corinthian "colts," as they soon came to be known throughout the Greek world, were a widely accepted currency, although they did not surpass the Athenian "owls" in popularity. On some of the smaller Corinthian coins minted during the fourth century B.C., Bellerophon himself made an appearance. A representation of Pegasus in a standing position, quite different from the usual flying image, also appears on some coins. According to ancient sources, this static pose was taken from that of a cult statue of Pegasus kept in the city of Corinth. In time the head of the goddess Athene changed in style, and during the fifth century B.C. a variety of symbols appear behind her head.

An unbelievable wealth of coinage developed in the Greek world, especially during the period when the Greek city-states enjoyed full autonomy. A few statistics speak clearly to this point. More than 1,400 Greek city-states or other autonomous groups issued their own coinages, and their mints were often active for centuries. Asia Minor alone contained over four hundred separate mints which were used by hundreds of kings and rulers who struck coins in their own names.

Greek coinage was basically a silver currency. Although gold was being minted in large quantities in Persia during this period, gold coins made a late appearance in Greece proper. In this connection, it is wrong to assume that the gold coins issued occasionally by Greek cities were signs of prosperity. On the contrary, the Greeks resorted to gold only when dire necessity forced them to supplement the silver coinage commonly used. Such supplementary mintings of gold coincided with times when emergency expenditures had emptied the treasuries of silver. Gold coins were thus a sure indicator of troubled times.

Greek Coins in Sicily

Beginning in the eighth century B.C., a string of Greek colonies sprang up along the coast of Sicily. The colonies maintained close ties with the mother country and especially with Athens and Corinth. Within a century some of these Greek colonies began minting their own coinage, even though Sicily had no silver mines and the metal had to be imported from Spain or northern Italy. Naxos, a little wine-producing town situated below the snow-capped peak of Mount Etna, was the first Greek colony to start minting coins. The

25. *The great range of Athenian silver coinage represented by a tetradrachm (17.46 gr.), a drachm, a triobol or three obols, an obol, a hemiobolon or half obol, a trihemitartemorion or 3/8 obol, and the minuscule hemitartemorion or 1/8 obol, weighing 0.09 grams. Largest: 24 mm.*

currency of Naxos was a heavy silver *drachm* dedicated to Dionysus, the god of wine; and the deity's profile, executed in archaic style, appeared together with a cluster of grapes. Zankle, the Messina of today, was proud of its control of the narrow strait between Sicily and the Italian mainland. Its first coin showed a dolphin, symbolizing the sea, swimming within a sickle-shaped enclosure, a representation of the city harbor. Syracuse was destined to become not only the leading power in Sicily but one of the most brilliant cities in the entire Greek world. Its coinage displayed the fondness of the Syracusan aristocracy for horses and racing. One design, showing a four-horse racing chariot, in some cases accompanied by a winged figure symbolic of victory, was utilized again and again throughout the city's history. In later periods the design inspired some of the greatest compositions in all Greek coinage.

At the time when the Athenians were fighting off the Persians, Syracuse won a war against Carthage. To celebrate their victory, the Syracusans minted a memorial coin — a 10-*drachm* piece — that is one of the great masterworks of Greek engraving. It was called the Demareteion, in honor of Demarete, wife of the tyrant of Syracuse. On one side is seen the head of the nymph-guardian of Syracuse, Arethusa, surrounded by four dolphins. But the head shows little Olympian remoteness and is more individualized than usual. It is impossible to say whether the head is, instead, that of Queen Demarete or, if so, how closely the artist dared to follow his mortal model in an era when coin images were reserved for the immortals. On the other side the coin shows, in addition to the traditional Syracusan four-horse chariot, a running lion — perhaps intended as an image of the defeated Carthaginians.

31. Examples of exquisite Greek coin engraving including miniature masterpieces often less than half an inch in diameter; drachm from Stiela (Sicily) and litra from Akragas (Sicily), late 5th century B.C. 15 mm.

32. Greek coins indicating value were very rare. These bronze coins of Metapontum, South Italy, late 4th century B.C., carried the word obolos on the reverse. 20 mm.

33

The coinage of Syracuse reached its artistic apogee late in the fifth century B.C. These were years of triumph and years of disaster. In 413 B.C. Syracuse succeeded in defeating the almost invincible Athenian fleet, but shortly thereafter the city once again faced a belligerent Carthage which by 410 B.C. had conquered virtually all Sicily except Syracuse. Many of the artists who designed the coins of this period, proud of their creations, signed their works. They either half-concealed their name or initials in the nymph Arethusa's hair or her hairband, or often displayed them more openly, on a tablet carried by the flying Victory figure in the chariot scene. Names such as Eumenes, Eukleidas, Euainetos, Phrygillos, and Kimon are therefore known to us today. The beauty of their work secured these artists the admiration of their contemporaries. Eukleidas, Kimon, and Euainetos in particular were deemed to be masters. Coins imitating their designs were minted as far distant as Asia Minor, and the black-glazed pottery of southern Italy carried the imprint of the nymph Arethusa's head as rendered by Euainetos.

Eukleidas was the first artist to attempt to create three-dimensionality in a full face portrayal on the shallow surface of a coin. His subject was a helmeted head of Athene. To model a face in such a way as to give the illusion of depth in shallow relief betokens great skill. Rivaling Eukleidas's work is Kimon's full-faced head of Arethusa; it can be regarded as one of the most accomplished and most beautiful coins ever created. Kimon added further 34

33. A four-drachm piece, struck in Akragas, Sicily (c. 420-415 B.C.), displays the crab which abounded in the waters of this harbor) and the mythical figure of the monster Skylla which guarded the straits of Messina. 25 mm.

to his reputation by producing a large commemorative 10-*drachm* piece celebrating the Syracusan victory over Athens in 413 B.C. The profile head of Arethusa on this coin is a thing of perfect beauty. Kimon's triumph may possibly be superseded by Euainetos's rendition of Arethusa on a similar 10-*drachm* piece; there a perfect work of art is made even more brilliant by the warmth and charm of the nymph's expression.

Gold was a metal rarely used for Sicilian coins, and its appearance mainly signified some emergency. During the siege of Syracuse by the Athenians in 415-413 B.C., the beleaguered city resorted to gold coinage in order to meet its military expenses. One gold piece, with a value of 20 *drachms*, struck a few decades later, is a coin of outstanding beauty. A graceful head of Arethusa appears on one side, and on the other Heracles wrestles the Nemean lion. Its superb workmanship demonstrates how important art was in the life of the early Greeks; even when under the stress of war they labored to produce perfect work.

The massive attacks of the Carthaginians in the late fourth century B.C. brought the period of great masterpieces to an end. During the rest of the century, Syracuse continued to issue a few coins that were remarkable for their quality, but most of the coins in circulation were Corinthian "colts" that the Syracusans imported in large numbers. Bronze coins, rare before, slowly made an appearance and replaced smaller silver coins in local trade. The style and execution of many of these bronze coins, especially those from Syracuse, were worthy of their counterparts in silver. As time passed, however, their images grew more dull and lifeless. Late in the third century B.C. the Greek colonies of Sicily finally ceased to be independent and became part of the expanding empire of Rome.

34. The imposing but aloof beauty of an archaic head of Apollo represented on a tetradrachm of Leontinoi in Sicily, c. 480 B.C. 26

35. The more human traits of the same god Apollo on a tetradrachm struck by the Sicilian city of Catana, half a century later. 25 mm.

36. *The ferocious looking man-faced bull representing the river-god Gelas on a tetradrachm of Gela in Sicily, c. 410 B.C. 28 mm.*

37. *"Black the one and brilliant in its radiance the other king of the birds . . . voraciously tearing the pregnant hare to pieces." These lines from Aeschylus' Agamemnon best describe this impressive composition on a tendrachm piece struck by Akragas eight years before its destruction in 406 B.C. 39 mm.*

38. A charming composition of a youthful hunter leisurely resting probably represents the god Pan or a local river-god, on a tetradrachm of c. 405 B.C. from Segesta, Sicily. 27 mm.

Greek Coins in Southern Italy

A second group of Greek colonies occupied still another area that was also destined to become Roman. This was southern Italy, and the Greek coinage there, from its earliest beginnings in the middle of the sixth century B.C., possessed a new and unusual form. The first of the cities in the area to introduce coinage—Croton, Metapontum, and Sybaris—lay in the fertile plains north of the Gulf of Tarentum.

A philosopher from Asia Minor named Pythagoras settled in Croton in 529 B.C. There he founded the religious order of Pythagoreans, who hoped to achieve an immense moral reform of society. Pythagorean philosophy paired fundamental opposites: rest and motion, light and darkness. Croton and other neighboring Greek cities struck coins which appear to realize in money that intellectual theory. The same image was engraved in two opposite forms: the obverse representing the image in relief while the back carried the same image in sunken form.

Croton is also said to have been founded according to the instructions of the celebrated oracle of Apollo who occupied the god's shrine at Delphi. The city therefore marked its first coinage with a tripod dedicated to Apollo. The reverse of the coin showed in some cases a similar tripod, in others an eagle, a bird sacred to Zeus. Following the Pythagorean ideal, the figure on the reverse was shown not in positive relief but in sunken form. The coins differed

from other Greek coinage not only in this respect but also in their shape; rather than being small and thick, they were comparatively large in diameter and thin. Made of silver, the *stater* of Croton weighed approximately eight grams and was equal in value to three *drachms*.

Metapontum, another of the cities of "Magna Graecia," as the colonists called southern Italy, let the world know of its wealth in grain by choosing barley as the blazon of the coinage. A simple barley ear, shown in relief and flanked by slender angular letters spelling "META," marked one side of the Metapontum *stater* and appeared in intaglio on the other side. The elegance of this design makes the *stater* of Metapontum, first minted in 550 B.C., one of the early masterpieces of Greek coinage.

The wealth of the oldest of the cities of Magna Graecia, Sybaris, was so great that even today the word "sybarite" is synonymous with luxurious living and self-indulgence. The city's first coinage, minted in the middle of the sixth century B.C., shows a bull with its head turned. The bull may symbolize the River Crathis, the stream beside which Sybaris stood.

A fourth city, which may have been founded by the Sybarites, is Poseidonia (the Roman Paestum) on the Gulf of Salerno. As its Greek name indicates, the patron of the city was Poseidon, the brother of Zeus, whose domain   38

40. One of the greatest coin creations of the ancients: the lovely head of the nymph Arethusa represented in a frontal view by the engraver Kimon who signed his name in her diadem. On a tetradrachm of Syracuse, c. 410-400 B.C. 28 mm.

41. The charm and near perfect beauty of the nymph Arethusa characterizes this profile created by the engraver Euainetos for a large ten-drachm piece of Syracuse (c. 380 B.C.). 36 mm.

42. The head of the Syracusan Arethusa imitated on a black-glazed kylix or cup from Cales, South Italy, 4th century B.C. Without handles: 110 mm.

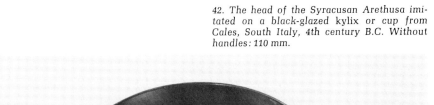

embraced all the world's waters. The first *staters* minted by the Poseidonians show a figure of the god in profile, characteristic in its archaic rigidity, brandishing a trident. The coins were minted shortly after 530 B.C.

The figure of Apollo is the blazon on the *staters* of a fifth Greek colony, Caulonia, situated at the southern extremity of Magna Graecia. Apollo appears in characteristic archaic form; the god's shoulders are seen in a frontal view while the rest of his body is seen in profile. A small running figure is poised on the god's outstretched left arm, a laurel branch is held in his right hand, and at his feet appears a stag.

Still a sixth city, Tarentum, was destined to become powerful and famous. Its wealth in fine wool, horses, and the murex shell, which was the source of an important purple dye, all contributed to the city's prosperity. For its trade, Tarentum needed coins, and a long succession of mintings in silver followed the city's first issues, struck around 500 B.C. The city's mythical founder, Taras, riding on the dolphin that was said to have rescued him from shipwreck, is an image that appeared again and again for more than 300 years, changing in style according to the trend of the times. The horses of Tarentum

46. An archaic figure of Apollo represented on an incuse stater (6th century B.C.) of Caulonia, another Greek colony in Magna Graecia or South Italy. 30 mm.

later became the city's great pride: a series of *staters* (first issued in about 425 B.C. and continuing for almost 200 years) displayed horsemen in various attitudes and attires. Some of the images clearly refer to sporting victories, whereas others allude to military activities; the young naked jockeys on the former coins are replaced by riders in full armor on the latter.

Early in the third century B.C., shortly before the start of the Punic Wars, the Tarentines quarreled with the increasingly powerful Romans to the north. Pyrrhus of Greece, the ruler of Epirus, came with squadrons of elephants to help Tarentum against the advancing Romans, and the appearance of elephants on the coins of Tarentum bears testimony to Pyrrhus's aid during the period. Even before this time of open war with Rome, military expenditures had forced Tarentum to mint gold coins. They are among the most perfect coins ever produced; the gold *stater* of 340-330 B.C., showing Taras with his arms raised in supplication to Poseidon, is one of the most striking. Scarcely 50 years later all Magna Graecia had fallen to Rome. Although the political power of the Greek cities was crushed by Rome, Greek culture ultimately vanquished that of the Romans, as the coins of Rome testify.

47. A sea-horse on a silver drachm struck by the Etruscans of Populonia in the 5th century B.C., similar in design to a sea-horse depicted on an Etruscan vase. Coin: 18 mm.

Coins of the Greek Mainland

We have already discussed the early coinage of Greece proper with its variety of blazons. During the fifth century B.C., however, many Greek cities became dissatisfied with the tradition of representing their divine protectors "frozen" in static poses. They wanted to bring the blazons to life by illustrating various events. For example, Heracles was worshipped in Thebes, and the city minted a series of *staters* showing different events in the Greek hero's life, as an infant strangling serpents or as a powerful youth stringing his bow. All the coins of Thebes also displayed, as a distinctive badge of the federation of Boeotian cities, the Boeotian buckler — probably representing an early kind of shield made from the hide of an ox.

On the sacred grounds at Olympia, site of the famous games, stood a statue of Zeus made by the great Athenian sculptor Phidias. This statue, 60 feet in height, was counted as one of the seven wonders of the ancient world. Formed of gold and ivory, it showed Zeus seated on a throne, his left hand resting on a scepter and his right hand holding a small statue of Victory. Some coin designs depicted Phidias's imposing figure of Zeus. Other coins showed his sacred bird (the eagle) and his weapon (the thunderbolt); still others, a winged

48. The city of Tarentum in South Italy often displayed exquisite compositions on its silver staters such as the mythical Taras riding on a dolphin (3rd Century B.C.) and a young rider crowning his horse, an allusion to a victory in the arena (430-380 B.C.). 20 & 22 mm.

49. Hercules fighting the Nemean lion represented on coins of Heracleia (above), as well as in a series of small diobols of Tarentum (4th century B.C.) showing various wrestling poses. Large coin: 23 mm; small coins: 12 mm.

43

Victory bearing a winner's wreath. The imposing head of Zeus that appears on the *staters* minted by Elis in the late fifth century is thought to be directly inspired by Phidias's statue. In this head, as in most of the coins of Elis, the artists have attempted to convey the lofty nature of that higher Olympus, the mountaintop abode of the gods, by emphasizing the serenity and eternal beauty of the world of the immortals.

Each Greek city tried to outdo the next in the beauty of its coins. The lovely head of Hera, Zeus's consort, graces the coins of Argos. Heracles, ready to destroy the deadly dart-feathered birds of Lake Stymphalus, stands doughtily on the coins from Arcadia. The fabled Chimera, part lion, part goat, part serpent, underlines the *staters* of Sicyon. These few pieces suggest the enormous wealth of coins struck by the Greek cities of Peloponnese alone. Pheneus, another of these southern cities, provides evidence of the close relation between coin engraving and sculpture. On the *staters* of Pheneus, minted in about 360 B.C., appears a figure of Hermes carrying the infant Arcas in his arms. The image shows similarities to the style of Praxiteles.

Before mainland Greece had at last to yield to Rome's power, the cultural

50. Fine engraving of a lion's scalp on a tetradrachm from Rhegion struck c. 410-400 B.C., reminiscent of South Italian sculptures of that period. 24 mm.

44

51. This fine composition on a tetradrachm struck c. 435-425 B.C. is dedicated to Jokastos, the mythical founder of Rhegium. 25 mm.

force known as Hellenism was destined to soar to a height of influence and brilliance hitherto unknown in the world. Hellenism carried a unified Greek heritage far beyond the borders of the earlier Greek realm and deep into the heart of Asia. Much of this expansion began during the brief reign of Alexander the Great and will be discussed later in this chapter. As one of the last glimmers of Greek glory, however, a revival of Athenian coinage that took place between the early part of the second century B.C. and the middle of the first century B.C. is noteworthy. With the benefit of Roman protection, Athens could once again command a considerable supply of silver from its rural mines, allowing the Athenians to strike large numbers of four-*drachm* coins. The traditional Athenian coinage was revived in a new and complex form. The face of the coin, a helmeted head of Athene, was a design no longer left to the discretion of the artist; instead, Phidias's colossal gold and ivory statue of Athene Parthenos served as the model. A complicated system of marking the names of magistrates responsible for each issue filled the reverse of the coin with inscriptions and symbols, while Athene's owl was depicted standing on a prize amphora.

Coins of Alexander the Great and the Hellenistic Period

The middle of the fourth century B.C. saw great changes in the Greek world. Powerful empires arose in the wake of Alexander's conquests and swallowed up most of the once proudly independent Greek city-states. Because many had their own well-organized mints, these cities continued to issue coins, but they bore neither the names nor the emblems of the cities that struck them. Many Hellenistic coins take their place among the finest contributions the Greeks ever made to art. The colorful world of Olympus, however, receded into the background. The gods served only as protectors; their place was on the reverse of the coin. The obverse was reserved for the image of the earthly ruler of the realm.

Portraits of rulers did not appear, however, on the coins of Alexander's day. The conqueror followed the traditions established by his father, Philip II of Macedonia (359-336 B.C.), who had minted the largest issue of gold coins ever seen outside the Persian Empire. Known as *Philippi*, the golden *staters* circulated throughout the Greek world, and imitations of them were minted by the barbaric tribes of Europe for centuries after Philip's death. Philip also issued silver coins; one of these, a *tetradrachm*, displayed the head of Zeus on the face. On the reverse was a horseman wearing the traditional wide-brimmed Macedonian hat, or *kausia*.

The coins that Alexander issued after succeeding his father in 336 B.C. included gold *staters* that displayed the head of war-wise Athene on the obverse and a winged Victory on the reverse. Alexander's silver *tetradrachms* bore on one side the head of Heracles, the mythical ancestor of the Macedonian dynasty, on the other a copy of Phidias's enthroned Olympian Zeus. The conqueror's coins were minted in all parts of his empire — in Sardis, Miletus, Tarsus, Alexandria, Damascus, Babylon, and in many other places, thus creating a universal bimetalic coinage. In all, 22 mints issued his coins. The coins that were first ordered struck by Alexander continued to be minted in many parts of the Greek world long after his death in 323 B.C.; some strikings took place as late as the first century B.C.

A handful of Macedonian generals, the companions of Alexander during his march through Asia, struggled with one another over the succession. Among them was Lysimachus, commander of the king's bodyguard. Thrace, a province in northern Greece which was menaced by unruly neighbors, was entrusted to Lysimachus. He emerged victorious in the many battles that first established his authority over Thrace and then allowed him to join forces with another of Alexander's generals, Seleucus, against still a third general, Antigonus. Lysimachus initiated a new coinage in gold and silver. On the fronts of his coins appeared an idealized head of Alexander, wearing a royal diadem adorned with the ram's horn of the Egyptian dual deity, Zeus Ammon. Lysimachus's coins were struck in enormous quantities in various mints and soon spread beyond the realms that he controlled in Greece and Asia Minor.

Lysimachus's power and prosperity came to a sudden end in 281 B.C. when he crossed swords with his old companion-in-arms, Seleucus, who had established himself in the easternmost part of Alexander's empire with his capital at Babylon. Seleucus forged a mighty empire, which stretched from Syria to the borders of India. His adventures in India were memorialized by

52. The image of the sea-monster Skylla used as decoration on the helmeted goddess Athene on a large silver double stater struck c. 400-380 B.C. by Thurium in South Italy. 28 mm.

53. A finely realized profile on a silver stater c. 380 B.C. depicts the nymph Terina, the patron divinity of Terina, a South Italy city eventually destroyed by the Carthaginians. 20 mm.

54. A tetradrachm of c. 430 B.C. showing an old, bearded man, wreathed with ivy, enjoying a cup of wine while taking a leisurely ride on a donkey. From Mende, in northern Greece, whose population wanted to depict an idealized scene of their patron divinity, Dionysus. 28 mm.

55. A local legend in Aenus, Thrace told of a wooden cult image of Hermes miraculously washed ashore. The head of this god was therefore chosen for their tetradrachm struck c. 450 B.C. 24 mm.

56. Apollo shown on a four-drachm piece of Amphipolis in Macedonia (5th century B.C.) symbolic of the Greek ideal of Olympic perfection and serenity. 23 mm.

very impressive coins minted at Pergamon shortly before his death. On one side is an Indian elephant, and on the other appears the horned head of Seleucus's favorite horse, the animal that had once saved his life.

The Macedonian general Antigonus lost his grip on a part of Alexander's empire in the battle of Ipsus in 301 B.C. His son, Demetrius Poliorcetes, "The Besieger of Cities," continued to resist, however, and his victory over Ptolemy of Egypt, one of his father's companions, was considered to be among the greatest sea battles ever fought. Demetrius memorialized his victory, the battle of Salamis in 306 B.C., with a silver *tetradrachm*. It shows a winged Victory standing on a ship's prow, announcing the success, and on the reverse of the coin Poseidon brandishes his trident as the king's protector. The Victory figure is one that was destined to be known to the world as the "Winged Victory of Samothrace." The famous sculptor Eutychides built a monument to celebrate Demetrius's triumph at Salamis. Many years later a copy of Eutychides' monument was built at Samothrace; the Winged Victory raised there is the one that stands today in the Louvre in Paris.

One of Alexander's greatest generals was Ptolemy, who succeeded in holding and enlarging Egypt as his share of the empire. Ptolemy's coinage reflected his determination to appear in the eyes of the world as Alexander's legitimate successor. After assuming the title of king in 305 B.C., Ptolemy minted a new *tetradrachm*. The obverse bears his own likeness, crowned with the royal diadem, and the reverse shows a majestic eagle with a thunderbolt in its talons. The *tetradrachm* continued to be struck unchanged by Ptolemy's successors for almost three centuries until, in 30 B.C., the last of the Ptolemies, Cleopatra VII, put an end to her life, and Egypt became a Roman province.

In the generations that followed the division of Alexander's empire, the dynasties that achieved some stability — the Ptolemaic in Egypt, the Seleucid of the Near East, and even the successors of Demetrius in the Antigonid dynasty in Greece — were in some instances divided and in others enlarged, until the Hellenistic world reached from Atlantic Africa in the west to the Black Sea and the Caucasus in the north and to the Indian subcontinent in the east. Names that are still familiar came into use at this time: Pontus on the shores of the Black Sea; Parthia, now an area in Iran; Bactria on the highway to India; and Mauretania, part of the Morocco of today.

Each of these kingdoms produced its own coins. These, although Greek in character and language, were distinctly individual mintings. They had one common characteristic: in each instance the portraits of the rulers took precedence over representations of the gods, and the gods, too, in some cases yielded what little they still held. Theirs was usually the reverse of the coin, where their divine presence added prestige to the ruler portrayed on the obverse, but now even the reverse was often devoted to a likeness of the founder of the dynasty. The coins of the Parthians, for example, invariably showed Arsaces I, the first Parthian king, on the reverse, regardless of which of his successors appeared on the front.

One notable monarch of a far distant Hellenistic kingdom was Mithradates VI (called the Great), the king of Pontus. Mithradates had silver *tetradrachms* and gold *staters* minted during his long rule. The fronts of the coins show the king's haughty features and loose-flowing hair; on the reverse appears either a drinking Pegasus or a stag surrounded by a wreath. The kings of Hellenistic

57. Ovid's saying "It would be easier to number the leaves of an oak-tree than the daily varieties of hair-styles" is confirmed by this selection of drachms of Corinth (4th century B.C.) displaying a great variety of hair-arrangements appropriately worn by Aphrodite, the goddess of beauty. 13-15 mm.

58. King Philip II of Macedonia (359-336 B.C.)
*selected the magnificent rendering of the head
of Zeus for the obverse of his silver four-
drachm piece. 23 mm.*

59. A real or imaginary portrait of Alexander the Great? We believe that the idealized head, bearing the ram's horn of Zeus Ammon, on the tetradrachm of Lysimachus (left) or possibly the features of the youthful Heracles on the posthumous tetradrachm (right) bear a closer resemblance to the great hero than his figure on the famous mosaic at Pompeii. 30 x 31 mm.

60. The coinage of Alexander the Great (336-323 B.C.) consisted of a double stater, a stater, a ¼ stater in gold, and a four-, two- and one-drachm piece with its fractions the half-drachm and the obol in silver. Top gold: 22 mm.

Parthia, a domain bordering on the Caspian Sea, struck silver coins that carried Greek inscriptions. A one-*drachm* piece was the most common. The coins bore portraits of the "king of kings" who had ruled Parthia. Among the portraits is one of a woman: the beautiful slave girl, Musa, presented by Caesar Augustus to King Phraates IV. Musa became Phraates' queen and later murdered him so that her son might rule.

Another farflung Hellenistic kingdom was Bactria, in what today is northern Afghanistan. This was once a wealthy land, and it is said to have contained nearly 1,000 cities. The coinage of Bactria clearly reveals the Greek character of the kingdom's ruling class. The exquisite portraits of Bactrian kings easily rival those of the finest mintings of Greece proper. The coins are inscribed with the names of kings that have a Greek ring to them; some of these rulers are known to history only from their coins.

Half a world away from Bactria were the Hellenistic kingdoms in Africa west of Egypt: Numidia and Mauretania. The boundaries of Numidia were approximately those of modern Algeria. Both African domains were ruled by kings who continued the traditions of Greek coinage. The names of such Numidian kings as Masinissa, Micipsa, Hiempsal I, and especially Jugurtha,

61. One theme, two art trends: the classical rendering of a horseman on a Macedonian tetradrachm of Philip II (first left), imitated by Eastern Celtic tribes who gave it their own interpretations. First left: 22 mm.

were familiar even on the streets of Rome as enemies or allies. Jugurtha and his two sons walked as prisoners before the triumphal chariot of the Roman consul Marius in 104 B.C. The Numidian kings minted coins in silver and bronze that bore Punic inscriptions and representations of men's heads that may have been intended as the rulers' portraits.

Among the kings of Mauretania was Juba II (25 B.C.-A.D. 24), whom Augustus married to Cleopatra Selene, the daughter born to Mark Antony by Cleopatra. Juba issued a series of small silver coins in the Hellenistic tradition that carried his and his wife's portraits. Mauretania's independent coinage came to an end when the kingdom was made a province of the Roman Empire in A.D. 40. Before then, or soon thereafter, most of the Hellenistic world, with its many mints, came under Roman rule. But the Romans, in a move of great political wisdom, recognized local autonomy in many instances, and not a few Greek cities continued, with Rome's blessing, to strike coins that incorporated their own language and their own images. Thus Roman colonial coinages actually represent a continuation of the Hellenic tradition. □ 52

62. The proud features of King Perseus of Macedonia (178-168 B.C.) on a tetradrachm issued in his homeland, and Perseus and his two sons as prisoners of Rome in front of their captor, represented on a Roman denarius struck a century later (c. 55 B.C.). Greek: 32 mm; Roman: 20 mm.

63. An especially gifted engraver's work on a tetradrachm struck by Ptolemy XII of Egypt during his second reign (55-51 B.C.) deviating from the common impersonal renderings of Ptolemaic portraiture. 25 mm.

64. This brilliant gold eight-drachm piece, although struck by Ptolemy VI of Egypt in 163 B.C., possibly in commemoration of the tenth jubilee of his wedding to Cleopatra II, depicts the veiled head of the deified Queen Arsinoe II, an ancestor who died in 270 B.C. The reverse shows a double cornucopiae, symbol of wealth and plenty. 28 mm.

66. The ancient goddess Isis Pharia, worshipped in Alexandria, holding an inflated sail on this large bronze drachm struck there in the name of the Roman Emperor Hadrian (98-117 A.D.). 35 mm.

67. Bronze coin struck in the Greek city of Aspendus in Asia Minor under Roman rule (c. A.D. 225) representing athletes drawing lots from an urn to determine their starting position in a contest. 35 mm.

65. The gracefully reclining figure of Tyche as city-goddess on this large bronze drachm struck in Alexandria, Egypt, A.D. 123/124 under the Roman Emperor Hadrian, reveals the high cultural level of Egypt when a Roman province. 35 mm.

ROMAN COINS

III: ROMAN COINS: POWER, GLORY, AND BELIEF

Roman coinage exuded confidence in victory, and a yearning for glory . . . for which she invoked the support of the gods.

Rome started her ascent to power during the late fourth and third centuries B.C. Coinage was already known in Italy. Indeed, some of the finest Greek coins were produced on Italian soil. But Rome resisted for a time the adoption of coinage, especially handy silver. Barter in nature, and especially cattle, dominated trade. The earliest currency of Rome consisted of irregular metal lumps of ore and ingots. Their place was later taken by brick-shaped ingots of bronze called *aes signatum* ("marked bronze") weighing from three to five pounds. Eventually a round, one-pound piece of bronze came into use. This was the *aes grave*, or "heavy bronze." The individual "coin," called an *as*, was the equivalent of 12 *unciae*, (a word that is preserved in today's familiar unit of weight, the ounce). An *as* corresponded in weight to a *libra pondus*, other Latin terms that are still in use today. *Pondus* survives in the word "pound," and *libra* in its abbreviated form as "lb."

The libral *as* of the third century B.C. did not bear Rome's name. Two-faced Janus, patron of the Roman people, appeared on one side, and a ship's prow, perhaps signifying Rome's decisive victory over the Latins at Antium in 341 B.C. when it secured its supremacy in Italy, appeared on the other. Eventually the *as* underwent several reductions in weight.

Soon Rome's expansion brought the young state into contact with the cities of Magna Graecia in southern Italy, and especially with Tarentum, a Greek colony noted for its well-developed monetary system. Rome soon found that its cumbersome bronze money was inadequate, especially in time of war, and was forced to introduce a silver coinage that was entirely patterned after coinages of Magna Graecia. The coins were minted on Rome's behalf by certain cities in Campania, a region in southwestern Italy. For this reason Rome's early silver coins are called the Romano-Campanian series. These coins, with a value of two *drachms*, are particularly beautiful and entirely Greek in character. Their images — a helmeted bearded Mars and a handsome young Apollo, with a classical profile — are strongly reminiscent of Greek coinages. The images on the later coins — a young Hercules, a helmeted young Mars, and a fierce Bellona — show a more pronounced Roman character. One single two-*drachm* coin bears a scene drawn from the Roman legend that tells of the founding of Rome: the figure of a she-wolf is shown suckling Romulus and Remus. Evidently the design was derived from the famous bronze statue that graced the Capitol in Rome more than two millennia ago and is still in existence.

Romano-Campanian silver coinage seems to have been introduced at some time around 269 B.C., shortly before Rome came face to face with its most tenacious enemy: Carthage. A few decades later Rome decided to increase its silver supply by striking a new *didrachm* or *nummus*, called a *quadrigatus*, a name derived from a quadriga (chariot with four horses abreast), driven by Jupiter, shown on the coin. This forceful image represented the new Roman confidence gained in their first war with Carthage. At the same time, the rather complex Roman bronze coinage was still being issued in many denominations, and the *as* was eventually reduced in weight from one

69. *Cast bronze as showing Janus, the two-faced god, beginner of all things, and patron who taught the Romans devotion to laws and justice (222-215 B.C.). 62 mm.*

pound to one ounce, while the bronze coins were not cast but struck. Years later, during a particularly difficult phase of the Carthaginian wars, Rome introduced a new silver coin, the "victoriatus," called after its reverse image: Victory crowning a trophy.

It was, however, a later minting in silver — the *denarius* — that was destined to become the pillar of both the republican and imperial Roman monetary systems. The coin contained approximately 4.5 grams of silver, was equal in value to ten *asses* and was marked with the Roman numeral X. Two other silver coins were associated with the *denarius*: a half-*denarius* known as the *quinarius*, marked with the Roman numeral V, and a quarter-*denarius*, known as the *sestertius*. The helmeted head of a goddess appears on the front of the *denarius*; it is generally taken to be the likeness of Roma or Bellona, the victorious war goddess of Rome. The reverse of the coin shows the "heavenly twins" of Greek myth: the Dioscuri, Castor and Pollux.

During the second century B.C. moneyers became more conscious of their responsibilities and started signing their issues, at first with initials or monograms, and later with complete names. As the bronze coinage of Rome became more and more devalued, the equivalence of the *denarius* rose from ten *asses* to 16; the numeral X on the coin was changed to the numeral XVI. The design of the coin was also changed. The Dioscuri were replaced by the image of a racing chariot, on some coins driven by Jupiter and on others by Mars or Hercules. Later the reverse of the *denarius* was adapted to convey a "story," a more complex scene, with a narrative element. These images bring us into close contact with the enormous wealth of Roman lore, transmitted

70. *Horse's head on a silver didrachm struck by the Roman Republic, early 3rd century B.C.*

71. *Among the coins of the early Roman Republic were the silver* quadrigatus *and various fractional bronze coins, of which the* uncia *and* semuncia *were the smallest (222-187 B.C.). quadrig.: 21 mm.*

72. *The Roman Republican* denarius, *marked with an X indicating its value of 10 asses, its half or* quinarius, *marked with a V or five, and its quarter or* sestertius, *indicated by an IIS. Largest: 19 mm, smallest: 12 mm.*

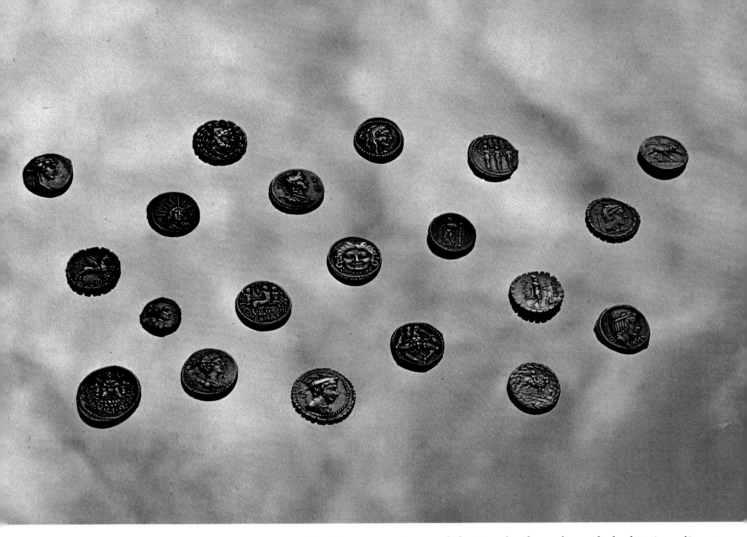

73. The Roman Pantheon included local divinities in addition to the many gods taken over from the Greeks, for example: kind nymphs and sibyls; fearsome monsters: centaurs, griffins and the terrifying Medusa. Aver.: 20 mm.

to us, not in the reserved way of the Greeks through symbols, but in a direct, colorful picture-language.

Gods, Monsters, and Myths of Rome

The coinage of republican Rome is one of the most amazing picture books of Roman mythology. By issuing coins with divine images, Romans honored the gods and hopefully placed themselves under divine protection. Such strong personalities as Caesar or Pompey were convinced that they acted under the guidance of patron-divinities. Jupiter was often represented as a victory-image driving a four-horse chariot and holding a scepter. Jupiter's consort, Juno (the Greek Hera), was represented on many Roman coins as Juno Moneta, protectrice of the Roman mint (the mint was housed in her temple).

Apollo, the patron of music and poetry, was as popular in Rome as in Greece. A Roman coin of 41 B.C. shows the god's head much as Greek coins did, with his long hair wreathed in laurel. Apollo's sister, Diana (the Greek Artemis), is often shown on coins as Diana Lucifera, "the bearer of light," or as the moon goddess, Luna, who guided mortals during the dark of night. In this role the virgin huntress carries two lighted torches instead of her usual bow and quiver.

The Romans also made Hercules, the guardian of Greek Tarentum, their own. He is shown on a *denarius* struck in about 100 B.C. accomplishing the first of his labors by strangling the Nemean lion. Mars, too, was often invoked by the belligerent Romans; shown as a helmeted youth, his image graces many coins. The divine patron of smiths, Vulcan, whose metallurgical skills would surely have allied him to those who mint coins, also appears. On a coin of about 101 B.C., he is seen wearing a conical cap and placed behind his head are a pair of pincers for handling red-hot metal. These are only a few of the divinities whose images appeared on the coins of Republican Rome.

Classical myth describes almost as many monsters as gods and goddesses. One such monster, with a human body that ends in a pair of fish tails in lieu of legs, has been identified as the fearsome Typhon whose life was ended by a shower of Jupiter's thunderbolts. A coin of republican Rome showing the monster's death at Jupiter's hand may have alluded to Caesar's power, the equal of Jupiter's in defeating a monstrous enemy of the fatherland, the army of Pompey. Other mythological monsters and marvels often appeared on the *denarii* of the Roman Republic. Among them were centaurs, griffins,

the dreaded Gorgo, Medusa, and the hideous pair of monsters, Scylla and Charybdis, who reputedly took a terrible toll of the seafarers passing through the Strait of Messina. The coinage also recorded legendary stories of Rome's past. For example, it is told of Romulus and Remus that the twins were found under a fig tree by the shepherd Fostulus as they were being suckled by a she-wolf. A *denarius* of the second century B.C. depicts the legend in a charming composition showing the twins, the shepherd, the wolf, and even the fig tree. Two other interesting legends depicted the rape of the Sabine women and the death of the treacherous Tarpea who opened the gates of Rome to the enemy in exchange for their golden armbands.

74. Many fascinating legends of Rome's early beginnings were illustrated on the denarii of the Republic such as the founding of Rome, the augury predicting Romulus' success, the rape of the Sabine women and the punishment of the treacherous Tarpeia. Aver.: 20 mm.

A Chronicle in Silver

Although the Roman coin engraver was artistically inferior to the Greek, he was one of the most skillful storytellers in the art of miniature bas-relief. The Republican *denarius,* a rather small silver coin, was entrusted with the task of memorializing important events in Roman history, and as a consequence, the coins comprise a veritable chronicle in silver. Romans rarely allude to contemporary events in their early coinages. The coins' account of Rome's rise is, of course, somewhat distorted, giving us the impression that Rome emerged almost effortlessly to grandeur and power. For example, the many humiliations suffered in the long struggle with Carthage, the battle-fields abandoned and the bitter truces accepted, all go unrecorded on the coinage.

75. Wars played a decisive role in Rome's growth. Moneyers often depicted important past deeds on their coins showing their belligerent neighbor King Bituitus of the Averni and the audacious Vercingetorix; Sulla accepting the submission of foreign kings; Pompey's wreaths received for his victories in three continents; and a rebellious slave being punished by flailing. Aver. 20 mm.

What is shown of the Punic Wars, instead, is the novel weaponry that the Carthaginians brought into battle. One hundred and twenty of Hasdrubal's elephants were captured by the Romans in Sicily; L. Caecilius Metellus brought them back to Rome to parade in his triumph. More than 100 years later, a member of the Caecilia family issued two *denarii* that proudly show elephants. On one, Jupiter, crowned by Victory, is in an elephant-driven chariot, while on the other the head of an elephant, seen beneath a chariot driven by *Pax* ("Peace"), may symbolize the peaceful conclusion of the first Punic War.

Rome's enemies to the north were also memorialized in the coinage of the

Republic. An example is the victory in 121 B.C. over Bituitus, ruler of the Arverni, a Celtic tribe, who, it was said, had huge dogs brought into the battle. A son of the Roman consul who conquered Bituitus issued a coin showing a warrior fighting a dog almost his own size. The conquest of Gaul was completed by Julius Caesar after many years of battle. The last Gallic resistance, under Vercingetorix, was finally broken in 52 B.C. Vercingetorix was eventually executed in Rome; his probable image, with an energetic but gaunt face, bearded and with loose-flowing hair, appears on *denarii* minted at this time. Caesar, too, had coins struck for this event (50-49 B.C.). They display a trophy of Gallic arms, distinguishable as such by the inclusion of a battle-axe and a typical Gallic war trumpet, and a bearded figure, hair flowing wild, evidently meant to be a vanquished Gaul. The man crouches at the foot of the trophy, his hands tied behind his back.

The alliance of the ruler of Macedonia with Rome's traditional foe, Carthage, brought the legions to Greece. Several Roman coins record the events of this war that won for Rome enormous booty in art, in treasure, and in slaves. One *denarius* memorializes the Roman sea victory at Aegina and the sale at auction of the Greek war prisoners whose fellow citizens later bought back their liberty. A series of *denarii* displays the figures of the nine Muses; their statues were brought to Rome as loot and were used to adorn a temple, dedicated to Hercules and the Muses, that M. Fulvius Nobilior built in Rome.

After previous defeats and humiliating treaties, the young Macedonian king, Perseus (179-168 B.C.), prepared for war but suffered a crushing defeat once again by the Romans in 168 B.C. The proud king and his two sons were captured and forced to march in the triumph of the victorious L. Aemilius Paullus. A coin issued in 55 B.C. depicted Perseus with his hands tied, his two sons facing the victorious Roman in front of a military trophy.

Roman arms destroyed the ambitions of more than one Greek ruler. Antiochus III of Syria had successfully waged war against his neighbors and enlarged his kingdom. When he turned toward Egypt, whose infant king, Ptolemy V, was under the protection of Rome, he erred fatally. In 190 B.C. in Asia Minor, Lucius Cornelius Scipio, brother of Scipio Africanus, completely destroyed the armies of Antiochus at Magnesia ad Sipylum. Scipio's triumph is said to have revealed to the people of Rome for the first time the immense riches of the Orient; according to the historian Pliny it was this war that introduced luxury into Italy. All these events were in due course recorded on coins. For example, a *denarius* minted in 66 B.C. by the young Marcus Aemilius Lepidus (who was later to share the triumvirate with Caesar and Pompey) shows one of his ancestors offering his protective hand to young King Ptolemy.

Republican generals celebrated their victories with great splendor. In 53 B.C. the powerful army of Marcus Licinius Crassus, a triumvir with Caesar and Pompey, and therefore one of Rome's magnates, was totally defeated by the king of Parthia. Proud Crassus was put to death. The year before this tragic event, Crassus's son issued a coin showing a fully armed, mounted warrior, one of the ill-fated horsemen who had enrolled in Gaul for his father's campaign. Pompey's son-in-law struck many coins devoted to Pompey's honor. One displays a terrestrial globe, surmounted by four wreaths; three of the wreaths refer to Pompey's victories in three continents — *Ex Europa, Ex*

76. Events of everyday Roman life often found their place on coins: corn-distribution to the population of Rome; casting of a vote-tablet into a basket; the passing of a law which protected civilians against military magistrates. Aver.: 20 mm.

77. Coining implements shown on a denarius of 45 B.C.: an anvil between a pair of pincers and a hammer topped by the cap of Vulcanus, the god of fire and patron of the smiths. 20 mm.

78. Sumptuous buildings of ancient Rome depicted on coins: (from left to right) the aque-
duct of the aqua Marcia; a sanctuary to the
Sabine goddess of love Venus Cloacina; the
splendid temple of Jupiter; the round temple
of Vesta; the Villa Publica, a guest-house for
foreign dignitaries; and the temple of Venus
erected on a mountain top in Eryx, Sicily:
the background drawing is by G. da Sangallo
(1445-1516) of the Basilica Aemilia. Aver.: 20
mm.

Africa, and *Ex Asia* — and the fourth represents the jeweled golden chaplet
conferred upon him by the Senate in 63 B.C.

Arabia was a province added to Rome by Pompey's arms, and the Arabian
king, Aretas, was forced to pay heavy tribute. Pompey's delegate in Arabia
had coins struck for the public games held there in 58 B.C. One of these
shows King Aretas in a posture of submission, kneeling beside a camel; it is
notable as the first coin known to record an almost contemporaneous event.

Roman Republican coinage is unique in that it provides such excellent
sources for the study of everyday life. The moneyers tried to depict whatever occupied the minds of their constituency: voting, public games in the
arena, horse races, and other contests in honor of such divinities as Apollo,
Saturn, Flora, and others.

A series of ancient Roman buildings were represented on coins. Two *denarii*
showed the most venerated of all Roman temples: Jupiter's. Among others
are the Basilica Aemilia, which served as a court of law and a meeting place
for merchants; the Villa Publica, a guesthouse for foreign dignitaries; aque-
ducts, columns, monuments, and wells.

Roman Minting

65   A coin of 45 B.C., honoring Juno in her role as mint-mistress, Juno Moneta,

shows on one side some of the implements used in coining: an anvil, a pair of tongs, and a hammer, along with the distinctive cap worn by Vulcan, the god of fire and metalworking. Juno was patroness of the mint, and Rome's coins were struck in a building attached to her temple on the Capitol. The office of moneyer was held by young members of the leading families of Rome at the beginning of their political careers. Often, the designs they selected for the coins served to draw the attention of the plebeian masses to the merits of the youths' respective families.

The coins of Rome bore numerous markings to indicate the authority responsible for their issue. Some were marked "EX S.C.," or "S.C.," meaning that the issue was authorized by the Senate: *Ex Senatus Consulto*. Other coins carried the letters, "EX A.P.," or only "A.P.," indicating that the silver for the coins had been drawn from the public treasury, that is, *ex argento publico*, and not supplied in the usual way by minting contractors who bought their bullion on the free market. The actual labor at the mint — casting coin blanks and striking the designs onto the blanks — was done by a staff of slaves owned by the state and supervised by a freedman. The dies were cut by trained artisans, in many instances Greeks versed in the art. With the exception of the earliest issues of heavy bronze, which were cast, all Roman coins were produced by striking.

Counterfeiting was a problem in Rome. Some supposedly silver coins actually consisted of copper cores covered with no more than a thin layer of sil-

79. Julius Caesar's story on coins: (from left to right) his patron-goddess Venus; the portrait of his opponent Pompey the Great (106-48 B.C.); Caesar's own portrait issued one year after his death; his follower Mark Anthony (83-30 B.C.); the elephant symbolizing Caesar's power to annihilate his enemies; his implements as supreme pontiff; the head of Vercingetorix; and the trophy commemorating his victories in Gaul. Aver.: 19 mm.

80. Denarius struck in Greece, 43-42 B.C., by Marcus Junius Brutus, one of Caesar's assassins; the reverse depicts two of the fatal daggers flanking the cap of liberty. 20 mm.

ver. Early in the first century B.C., counterfeiting was so prevalent that public confidence in the coinage became badly shaken. Punch marks were then introduced as a means of demonstrating whether or not a coin had a copper core. Soon *denarii* with serrated or dented edges were issued. This innovation, in a sense a precursor of the milled edges of modern coins, might have deterred counterfeiters, although some serrated *denarii* have been discovered to be counterfeits with copper cores.

From Triumvirate to Principate

The great Roman civil wars that began in 49 B.C. immensely enlivened the coinage of Rome. Many of the contestants were forced to issue their own coins to pay their troops, and often these coins were struck far from the Eternal City. The coins, moreover, were supposed to popularize each cause, especially among the soldiers who received them as pay. In consequence special care was given to the imagery on those coins.

The principal figures in the civil wars were Pompey the Great; his two sons, Gnaeus and Sextus Pompeius; his colleague, Julius Caesar; the third triumvir, Marcus Aemilius Lepidus; Caesar's then favorite, Marcus Antonius (better known in English as Mark Antony); Caesar's erstwhile favorite, Marcus Junius Brutus; the brother of Brutus, Decimus; a fellow conspirator, Gaius Cassius Longinus; another conspirator, S. Casca Longus; and Caesar's adopted heir, Octavianus. The individual coinages they authorized must

83. Emperor Claudius (41-54 A.D.) seen within the walls of the camp of the Praetorian guards, thus acknowledging the fact of his election by them; aureus, A.D. 44-45. 19 mm.

have been numberless, and only a small selection from among these can be discussed here.

Caesar first defeated Pompey at Pharsalus in Greece in 48 B.C. The battle cry of Caesar's troops was "Venus Victrix," and a coin that was struck by Caesar after the victory depicts the head of his divine protectress. (Why Venus? Students of Virgil will recall that Aeneas, the supposed Trojan immigrant-colonist of Italy, was born of a union between Venus and his royal father; Caesar's family claimed its descent from Aeneas.)

Pompey had been a brilliant strategist; when given the task of clearing the Mediterranean of pirates, he swept the sea free of them in barely a month's time. One particularly fine coin portrait depicts the great Pompey as unflattering history describes him: boring, dry, dignified, and formal. Pompey's sons, Gnaeus and Sextus, struck coins that memorialized their own careers. Some of them depict the head of Neptune, the god that granted them victory at sea. Others show the famous lighthouse of Messina, and an image of Scylla, the monster who, legend claims, imperils the Strait of Messina jointly with the monster Charybdis.

"On the Ides of March I devoted my life to my country, and since then I have lived another life which is free and glorious, for her sake." These are Brutus's words spoken after Caesar's assassination as reported by Plutarch. On a coin he had struck in Greece almost two years after Caesar's assassination, Brutus had his portrait placed on one side; on the reverse are seen two of the daggers used by the assassins, flanking a liberty cap. A contemporary

84. Roman coin portraits attained a high degree of artistic accomplishment under Emperor Nero (A.D. 54-68) who considered himself a great artist; bronze . 30 mm.

85. Judaea capta — the conquest of Judaea by Vespasian (69-79 A.D.) and Titus (A.D. 79-81) was widely commemorated on coins; denarii struck by both emperors depicted captive Jews and Jewesses at the foot of trophies constructed from their captured weapons. Larger coins: 28 mm., smaller coins: 18 mm.

86. *Victory recording the glorious conquest of Dacia by Emperor Trajan (A.D. 98-117) as seen on the column erected in Rome and on a silver denarius; other denarii show the column; a military trophy with the enemy weapons; and the subdued province mourning. Aver.: 19 mm.*

account states that Brutus struck these coins "to show that . . . he had in concert with his fellow conspirator Cassius given liberty to his country." Another coin struck by Brutus similarly documents this belief. On a *denarius* he and Casca issued in Greece is shown a Victory triumphant over tyranny, a broken diadem in her hands and a smashed scepter at her feet. Only a few months after the coins were struck, the forces of Brutus and Cassius were defeated at Philippi (42 B.C.). The surviving conspirators then put an end to their own lives.

The robust, slightly vulgar face of Mark Antony, not without the charm of carefree character, appears on a series of coins the great general had struck, either in his own name or together with his colleagues in the second triumvirate, Lepidus and Octavianus. As he is seen on one *denarius*, wearing a slight beard and with his head veiled, both signs of mourning for Caesar, may be exactly the way the people of Rome saw him when, standing beside Caesar's bier in the Forum, Antony delivered his celebrated funeral oration. The coins that bear testimony to Mark Antony's many deeds tell also of his ventures in Egypt. A *denarius* struck in Asia Minor carries on one side a portrait of Antony and on the other a portrait of Cleopatra. The artist who cut the dies for this coin was evidently not particularly fond of either figure; Antony's face shows a caricature of a grin, and Cleopatra's profile is sharp, almost birdlike.

The last chapter in Antony's life, the decisive sea battle at Actium in 31 B.C. that witnessed Octavianus's triumph over the alliance between Antony and Cleopatra, involved extensive preparations. Antony had minted an enormous

87. Head of one of the most enlightened men to achieve the throne of Rome, Emperor Hadrian (A.D. 117-138) who made long and exhausting trips to most of his far-off provinces; aureus. 20 mm.

88. Emperor Marcus Aurelius (A.D. 161-180) was not only an eminent philosopher but also a victorious general. His victory over Germanic tribes was commemorated on coins. Bronze sestertius with German captives, (A.D. 172-173), as well as the column erected to him which still stands in the center of Rome, seen here in an engraving by G. B. Piranesi of the mid-1700s. Bronze coin: 33 mm.

89. A gallery of imperial ladies; wives, daughters, mothers and even grandmothers of ruling emperors. Background stucco from Pompeii. Large green coin: 30 mm. ▷

quantity of coins, the so-called legionary *denarii*. On one side appeared a war galley and on the other three Roman military standards. The issues carried names and numbers of 30 separate legions, equivalent to a force of 180,000 men. The great wealth represented by these coins did not secure victory for Antony, but they have contributed to the perpetuation of his memory; to this day they remain among the most frequently discovered Roman Republican coins.

90. Four rulers of the Roman Empire: Nero (A.D. 54-68); Marcus Aurelius (A.D. 161-180); Maximianus I (A.D. 286-305); and Constantius II (A.D. 337-361). First: 20 mm.

Coins of the Empire

One of the first acts of Octavianus, called Augustus on his accession to power, was to establish a centrally administered system of money issuance; it was a key element in his system of centralized control. Augustus had to challenge the authority of the senators to achieve his goal. To avoid an open clash, he left the authority to issue bronze coins under senatorial control. As a result the bronze coins issued in Imperial Rome, from the time of Augustus to that of the Emperor Gallienus (A.D. 253-268) carry with rare exceptions the letters "S.C." (*Senatus Consulto*), indicating that they were struck by authority of the Senate. The important coins — silver and gold — were issued under the authority of Augustus.

The features of the Emperor Augustus appeared on most of the coins of Rome for more than 40 years. We hear from Suetonius that the emperor's "outward appearance was distinguished by remarkable beauty and always by extreme grace." His many coin portraits continued almost unchanged over the years; the head we see is that of a young man with regular, fine features but an aloof, impersonal expression. The coins do more than display the portrait of Augustus; many illustrate the important events of his reign. A crocodile was the symbol used to confirm his conquest of Egypt — *Aegyptus capta*. A tiara and a bow, quiver, and arrows from Armenia refer to the submission of that mountainous principality. The emperor's agreement with the king of Parthia, which obtained the return of the Roman legionary standards seized from the fallen Crassus in 53 B.C., was greatly celebrated in a number of mintings. One of these shows a kneeling Parthian

91. Portrait of Emperor Severus Alexander (A.D. 222-235) on a bronze sestertius which acquired an aqua-colored patina over the centuries. 28 mm.

92. Julia Maesa (died A.D. 225) was politically very active during the rule of her grandsons Emperors Elagabalus and Severus Alexander; sestertius struck under Elagabalus (A.D. 218-222). 30 mm.

and another the circular Temple of Mars that Augustus had built in Rome to house the long-lost standards.

After ruling for more than four decades Augustus died in A.D. 14 at the age of 77. The coins of his successors continued to illustrate imperial history. The Emperor Claudius (A.D. 41-54), for example, transformed Britain into a Roman province. A silver *denarius* struck in A.D. 46 shows the triumphal arch raised in Rome to commemorate the event. His successor, the Emperor Nero (A.D. 54-68), ordered the minting of a large bronze *sestertius,* showing a bird's-eye view of the harbor of Ostia, built by his predecessor. The scene includes the harbor lighthouse, the surrounding buildings, ships coming into port, and a figure symbolic of the River Tiber.

The system established by Augustus was continued by his successors almost unchanged, except that, a few decades after Augustus's death, the minting of the imperial coinage was moved back to Rome and thereafter most Roman coins were struck at the Capitol. The greater part of the operation, as in Republican days, was in the hands of slaves or freedmen; these "unskilled" workers included casters, trimmers, strikers, and those who held the dies in position for striking. In addition the mint employed skilled die engravers and supervisors, and a superintendent oversaw the entire operation. During the late empire, such "moneyers," as they came to be known, formed a hereditary caste, the post passing from father to son. The supply of raw metal was drawn from mines or from old coins that were melted down. Often procurement of the bullion was assigned to contractors who even undertook to cast the blanks for the coins. Accountants kept the mint books,

and state bankers, or *nummularii,* called in obsolete coins and distributed new ones.

Aesthetically the coins of Imperial Rome excelled in fine portraiture. The artists concentrated on the facial features of various emperors. The Roman portraits are characterized by a strong touch of realism, a tradition that encouraged the artists to try to capture the personalities of their imperial models. It may not be merely a coincidence that under Nero, a tyrant who nonetheless greatly admired things Greek and considered himself a great artist, the imperial coinage reached its artistic apogee.

Initially, the imperial coinage had as its highest unit the gold *aureus,* a coin that weighed about 7.96 grams and was valued at 25 *denarii.* A second gold coin, the *quinarius,* was half the value of the *aureus.* The gold used for both coins was almost pure, not alloyed with lesser metals. Gold was issued in very large amounts and together with the silver *denarius* soon was accepted as a world coinage. The silver coinage consisted of *denarii* and their halves, the *quinarii.* A subsidiary coinage of bronze and brass consisted of *sestertii, dupondii,* and *asses.* To help distinguish between the *dupondius* and the *as,* which were about the same size, the portrait of the emperor, (which both coins bore) appeared on the *dupondius* wearing a crown of rays, like an immortal.

The Augustan system remained unchanged until the time of Nero, although unofficially the weight of the *aureus* and of the *denarius* was gradually reduced. To keep pace with inflationary trends, Nero in A.D. 64 lowered both the gold and silver coinage in weight and the purity of the metal. The debasement of the *denarius* which was only some 10 per cent in Nero's time, steadily increased under his successors; by the turn of the second century its value had fallen nearly 40 per cent.

In A.D. 215 the Emperor Caracalla further reduced the value of the *aureus* and minted a new silver coin valued at two *denarii* and therefore it was called an "antoninianus" (one of the emperor's names was Antoninus). By the middle of the third century the *antoninianus* had completely replaced the *denarius,* and by the time of Emperor Gallienus (A.D. 253-268) the only silver left in the coins was a thin surface wash, so that the *antoninianus* was barely distinguishable from a copper piece. As for gold, by the second half of the third century coins made of gold were for the most part issued only to buy the loyalty of the troops. Gifts of money to the army had increased steadily in imperial times, and the soldiers considered such payments rightful recompense. These expenses and the distribution of food and money to the plebeians of Rome contributed greatly to the draining of the Empire's resources. The cry of the City mob — *"panem et circenses"* — ultimately was to bring Imperial Rome to the brink of bankruptcy.

Flavius Vespasianus, a man of humble origin but a brave general, had distinguished himself under Nero by quelling a rebellion in Judaea. As emperor, Vespasian and his son Titus celebrated a triumph that showed the people of Rome the riches of conquered Jerusalem. Gold, silver, and bronze coins were struck, announcing to the world that Judea had been defeated (*Judaea devicta*) and captured (*Judaea capta*). Most of the coins showed a palm tree and, at its base, a Jewess, symbolizing the province, and a standing captive Jew, mourning beside a heap of arms.

94. *Small bronze coin (c. 317-337) with the youthful bust of the Caesar Constantine II, son of Constantine the Great, holding globe surmounted by Victory which crowns him. 20 mm.*

93. *Constantine the Great (A.D. 307-337) and his family. Surrounding his colossal marble head are coins struck by Constantine, his father Constantius Chlorus (lower right side) and his son Constantine (second at left). Below are coins of Licinius I, his brother-in-law; Helena, his mother; Fausta, his wife; and Crispus and Constantine, his sons. Aver.: 20 mm.*

Two later emperors, Trajan (A.D. 98-117) and Hadrian (A.D. 117-138), ruled during one of Rome's most brilliant periods, and once again history was reflected in a rich and varied coinage. The gold and silver coins of Trajan's day not only celebrated his victories over the Dacians but also recorded his feats of peace, most notably his construction of the Forum of Trajan, the Basilica Ulpia, and the Hippodrome, or Circus Maximus, the scene of one of Rome's most popular amusements, chariot racing. A bronze coin, struck by the order of the Senate, gives us an excellent picture of the Hippodrome, its walls supported by arches, the great obelisk in its center, and its *metae*, or "goal pillars." Trajan's successor, Hadrian, was perhaps the foremost lover of Greek culture to rule in Rome. The coins struck during his reign, particularly a series dedicated to the various provinces of the empire, reflect this philhellene's humanitarian ideals.

The year A.D. 193 was one of infamy in Roman history, but it is notable from the numismatic viewpoint. This was the year when the men of the Praetorian Guard assassinated the Emperor Pertinax after a rule that had lasted only three months and 25 days, and then put the imperial throne up at auction. The highest bidder, M. Didius Julianus, promised to pay 6,200 *denarii* to each man of the Praetorian Guard. It was no very great bargain: the reign of Didius

95. Late Roman coins tried to present the emperor as supporter of Christendom, holding the standard with Christ's monogram, and as defender of the empire by showing him setting his foot on a fallen enemy while holding a Victory; gold solidus of Arcadius (A.D. 383-408). 21 mm.

lasted only 66 days. Within that brief time, however, the imperial mints somehow were able to strike 19 different kinds of coins that portrayed Didius and another 12 kinds either his wife, Manlia Scantilla, or his daughter, Didia Clara. The brashness of the coins' inscriptions is amazing; one of the coinages grants Didius the epithet *Rector Orbis* — "leader of the world." The design shows the short-lived emperor holding a terrestrial globe.

The high priest of the Syrian sun-god, Heliogabalus, was the cousin of an emperor mentioned earlier — Caracalla (A.D. 211-217) — and followed Caracalla on the throne at the tender age of 14. The youth ruled for four years under the name of Elagabalus. As the new emperor entered Rome, a conical black stone sacred to the Syrian deity was borne in his procession by a chariot yoked to milk-white horses; the stone was later housed in a temple on the Palatine Hill. The coinage of Elagabalus's rule depicts the black stone, "fallen from heaven," that the emperor worshipped, and also shows him in his pontifical robes, sacrificing at an altar; a star, placed above him, may symbolize the sacred sun.

Near the end of the third century A.D. the condition of the imperial Roman coinage approached the catastrophic when Emperor Diocletian (A.D. 284-305) intervened. He issued an edict on price ceilings—*De maximis pretiis*—in A.D. 301 in an effort to stem the rising cost of living by setting the top prices that could be demanded for various commodities; the edict imposed severe penalties on violators. Diocletian also undertook a reform of the coinage. The Senate was forbidden to mint coins, as were local and provincial authorities. All such coins were replaced by a unique imperial coinage, supplied by authorized mints throughout the empire. Each mint marked its coinage with the first letter or letters of its name; for example, "L" meant Londinum (modern London), "R" meant Rome.

In his reform Diocletian ordered the minting of gold coins that were quite pure in metal and exact in weight and equivalent to 25 silver coins each. The silver coin, also unalloyed, was first known as an *argenteus,* and later called a *siliqua.* Diocletian's bronze coinage came in three denominations; the largest, the *follis,* was about one inch in diameter. Bronze coins were raised in value beyond the worth of their metallic content by means of a very thin silver plating.

A scant decade later, in A.D. 312, the successor to Diocletian, Constantine I, expanded his predecessor's monetary system by adding a lighter gold coin, the *solidus* and its fractions, the *triens* and *semis.* The coins remained in use

96. Payment of land rent, Roman bas-relief (A.D. 2nd-3rd century), found near Trier, Germany.

97. Along the borders of the Roman Empire there were nations and tribes which struck autonomous coinages: (clockwise) on the Danube large silver coin struck by the Eastern Celts; in Asia, bronze coin from Judaea and a silver drachm from Arabia (1st century A.D.); in North Africa silver drachms of the Kings of Mauretania and Numidia (1st century B.C. – 1st century A.D.); in Spain large bronze coin from Obulco (Cordoba); in Britain low-silver drachm of the Celts. Large bronze Judaea: 30 mm.

well into later Byzantine times. The revival of gold and silver coinage in the fourth century may in part have been due to the supply of precious metal gained from the Christian takeover of "pagan" temples.

Under the continuous blows of assaulting enemies, fissures within the Roman state clearly forecast a formal partition of the old empire between an imperium of the west centered on Rome, and an imperium of the east with its capital at Constantinople, the city founded by Constantine on the remains of Greek Byzantium. The coinage of the late empire is basically different in concept from previous coinages. Although the early rulers of Rome were autocrats and tyrants, they lacked the godlike nature ascribed to them from the fourth century on, after the model of the Oriental potentates. Portraits of emperors become standardized, individual features being sacrificed for the exterior attributes.

The coinage of Constantine (the first Christian emperor as a consequence of a conversion on his deathbed) bore his bust, the head on some coins helmeted and on others crowned with laurels. The reverses of the coins gave evidence of the emperor's earlier beliefs; they often depicted a sun-god cult figure. In fact, it was some years before the new official state religion was represented on the coinage. The *labarum,* or imperial standard, raised only when the emperor himself was with the army, had been altered by Constantine by his adding the Greek monogram of Christ: the letters *chi* (X) and *rho* (P), flanked by an *alpha* (A) and *omega* (Ω), symbolizing "beginning" and "end." The image of the altered standard appears on coins struck by Constantine's successors. These emperors are seen holding a Victory figure in one hand, with the other hand supporting the *labarum.* In most instances the Victories on the coins were the only victories the later empire knew. The pagan goddess had served old Rome faithfully for centuries, but she had become elusive now, and the power of the empire traveled a downward path.

78

Coins of the Imperial Frontier

Along all the borders of Imperial Rome were found kings of nations and chieftains of tribes. Some were "clients" of the empire, or rulers who had accepted Rome's patronage and owed the empire a certain deference. Other rulers were only semi-dependent and still others were, at best, friends or neutrals. Throughout these frontier areas Roman gold and silver coins circulated widely. The coins of Augustus and his successor, Tiberius, have been found as far distant as Mysore and Travancore in India, the almost mythical land whence came precious stones and spices (above all, pepper), commodities in great demand among luxury-loving Romans. Long and perilous roads across the Caucasus led to northern Afghanistan, where traders could purchase the silks of China. A wealth of metal ores in Spain and in Britain first drew traders and at last the armies of Rome to these far regions.

Throughout the frontier there circulated a strange assortment of coins; not only were Roman coins to be found, but also local imitations of Roman coins and entirely independent local mintings. In Spain as early as the days of the Roman Republic, native silver coins with Iberian inscriptions were struck with the permission of Roman governors. Many of these attractive coins acquaint us with the names of Spanish tribes, such as the Celsitani or the Arsenses, and with place names such as Osca (modern Huesca) and Gades (modern Cadiz). Under the empire the practice continued, and many Spanish cities issued their own bronze coinages.

98. "The thirty pieces of silver" of Judas, medieval wallpainting in Puy Chalvin, France, and silver shekels struck in Tyre, Phoenicia, probably the coins used in the payment of Judas' betrayal money. Coin: 30 mm.

Gaul, a vast and turbulent area continuously at war with Rome until it became a Roman province in 42 B.C., and the Celtic tribal areas along the Rhine and Danube all used imitations of Greek coins, especially silver *tetradrachms* and gold *staters* of Philip and Alexander, in vast numbers. These adaptations often bore bizarre designs, highly interesting expressions of a primitive but vigorous art. Horses and riders, speeding chariots, and human heads stylized almost beyond recognition are the most frequently encountered motifs. Of particular interest among the coins of Gaul is a gold coin struck by the Arverni that bears a portrait and the name of Vercingetorix, the famous chieftain whose life was ended soon after he marched as a captive in Caesar's triumph at Rome. One gold coin of nearby Britain would not have put any Greek artisan to shame. It bears, in addition to the images of an ear of grain and a prancing horse, the name of Cunobelin (A.D. 5-40), a ruler in southeastern Britain. As Cymbeline, he was known both to Boccaccio and to Shakespeare, who based his play on Boccaccio's account of the early British king.

In Asia Minor and beyond, the rulers of many states advertised their relations with Rome by striking coins that combined their own portraits with those of the ruling Roman emperor. Princes of Thrace and kings of Cimmerian Bosporus farther to the east (the Crimea of today) were vassals of this kind. The Bosporan kings were even given the right to issue gold coins — the only gold coinage in the empire other than the imperial *aureus*. The Bosporus coins bear, in addition to the king's portrait, the likeness of the reigning Roman emperor.

The client kingdom of the Nabataeans in the northwest of Arabia was another state that maintained friendly relations with Rome. The Nabataeans controlled the route to southern Arabia, or *Arabia Felix*, whence came frankincense, a commodity in great demand in Rome. The silver coins of this kingdom bear the portraits and names of its kings and queens. The Semitic inscription on the coins struck by one Nabataean ruler, King Aretas IV (9

99. The images which adorn Judaean coins produced during the second revolt (A.D. 132-135): grape leaves, palm-trees and amphoras can also be found on capital-fragments from the Synagogue in Capernaum. Large bronze: 30 mm.

B.C.-A.D. 40), reads in translation "lover of his people." In those troubled days perhaps King Aretas was the only monarch who could sincerely publish such a claim.

Coins from the Land of the Bible

Judaea had a fairly long coining tradition going back to the 5th and 4th centuries B.C. before she became a client-kingdom during the reign of Herod the Great (37-4 B.C.). Herod tried to prove his loyalty to Rome by striking only bronze coins, inscribed with Greek letters. But in A.D. 6, during the rule of Herod's son, Herod Archelaus, Judea became a Roman province under the control of Roman procurators. These procurators kept to an earlier tradition, issuing small bronze pieces called by the Greek name *lepta*, or mites (the famous widow's mite of the Bible). Inscriptions indicating the name of the current Roman emperor, were in Greek. Designs tried to take into account the Mosaic sensitivity of the Jewish population to conform to the Law, and excluded, therefore, any portraits, concentrating instead on inanimate objects and symbols such as palm trees and cups. The coins of Pontius Pilate, Judaean procurator from A.D. 26-36, during the reign of Emperor Tiberius, are included in this group. Other coins directly connected with the life of Jesus circulated during those years. For example, the "tribute penny" which Christ referred to when he answered the Pharisees on whether it was lawful to pay tribute to Caesar by saying: "Render unto Caesar the things that are Caesar's and unto God the things that are God's," was a *denarius* of the Emperor Tiberius. Among the large silver coins which circulated in the eastern Mediterranean area during the first century A.D. were silver *tetradrachms* of Tyre showing the head of Hercules, Melkhart on one side and an eagle on the other. It was with these coins that Judas must have been paid his betrayal money, the thirty pieces of silver.

A revolt of the Jewish people broke out against Rome in A.D. 66. Jerusalem was destroyed, the Temple fell, and its treasures were carried away to Rome. During the four years of the war, the Jews issued a series of five silver coins — *shekels* and half *shekels*, as well as bronze coins — inscribed with the words: *yerushalayim hakedoshah* ("Jerusalem the Holy"), each bearing a numeral indicating in which year, since the beginning of the revolt, they were issued. Sixty years later, when Emperor Hadrian decided to build a Roman temple dedicated to Jupiter Capitolinus on the site of the old Temple, a new revolt broke out under the leadership of Simon Bar-Kochba, "Son of the Star." The war raged three years. Many coins with a rich iconography were struck in silver and bronze. Old Roman silver coins were used as a silver supply and were carelessly overstruck, often showing, under the new design, parts of former Roman coin images complete with portraits of emperors.

Large silver *tetradrachms* were issued as manifestoes depicting the façade of the Temple of Jerusalem which Bar-Kochba started to rebuild, showing the Torah shrine between the columns. The coins spoke of the freedom or redemption of Israel, but this dream was crushed by Hadrian's legions. The Jews were then dispersed throughout the world. A new Roman city, called Aelia Capitolina, was erected on the ruins of the Holy City, and the Jews were prohibited entrance under penalty of death. □

81

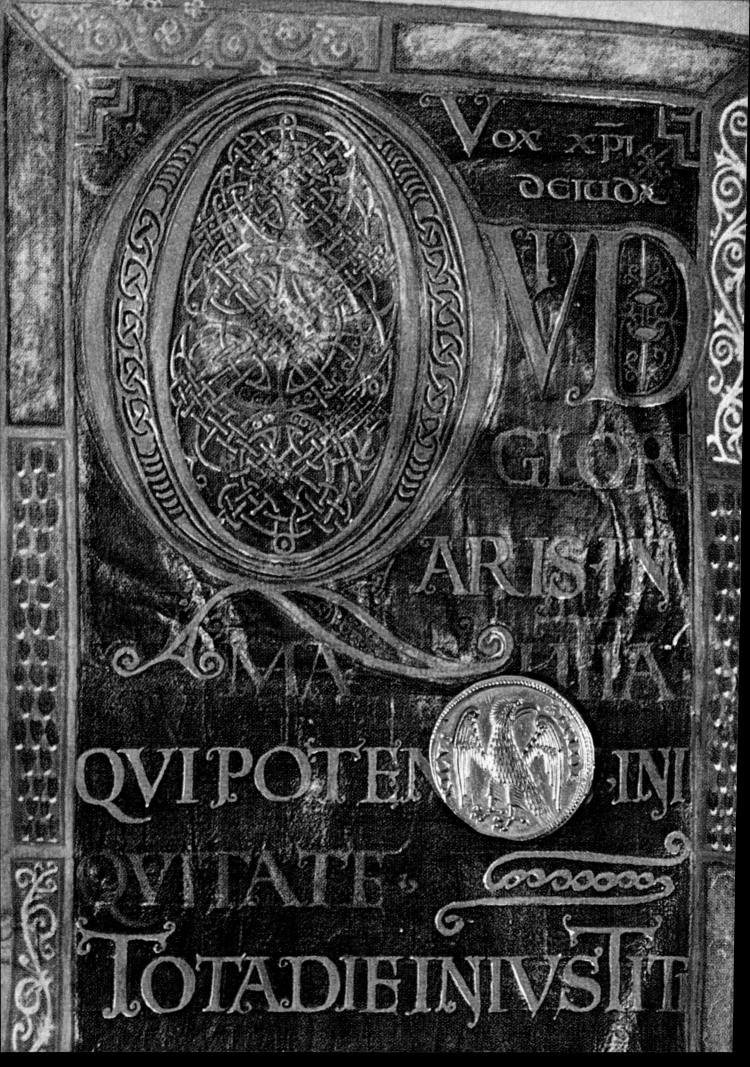

Dilexisti maliciam super be...

iniquitatem magisquam loq...

Dilexisti omnia uerba praeci...

lin guam dolosam:

Propterea ... destruet te in finem.

... migrauit te de taberna

co... em tuam de terra uiuentium, ...

Vide... ... & timebunt. & super

eum ridebunt & dicent. ecce homo

qui non po...

Sed speraui in multitudine diuitiarum

suarum. & praeualuit ... in uanitate sua.

Ego autem sicut oliua fructifera in domo

dei. speraui in misericordia ... ... mae

ternum & in saecu...

Confitebor tibi in sae... ... quia fecis

ti. & expectabo nomen tuum. quoniam

bonum in conspectu sanctorum tuorum.

IN FINEM PRO MELECH. INTELLE...

IV: MEDIEVAL COINS: IN SEARCH OF THE CITY OF GOD

A chaotic time when triumphant newcomers honored Roman law, Christian faith and the imperial artistic tradition.

Coins of the Byzantine Empire

Rome was slow in dying. While the empire in the west reeled beneath the onslaughts of successive invaders, the empire in the east — the Byzantine Empire — perpetuated the legacy of Rome in its own way. For example, the coins of the early emperors in the East continued to bear Latin inscriptions, and the use of Latin gave way to Greek only gradually. Even then, although the words were Greek, the emperor's title — *basileus Romaion* — still meant "King of the Romans."

The Byzantine Empire survived for a millennium and left behind a rich numismatic heritage. Yet the imposing sequence of imperial gold, silver, and bronze coins constitutes only a pale reflection of the empire's historical and artistic achievements. With few exceptions, the coins bore either a bust of the ruling emperor or showed him in full figure, in some instances accompanied by members of his family. For example, Constantine VI, who shared the rule with his mother, Irene, at the end of the eighth century, marked his coins not only with both their portraits but also with the figures of his father, Leo IV, his grandfather, Constantine V, and even his great-grandfather, Leo III. If Byzantine coin engravers had attempted, as did their Roman predecessors, to produce realistic portraits, the Byzantine coinage could divulge many intriguing secrets. From the very beginning, however, the images were conventional and symbolic instead. The coin design had essentially a two-dimensional character.

101. Large bronze coin of 40 nummia displaying the crowned bust of the Byzantine Emperor Justinianus I A.D. 539-540. 43 mm.

While the fragmented western empire entered a period of gold scarcity, the Byzantine Empire continued to mint gold coins. The late Roman gold *solidus* was the model followed; it was now usually called a *nomisma* or was sometimes known by a nickname such as *michalatus* if, as in this example, the *nomisma* had been struck by an emperor named Michael. When, as during the Crusades, these coins were brought to western Europe, they were known as *bezants,* that is, "coins of Byzantium." The *nomisma* kept its high gold content until the beginning of the eleventh century when it began to be degraded until it reached the level of an *electrum* coin. During the eleventh century strange, cup-shaped gold coins, called "scyphates" appeared.

Comparatively little silver was minted under the Byzantine Empire. One such coin, the *miliaresion,* was taken over from the Roman. Later in the seventh century a new heavy silver coin, the *hexagram,* did not stay in circulation for much longer than half a century. Silver and copper pieces of a very crude design were among the last issues of the empire. In 498 Emperor Anastasius I ordered a most important reform establishing a copper coinage which had to carry exact indications of value. Now, wide distribution of the coinage required a vast diffusion of minting facilities throughout the empire.

Justinian I (527-565) and his wife Theodora presided over perhaps the most brilliant period known to Byzantium. Close by the famous cathedral of Santa Sophia, which Justinian rebuilt after its destruction in 523, stood an

equestrian statue of this Christian emperor, helmeted and clad in military

102. The sumptuous costume of the Byzantine emperor. The richly embroidered long robe and the loros draped over his arm, the crown, and the orb are minutely depicted on this gold nomisma of Romanus III Argyrus (1028-1034). The Virgin is seen beside the emperor. 24 mm.

garb. "In his left hand he holds a globe," wrote a pious chronicler, "by which the sculptor signifies that the world and sea are subject to him, yet he has neither sword nor spear nor any other weapon, but a Cross stands upon the globe which he carries, the emblem by which he had obtained both his Empire and victory in war." Some of the coins minted for Justinian may have been inspired by this statue. They show him wearing a cuirass and a plumed helmet and holding an orb topped by a cross.

The rulers who followed Justinian, however, were weak or incompetent, and new wars with the Slavs, the Avars, the Lombards of Europe, and the Sasanians in Asia caused the empire great hardship. Large quantities of Byzantine gold were spent in buying off some of the enemies. The Avars received tribute, and Franks were hired as mercenary troops to oppose the advancing Lombards. Tiberius II Constantinus (578-582) sent the required fee to Chilperic, the king of the Franks; the gold was in the form of one-pound medallions, but none is known to have survived. Some remarkable changes took place in coin iconography after Justinian. Tiberius II had a cross shown on the reverse of the coins, possibly a Calvary Cross on Golgotha richly ornate with gold and precious stones. Byzantine coinage also showed sumptuous imperial costume, consisting of tunics or shirts and "loros," long, broad, richly embroidered scarves. The image of the emperor showed him holding, in his left hand, a scepter surmounted by an eagle and a cross; and in his right hand the "mappa," a folded piece of white cloth with which he would give the signal for the beginning of the arena games. His crown was encrusted with jewels and pearls and bore a cross on top with two long pendants hanging alongside his face.

103. Rex Regnantium — "King of Kings". By using His image, Byzantine emperors paid homage to Christ, considered the true guiding light of the empire. Gold and electrum nomismata of Nicephorus II Phocas (963-69); Romanus III (1028-34); Michael IV (1034-41); Alexius I (1081-1118); and John II (1118-43). Center coin: 34 mm.

In 685 Justinian II ascended the throne, and soon thereafter the figure of Christ appeared on Byzantine coins. He holds the Gospel and makes the sign of benediction; the Latin inscription, Rex Regnantium, "King of Kings," accompanies the image. The Emperor Leo III (717-741), known in history as a great reformer and outstanding soldier, nonetheless initiated a period of great internal dissension in Byzantium. In 726 he ordered all Christian images, so-called icons, removed and destroyed. Thus began the "iconoclastic controversy," supported by the army but otherwise strongly opposed. Uncounted works of art were destroyed; the recently introduced image of Christ was replaced by the busts of the rulers; only the Cross continued to be displayed on coins.

One hundred years later, the image of Christ once more appeared on Byzantine coins. It was not until the rule of the Emperor Leo VI (886-912), however, that the Virgin Mary appeared on a coin. She is seen with both hands raised in a typical posture of prayer. The simple but very graceful figure, wrapped in a mantle and shrouded by a plain Syrian veil, apparently was copied from one of the most popular religious images in Constantinople: the Virgin as special protectress of the imperial city. Representations of Christ, of the Virgin, and of various saints, either crowning or blessing the emperor, were now often copied from similar works of art and reproduced on coins. "Mother of God, full of glory, he who sets his hopes on thee shall never fail to prosper in his work." These were the fervent words that the Emperor John Zimisces (969-976) addressed to the Virgin Mary in thanks for his victory over the Russians in 972. He had the words, written in Greek, placed on the face of a silver coin that for the first time showed Mary holding

the infant Jesus. On a gold coin the same emperor ordered displayed another innovation; he is seen being crowned by the Virgin, while the "hand of God" reaches down from heaven to bless him.

The defeat of the Emperor Romanus IV Diogenes (1068-1071) by the Seljuk Turks at Manzikert dealt a terrible blow to the Byzantine Empire. It alerted Christendom in the west to the extreme dangers that the infidel represented. Although the Pope disagreed with Byzantium on religious grounds, he did what he could to induce the kings and princes of Europe to rally to its cause. Thus began the Crusades. Byzantium felt their impact as much as, if not more than, the advancing infidels did.

The Emperor Alexius I Comnenus (1081-1118) ably defended Byzantium from the Turks with the help of a newly reorganized army and adroit diplomacy. To meet the heavy demands on his realm, however, he had to adopt a ruthless monetary policy. He obtained bronze by melting down public monuments and multiplied the supply of gold coins by debasing their gold content. The gold *nomisma,* which had already undergone steady depreciation, was further debased. The coin was not struck flat but cup-shaped, the concave face bearing the imperial portrait. The coins of his successors, John II (1118-1143), Manuel I (1143-1180), and Andronicus I (1183-1185), had much in common with those of Alexius. Their cup-shaped gold and electrum *nomismata* displayed the figure of the emperor, being crowned by the Virgin, while on the other side appeared Christ enthroned. On some of the coins, saints — such as St. George, St. Theodore, or St. Demetrius — took the place of the Virgin.

The year 1204 proved nearly fatal to the empire; in April a force of knights from Europe, ostensibly en route to fight the "infidel" in Egypt, instead stormed and sacked Constantinople. Beyond the imperial city itself only a few small, far-flung components of the shattered Byzantine Empire, among them Trebizond on the Black Sea, continued to be viable. The Empire of Trebizond, which claimed authority over the Crimea, parts of the Caucasus, and the southern shore of the Black Sea, held out against the Turks until 1461. Trebizond developed its own coinage. One silver coin, called an *asper*, maintained the Byzantine tradition of showing the figure of the ruler along with that of a saint, but the style of execution was distinctly local. Later Trebizond pieces that show both saint and emperor on horseback may reflect Asian influences.

The lives of the last rulers of Byzantium were occupied by efforts to redress the defenses of Constantinople, by now the empire's last bastion and nearly its sole possession. They tried to rebuild the city's fortifications to withstand the inexorable advance of the Turks, who, by their conquests in Asia Minor and the Balkans, were closing an ever-tighter ring around the metropolis. Ironically, Byzantium was saved for a brief time not by help from other Christian states but by the wild hordes of the Mongols. In 1402, at the battle of Angora, the Mongol leader Tamerlane decisively defeated the Turks and thereby won Constantinople a temporary and unintended respite.

The Byzantine emperors, once proud "autocrats of the Romans," were now reduced to pathetic dimensions. They humbled themselves by seeking help from their Christian brothers in the west. The Emperor Manuel II (1391-1423) traveled to France and to the court of Henry IV of England; Emperor John VIII (1423-1448) visited Italy in 1438 to attend the Council of Ferrara. The coins of Byzantium's last centuries show how the old splendor had vanished. A contemporary chronicler declares: "The jewels in the crown were glass, the robes not real cloth-of-gold but tinsel, the dishes copper, while all that appeared to be rich brocade was now only painted leather." The cup-shaped *nomisma* was now of debased metal rather than gold, and quite

105. Gold nomisma showing the Emperor Andronicos II Palaelogus (1282-1328) on his knees imploring the blessings of Christ. 22 mm.

106. Silver groats displaying a cross and a city-gate, struck by the Norman princes of Tripolis (late 13th century), were exceptionally fine strikings compared to other deniers and obols issued by other Crusaders. The fine silver groats of the Grandmasters of the Order of St. John in Rhodes (14th century) and those issued in Cyprus by the Lusignan princes (13th — 14th century) have a special charm. First large: 25 mm., last: 28 mm.

crudely made. Coins from Venice and Genoa, were often the only reliable money to be had.

The last emperors of Byzantium had some silver and bronze coins minted. They were very crude, and their design seems as if it had been traced in clay by an old and shaky hand. One can dimly discern a bust of the emperor and a bust of Christ; these pathetic tokens were the final coins of a once glorious and mighty empire.

On May 30, 1453, the last emperor of Byzantium, Constantine XI, died among the defenders of the city. That same day the Turkish victor, Mohammed II (1430-1481) entered the city.

Coins of the Crusades

The Crusades began after the Saracens captured Jerusalem in 1071. Thousands of Christian believers fought to free the Holy Land and, after great sacrifices in blood and treasure, arrived at the gates of Jerusalem in 1099. Once triumphant, the Frankish princes established a number of principalities such as Edessa, Antioch, Jerusalem, and Tripoli. The coinages struck by these princes show the influence of many conflicting cultures and beliefs — French, Venetian, Byzantine, and Arab. Some issues were small, unassuming, base silver coins, *deniers* and *obols*, bearing a cross surrounded by a circular inscription. A few represented such famous landmarks as the Holy Sepulchre, the Tower of David, and the Temple of Jerusalem. The most attractive coins in this series are from Tripoli struck by the Norman Princes, Bohemund VI and Bohemund VII.

107. The so-called "Saracenic besants" struck by some Crusaders in the 13th century bore Arabic inscriptions expressing the Moslem profession of faith (left). Later they changed to the Christian profession but maintained Arabic letters. Sometimes a small cross was added in the center. Aver.: 22 mm.

90

The Crusader coinages include the so-called Saracenic *besants,* gold pieces struck by the Crusaders in Syria and Palestine imitating Arabic gold *dinars* and silver *dirhems,* ironically publicizing the Moslem profession of faith. Others carried statements of Christian belief although expressed in Arabic letters. These coins demonstrate once again the power of money: commercial interest proved stronger than the Crusaders' religious fervor.

Cyprus, the Mediterranean crossroads of this epic period, issued a fine silver *groat* from the late thirteenth to the fifteenth centuries. Rhodes issued one depicting a kneeling figure of the Grand Master of Rhodes in front of the Calvary Cross. These *groats* of Rhodes struck by the Order of St. John in Jerusalem memorialize the brave knights who dedicated their lives to the care of the sick and the wounded.

Coins from the Barbarian Invasions to the Fall of the Merovingian Dynasty

The year 1453 saw the eastern empire fall at last. Rome's western empire, of course, had fallen nearly 1,000 years earlier, in 476. In that year, Odoacer, leader of the Heruli (a Germanic tribe), deposed the last Roman emperor in the west, Romulus Augustulus. The western empire's defenses crumbled, and other "barbarous" tribes — Vandals, Ostrogoths, Visigoths, and Lombards — soon ruled over various fragments of the former Roman domain. The kingdoms that arose from the ruins of Rome nonetheless inherited a good part of the western empire's culture and even some of its administrative machinery.

The kingdoms' coinages give us a glimpse of a chaotic time when the triumphant newcomers continued to honor both Roman laws and customs and the imperial artistic traditions. The new rulers preserved Rome's monetary system and the iconography of the coinage. With one eye always turned toward Byzantium and the continuing power of the eastern empire, these "barbaric" kings produced coins that imitated late Roman and Byzantine models. The faces of such Byzantine emperors as Anastasius and Justinian (their names given in Latin) are seen on many of these coins. In general, some decades were to pass before these "barbaric" rulers placed their own images

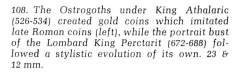

108. The Ostrogoths under King Athalaric (526-534) created gold coins which imitated late Roman coins (left), while the portrait bust of the Lombard King Perctarit (672-688) followed a stylistic evolution of its own. 23 & 12 mm.

and their names, in some cases only as a monogram, on the gold coins they issued.

Gold was relatively abundant in the West, often forming part of the tribute paid to the tribes by the emperors at Byzantium or being acquired during looting expeditions. The old Roman *solidus* and a smaller gold coin, the *tremissis* (one third of a *solidus* in value), were the chief denominations used. Theoderic, the Ostrogoth king (454?-526), ruled in central Italy after 493, with Ravenna as his capital. A ceremonial triple *solidus* shows Theoderic uncrowned but holding, in Roman fashion, a terrestrial globe topped by a Victory figure. The image probably reproduces one of the statues of the Ostrogoth ruler.

The Vandal kings also issued imitations of Roman *solidi* and lesser *tremisses* and put their own portraits and names on coins made of bronze and silver. The Vandal capital was Carthage, and certain ancient traditions, such as the representation of horses — animals greatly favored by the Phoenician goddess Tanit — on coins, were continued by the Vandal kings. One bronze coin bears a horse's head, for example, together with a figure symbolic of the ancient Punic city itself.

From the kingdom of the Visigoths, which endured in Spain for almost three centuries, come small gold *tremisses*, bearing the name of King Leovigild (572-586). A highly stylized image of his face appears on both sides of the coins. Stylistically related to the Visigoth coins are certain silver and gold coins minted by the Lombards, who established a powerful kingdom in northern Italy. On the reverse of the thin Lombard *tremissis* appears a winged figure that may represent their patron saint, the Archangel Michael.

The Byzantine sixth-century historian Procopius notes with indignation that the Franks "organized horse races . . . [and] struck [on metal] from the mines of Gaul a gold coin, and did not place on it the image of the Roman emperor, as it was customary, but their own." As Procopius points out, this was an act that not even the kings of Persia would have risked: "For that neither he (the Persian king) nor any other king of the barbarians had the right." Procopius was referring to a gold *solidus* issued by the Merovingian King Theodebert I (534-548). After entering Italy in 539 Theodebert issued coins that bore his face, in imitation of the Byzantine gold pieces minted by Emperor Justinian. The Frank added as an inscription his own name and the proud epithet "Victor."

109. The Merovingian small gold *triens* often depicted a highly stylized bust in profile and a Victory or a cross on the reverse side. 10 mm.

110. Charlemagne's name, written in the finely designed letters of the period, is often found on his coins. The Carolingian monogram is shown in the center of the coin. 17 mm.

111. Silver deniers of the French and German lands later changed their design, Churches were often used as motifs: (clockwise from top) France, Louis the Pious (814-40); Archbishop Hermann II of Cologne (1036-56); Siegfried of Soest (1275-97); denier of the Bishops of Munster (12th century); the deniers of Archbishop Thibaut of Vienne, France (952-1000) displayed a head in profile while a cross adorned those of Bertrand of Toulouse (1105-12). 17-19 mm.

112. The good silver content and the elegance of the French gros tournois, struck since 1266, induced other countries to imitate it: groats struck in Provence for Charles II (1307-09), in Cologne by Walram of Julich (1332-49) and in the cities of Metz and Basel (1499). Upper left: 25 mm.

113. The medieval gold coins of France and England often represent masterworks of Gothic art. Grouped around an English noble of Henry VI are (clockwise): a mouton d'or, (1354) and an ecu (1422-61), both of France; an angel of England; a leopard struck by the Black Prince for Aquitaine (1355-75); a salut d'or (1423) and a franc a cheval of John II (1360-1364), both from France. Upper center (lamb): 30 mm.

The Merovingian kings, imitating Romano-Byzantine coinage, issued small, one-third *solidi* designated a "trientes". These small and unassuming gold pieces carried a highly stylized and rather crudely executed profile of the ruler, associated with a Victory figure or, more often, with a cross. The minters who produced the coins followed the court in its peregrinations. Gradually the right to issue coins, heretofore entirely a ruler's close-guarded privilege, slipped out of the hands of the Frankish kings and was assumed by the principal nobles and prelates in the kingdom. Moneyers were recruited from among the goldsmiths of the country. As they saw the potential for profit, the moneyers also went into business on their own, striking coins when and where the need arose. Soon coins were being produced in important trading centers, at places of justice where fines had to be paid, and in the centers of authority where taxes were collected. The Merovingian gold *trientes* give evidence of the trend. Each was marked with the name of its minting place and that of its maker. The *trientes* that have come down to us bear the names of some 900 minting places and more than 2,000 moneyers.

The seventh century saw a decline in Merovingian power. Gold coins were gradually replaced by silver ones, and the trend accelerated after the opening of the rich silver mines at Melle in Poitou in western France. It was the *denarius,* a small silver coin exchanged at the rate of 40 for one *solidus,* that became the basic currency. Thus silver was introduced as the main coining metal of the Middle Ages.

114. High, French Gothic art is expressed in this gold coin struck since 1296 by King Philip IV. It was called masse d'or — "golden mace" from the mace or scepter topped by the "hand of justice" which is held by the enthroned king. 34 mm.

Carolingian Coins

The last Merovingian king, Childeric III, was deposed by Pepin the Short in 751. Crowned King of the Franks, Pepin founded the Carolingian dynasty. An outstanding ruler, he completely reorganized the coinage and brought minting once more under the authority of the crown. The names of the moneyers disappeared from the coins, and the number of mints was greatly reduced. Pepin introduced a new coin, the *denarius argenteus.* Popularly called the *denier,* it became the basic unit of medieval European coinage.

115. This bracteate, struck by the Margrave Dietrich of Meissen in Saxony (1197-1221), is indeed as thin as a leaf — bractea — as the profile-view shows. 41 mm.

Pepin put no images on his coins, but only inscriptions. Elegant Roman capital initials, signifying his titles, gave the thin but well-struck *denier* a handsome appearance. Occasionally some small symbols such as a cross, a star, a crosier, or the Frankish battle-axe was added to the basic design.

Under Pepin's son and successor, Charles the Great (Charlemagne), the work of Pepin continued. The coinage reform made 12 *deniers* equal to one silver *solidus* and 20 *solidi* equal to one pound of silver bullion. This relation of 12 smaller coins to one larger coin, and of 20 of the larger coins to one still larger unit, survived in the west for more than a thousand years; it came to an end only when England decimalized its *pence, shillings,* and *pounds* in the 1960s.

Charlemagne increased the weight of the *denier.* With the greater weight came a change in design: Charlemagne's own monogram and the cross became its main components, replacing the design on earlier coins that showed his monogram on one side and the name of the mint on the other.

Charlemagne's coronation as emperor took place in Rome. He had been proud to be a Frank and dressed and behaved according to his people's customs, but after setting foot on Roman soil Charlemagne bowed to the grandeur of the ancient city. No more convincing demonstration can be found than Charlemagne's portrait *denier* where he is shown wearing a laurel wreath on his head, in the fashion of Roman emperors, and an inscription declares him to be *Imperator augustus.* The reverse of the coin bears a simple linear design: a templelike church, with a cross in the center, and the inscription *Christiana Religio.* The church is probably meant to represent St. Peter's Basilica, where Charlemagne was crowned.

Coins of Medieval France

The monarch who established the dynasty that followed Charlemagne's was Hugh Capet (987-996). The first of the Capetian kings, he issued *deniers* that bore his name and title on one side and, on the reverse, a cross and the name of the mint. This kind of simple coinage was continued by his succes-

116. Master-works of German Gothic: bracteates from the Abbeys of Gandersheim and Hersfeld, from Reichenau, Brunswick-Luneburg and from Falkenstein (12th and 13th centuries). Left first row: 32 mm., right first row: 23 mm.

sors with very few changes; a cross and a monogram of the ruler's name comprised a constant element in each design. A similar lack of elegance characterized the many coins minted by feudal lords and prelates who provided the currency required by local commercial needs. The portraits are crudely designed, or stylized beyond recognition. Crosiers, miters, and a blessing hand characterized the coins issued by many princes of the Church.

Philip II Augustus (1180-1223), one of the great Capetian kings, succeeded in strengthening royal power and securing for France an important role in European affairs. Under Philip trade was greatly encouraged and the coinage was reformed. Two types of *deniers* were issued: the *denier parisis*, characterized by a cross on the reverse side, and the *denier tournois*, which displayed the so-called "castle of Tours." They became the most widely circulated coins in the entire country.

Another of France's most revered medieval kings, Louis IX (1226-1270), took part in two of the Crusades that were now capturing the imagination of European Christendom. Saint Louis, as he became known after his death, returned from captivity in the Holy Land in 1254 and promptly undertook a reform of the coinage. He issued a new coin: a piece of fine silver that was equal in value to 12 *deniers*. The new coin was called a *gros tournois*, a name combining part of the name of a coin, the Roman *denarius grossus*, with the name of the familiar design, the "castle of Tours," which appeared on the reverse side. The *gros tournois* bore the legend *Benedictus sit nomen Domini Dei Jhesus Christi*, that is, "Blessed be the name of our Lord, Jesus Christ." Its value — the equal of 12 *deniers* — was indicated by a circle on the reverse of the coin consisting of 12 lilies, each framed in a scallop. The high silver content and the elegance of this well-designed coin assured its great popularity both in France and abroad.

As a companion coin to the *gros tournois*, Louis IX had a gold coin minted; it was called a *denier d'or a l'ecu*, after the *ecu*, or shield, that appeared on the coin. The two handsome coins reflect the advanced art of the Gothic period. Not only do they mark the re-establishment of a viable silver coinage and the reintroduction of bimetallism, but they also show a revival of the use of coins as a medium of aesthetic expression.

A successor to Saint Louis, Philip IV (1285-1314), simultaneously debased the coinage (a crime for which Dante relegated him to the *Inferno*) and was responsible for some of the most brilliant of all French medieval coins, rivaling in elegance and beauty the finest French Gothic work in ivory and gold. Some of the French gold coins show later kings enthroned, standing or sitting under a richly embroidered canopy, while others show them on horseback wearing the harness of a knight. A wealth of minute details of costume and architecture transforms the coins into a dazzling miniature record of medieval royalty and knighthood.

Names as varied and colorful as the coins themselves were given many of these pieces: *masse d'or* ("golden mace"), *chaisse d'or* ("golden throne"), *agnel d'or* ("golden lamb"), *pavillon d'or* ("golden tent"), and *ange d'or* ("golden angel"). On the *masse d'or* was seen the enthroned king holding the mace or scepter of office, topped by a "hand of justice." The *agnel d'or* showed the divine Lamb, halo around head with banner and cross behind, a bit of iconography well known on ecclesiastical seals of the preceding century. The most

117. Gold gulden struck in the German city of Nordlingen in the name of the Holy Roman Emperor Frederick IV (1440-93). 24 mm.

118. The very popular Meissen groat struck by the Margrave Frederick IV (1382-1428) of Meissen in Saxony imitated the famous groat of Prague. 28 mm.

119. The amazing wealth of coinages in medieval England: (from left to right) Celtic stater of pale gold, (1st century A.D.); an Anglo-Saxon silver sceat, (6th to 8th century); silver pennies of Edward the Confessor (1042-1066) and William I (1066-1087); silver long-cross pennies of Henry III (1216-72) and Edward I (1272-1307); and groat and half-groat of Henry VI (1422-61). Lower left: 25 mm.

sumptuous coins of the series are the *pavillon d'or*, showing Philip VI beneath a rich canopy, and the *ange d'or*, showing the winged and crowned Archangel Michael, holding the shield of France and a sword. Philip, the first of the Valois kings, issued an even more exuberant gold coinage, even though the wars with the English were then racking France. Crushing defeats at Sluys (1340) and at Crécy (1346) introduced the Hundred Years' War, when Edward III of England and his son Edward, the Black Prince, took control of large territories in the southwest of France. Philip's son, John II (surnamed the Good), was captured by the Black Prince in the battle at Poitiers in 1356. After years in captivity, John was released. A payment of three million "crowns" was promised, and a beautiful gold coin, the *franc d'or*, was struck to provide some of the required fee. It represented the king dressed in armor, riding a caparisoned horse and brandishing a sword. The word "franc" is synonymous with "free," and the coin was intended to proclaim the king's release. France could not raise the full three million crowns, however, and John returned of his own free will to captivity in England where he died.

During these troubled times the people of France seldom saw any of these graceful gold coins. What came into their hands were mostly middle-sized

120. "RICARDUS" on a denier of Aquitaine on French soil is the only instance of a coin bearing the name of Richard Coeur de Lion (1189-99). 18 mm.

121. The pennies struck by English kings beginning with Edward I (1272-1307), were eagerly accepted and often imitated: (above) long-cross penny of London (1278-1307); (from left to right) penny of Dublin in Ireland (1272-1377); esterlin anglais struck in Namur, Low Countries (1263-1297); and ortug struck in Sweden (1396-1439). 18 mm.

or small coins made of more or less debased silver. Of these the *gros blanc*, the *blanc* and the *denier parisis* or *denier tournois* (and their multiples or fractions) were the most common. So-called "secret points" were placed under certain letters in the coin's inscription to indicate its place of minting. A great many different silver and particularly fine gold coins were issued by Charles VI (1422-1461), who became king of France when its lands were largely in English hands. Charles was the monarch who, inspired by Joan of Arc, reconquered his lost provinces until the English held only the port of Calais, re-establishing the unity of the country and the dignity of the French monarchy.

Coins of the Germanic Lands

The Germanic lands during the Middle Ages present a complex and often confused picture when kings and emperors were held in check by powerful church and feudal lords. Many of the princes and prelates were granted minting privileges. Similar rights were often usurped, and in time, some

122. The gold noble, one of England's most beautiful coins, represented the king standing on a ship, a reference to the great sea-victory against France at Sluys in 1340. 39 mm.

princes instituted their own, autonomous coinage. This confused situation produced an enormous minting of money. Numerous *pennies* and their halves, the *obols*, were deteriorated constantly in size, weight and fineness. Beginning in the 10th and 11th centuries, some regionally minted *pennies* became very popular and circulated widely, as were the *pennies* of Cologne, and the Regensburg *penny*, another popular coin, which circulated throughout southern Germany. Very unattractive small silver coins, called Saxon or Wendish *pennies,* also circulated widely, as did the coins known as Otto-Adelheid *pennies*. These imitated a minting showing the Emperor Otto I and his bride Adelheid, and a wooden church. This *penny* was particularly abundant, because the mints that produced it drew their silver from rich mines in the Harz Mountains.

The iconography of the *penny* is fascinating although designs are often rather naïve and coarse in execution. Religion was the key theme since coinage followed soon after the conversion to Christianity. Coins therefore often have the character of a profession of faith by using religious symbols and honoring

123. Medieval minter on a capital from the Abbey of St. George in Bocherville, Normandy, France (11th to 12th century). High: 455 mm.

124. Interior of a Swiss mint as illustrated by Diebold Schilling the Elder in the late 1400s.

125. Medieval coiner at work, from a mural in St. Barbara's church in Kutna Hora, Bohemia, c. 1470.

numbers of saints. Great emphasis was given to architectural representations especially churches.

The period of the Hohenstaufen dynasty not only ushered in the most brilliant of German medieval cultural and artistic attainments but also saw one of the most remarkable coinages in world monetary history: the *bracteates*. The exterior appearance of the *penny* had undergone considerable change. The coin blank had spread, growing larger in diameter and thinner. The images on many of these so-called *Dunnpfennige*, or "thin *pennies*," struck in Lower Saxony, Hesse, Franconia, and Bavaria, were blurred because the figure on the obverse of the coin showed through on the reverse. In spite of this, a series of highly interesting images were minted on thin *pennies*. For example, a number of them featured exotic hunting scenes, with lions, creatures of fantasy such as centaurs or dragons. These fabled beasts in part reflected the tortured mind of medieval man haunted by demons and monsters.

For practical reasons the manufacture was modified by using only one die in striking these thin *pennies*; the die image would thus appear in relief on the

126. The great variety of medieval deniers and groats from Trento, Aquileia, Venice, Milan, Bologna, Mantua, Lucca, Ancona, Rome, Naples and Messina underline a period of great political struggle in Italy but show, as well, an economic and cultural awakening. The iconography is varied and often aesthetically pleasing. First upper left: 20 mm. ....

face of the coin and in negative relief, or intaglio, on the reverse. The use of this minting technique won for the coins the name *Hohlpfennig* ("hollow penny") or *bracteates*, from the Latin word *bractea*, meaning leaf. Given the increased diameter of the coins, the diemakers could embellish their designs, and this series of *Hohlpfennigs* was minted for some 200 years: from the mid-12th to the mid-14th century. *Bracteates* were struck in central, northern, and eastern Germany, and in Bohemia, Poland, Hungary, and Austria. Many of the coins were of great beauty. In general, an ornate frame bearing a brief inscription, or no inscription at all, may enclose an exquisitely rendered full human figure or figures, or a bust may be presented seen against a very detailed architectural background.

A *bracteate* of Merseburg, in Saxony, shows the martyrdom of St. Lawrence, roasting on his gridiron, attended by two torturers. St. Stephen's martyrdom by being stoned to death is depicted on a *bracteate* issued by the Bishop of Halberstadt. Other coins depict the towers of a castle in Brunswick or the Lion Monument erected there by the famous Duke of Saxony, Henry the Lion (1129-1195). The counts of Falkenstein struck some *bracteates* showing Adam and Eve standing before the Tree of Knowledge, and others depicting a falcon, the family blazon.

In some areas of Germany, such as the Rhineland and Bavaria, *bracteates* were never struck, and two-sided coins continued in use. By 1248 the need for a larger silver coin had brought about the minting of the Tyrolean *Kreuzer*, named for its cross *(Kreuz)* and equal in value to four ordinary *pennies*.

127. *This banking scene, probably from Genoa (late 14th century), shows some of the functions of the Italian bankers. Coins in money sacks were counted and then stored in chests.*

Later, in imitation of the French middle-sized *gros tournois*, authorities in both the Rhineland and Westphalia started striking their own *Groschen*, or *groats*. Later still, the *groat* or *Groschen* became very popular and was soon minted in various parts of Germany. The Margraves of Meissen, in Saxony, imitated the famous *groat* of Prague, one of the most popular coins of the late Middle Ages. The Saxon *groat* enjoyed an almost equal popularity in northern Germany. Some of these coins went by different popular names, according to the images on them: one minting, known as the *Judenkopfgroschen*, shows a man's head with a pointed hat, a typical Jewish costume in those days.

Coins of England

Roman coins did not disappear from Great Britain even after this frontier province severed its ties with the western empire. By the end of the seventh century the Anglo-Saxon invaders replaced their gold coinage by small silver coins called *sceattas*, which changed to bronze during the eighth century.

One notable Saxon king, Offa of Mercia (757-796) maintained contacts abroad. He was in touch with Charlemagne and even with the Moslems. Both influences are evidenced on his coinage. Offa put into circulation a silver *penny*, a coin patterned after Charlemagne's *denier*, and also struck a gold coin that copied the gold *dinar* of the Caliph Al Mansur. As a reflection of the classical influences that Offa had encountered at the court of Charlemagne, the Saxon king's coins showed his bust and that of his queen, Cynethryth, clad in Roman garb.

When the next invaders of England, the Danes, established their rule in northeastern England during the ninth century, they, too, struck a series of silver *pennies*. In general these coins bear only various forms of crosses, together with inscriptions: the name of the king and the name of the minter. Alfred the Great (871-899), one of the line of Anglo-Saxon kings of Wessex, proved to be a strong enemy of the Danes. Among other accomplishments, Alfred liberated London; some of his *pennies* bear his image, wearing a diadem, and the name of London in monogram. Eventually the kings of Wessex became kings of the entire realm, with the title *Rex totius Britanniae,* or "King of all Britain." Under Ethelred II (968-1016) more than 70 mints, employing large numbers of minters, produced coins with a wide variety of designs. The majority of these coins appear to have been needed in order to pay the overseas Danes a subsidy that sufficed to keep them from invading England. In 994, for example, Ethelred established the "Danegeld," a land tax which provided the revenue for these payments. The discovery of hoards of English coins in Scandinavia in recent years supports the historical accounts of these large subsidies; one such account states that 155,000 pounds of silver was paid the raiders in six installments. In 1066 King Harold battled against still another invader of England — William, Duke of Normandy.

128. *The world's most popular gold coin, the ducat. Venetian ducats struck by the Doge Pietro Gradenigo (1289-1311) and Antonio Venier (1382-1400). 20 mm.*

William and his successors issued silver *pennies* showing the king holding either a scepter or a sword. The first of the Plantagenets, the royal line that succeeded William, was Henry II (1154-1189). His reform of the coinage in 1180 introduced a new issue, the so-called "short-cross" *penny.* The coins bore the king's head seen full face on the obverse and, on the reverse, a cross set inside a circular inscription. At this time, as in past eras of history, people were in the practice of "clipping" coins, that is, cutting off slivers of the edge in an unobtrusive fashion and melting down the clippings for sale as bullion. This fraudulent practice had become so common by 1247 that the short-cross *penny* had to be replaced by a new coin, the "long-cross" *penny;* the long arms of this cross extended to the very edge of the coins, which made clipping impossible. Henry III (1216-1272) issued the long-cross coins and is known to have struck the first English gold coin. It imitated the gold *florin* of Florence. Henry's attempt to establish a bimetallic currency did not work. The minting of the gold coin was soon discontinued, because the people had confidence only in silver.

Almost a century passed before gold was minted again. Under Edward III (1327-1377) three gold coins were struck: a *florin,* equivalent in value to six *shillings,* a half-*florin* and a quarter-*florin.* All three bore the figure of the king seated under a canopy on his throne. The inscription included Edward's claim to the throne of France. England's great naval victory at Sluys in 1340 gave Edward a reason for replacing his earlier gold issue with a new coin that was destined to become one of the world's famous pieces. This was the gold *noble,* equivalent in value to six *shillings,* eight *pence.* The coin showed the king standing on shipboard; on the reverse was an inscription in Latin, a text from the Gospel of St. Luke: "But Jesus, passing through the midst of them, went His way."

129. *The figure of St. John the Baptist and the city badge, the fleur-de-lis, represented on the silver and gold fiorini of Florence. 20 & 21 mm.*

The Wars of the Roses (1455-1485) brought the house of York to England's throne; the white rose of York was added to the gold *noble,* and the coin was thereafter known as the *rose-noble.* Another famous coin of the period, the *angel,* displayed the Archangel Michael killing a dragon. It carried the inscription: *O crux ave spes unica* ("Hail! O Cross, our only hope").

130. *The imposing eagle of Frederick II of Hohenstaufen (1198-1250) adorned the reverse of his augustalis struck since 1231 in Messina and Brindisi, Italy. 20 mm.*

Coins of the Italian Lands

No area of Europe can claim a more eventful history during the Middle Ages than the Italian peninsula. This land not only endured the invasions of bar-

baric peoples as dissimilar as the Moors and the Normans, but also felt the heavy hand first of Byzantium and then of the Germanic Holy Roman Emperors. The coins of Italy are numerous and varied; they reflect at once a period of constant struggle and an awakening, both economic and cultural, that was felt in Italy long before it reached the other nations of Europe. Many cities in northern Italy — Milan, Verona, Bologna, Lucca, Pavia, and others — struck their own coinages. The small silver coins bore simple motifs: a cross and the names of the current Holy Roman Emperor and of the city that minted the coin. In the hands of skilled die-cutters, the motifs evolved into exquisite designs. An example is the *bolognino,* a *denier* first produced in Bologna in 1191. Lucca selected a very illustrative design for its small silver coin. It was inspired by the legend of St. Veronica and showed the face of Christ imprinted on her veil. Mantua chose to honor the Latin poet Virgil, who was born in that city; although a pagan, Virgil was esteemed by Christians of the Middle Ages.

Genoa, a city that received its coining privileges from the Emperor Conrad III in 1139, kept Conrad's name on its coins for centuries, as it did the city's blazon, a stylized gate (*janua* in Latin). A great maritime power in the Middle Ages, Genoa in 1252 minted one of the earliest known medieval gold coins, the *genovino d'oro.* Genoa's great rival, Venice, was destined to play an important role in the monetary evolution of Europe. In 1202 under a famous doge, Enrico Dandolo, the city's mint started to produce a medium-sized silver coin, the *grossus Venetianus,* popularly called the *matapan,* equal to 12 *denarii* in value. The *matapan* soon gained wide circulation, and imitations of it were minted in both Byzantium and the Balkans.

On October 31, 1284 the Great Council of Venice voted in favor of minting what has become perhaps the most familiar of all medieval coins, the *ducat.* A gold coin similar in design to the *matapan,* it bore the Latin inscription: *Sit Tibi Christe datus quem tu regis iste ducatus,* "To thee, O Christ, be dedicated this duchy, which thou rulest." Known in Italy as the *zecchino,* from the Italian word *zecca,* or mint, the *ducat* has proved to be the most long-lived coin yet known: it remained in circulation from the 13th century until World War I. Originally weighing 3.559 grams, the *ducat* was later struck in fractional values and in multiples that went as high as 100 and even 105 *ducats;* the latter coin weighed 367.41 grams.

A coin with almost as familiar a name, the *florin,* was first minted in the 1230s in Florence. It took its name, *fiorino,* from the city's blazon — a lily — which appeared on the coin together with the image of Saint John the Baptist. The silver *florin* or *fiorino d'argento,* was followed in 1252 by a gold *florin* or *fiorino d'oro.* Weighing 3.53 grams, this gold coin was widely imitated; the German version, for example, was called the *Gulden.* Bologna was one of the great centers of learning in Europe; its university was founded late in the 11th century. The city minted some silver coins inscribed with the words *Mater studiorum,* or "Mother of studies," and gold coins with the words *Bononia docet,* "Bologna teaches." A rich and varied coinage was also produced in southern Italy, where the Normans had established principalities in Apulia and Sicily. In 1130 Roger II was crowned as King of Naples and Sicily. A silver coin, cup-shaped in the Byzantine manner, shows King Roger and his son portrayed in the stylized Byzantine iconographic tradition.

131. *The arms of Castile and Leon on a silver real of Peter I, the Cruel (1350-69) and the crowned bust of the king on a real from Valencia of Alfonso V of Aragon (1416-58). 26 mm.*

132. *This rare and large gold coin of 20-excelentes de la Granada, struck after 1497, bears the portraits of Their Catholic Majesties Ferdinand and Isabella who were celebrating their victory over the Moors. 53 mm.*

104

133. These three medieval, Bohemian coins, against the background of the Karlstein castle, typify the evolution of the coinage from the denier of Odalricus (1012-37) and the minuscule deniers of the 12th century, to the fine gold ducat struck during the 14th century. First top: 21 mm.

After the extinction of the Norman line, a German dynasty, the Hohenstaufens, ruled over southern Italy. The greatest of the Hohenstaufens was Frederick I, who was simultaneously Holy Roman Emperor (1215-1250). Frederick contributed greatly to a revival of classical ideals. His ideals were summed up in the design of a gold coin he introduced, the *augustalis*, which represented him gowned and cuirassed in the fashion of the Roman emperors and bore the inscription *Caesar Augustus Imperator Romanorum*. The reverse, equally fine in its engraving, showed an imperial eagle, the symbol not only of ancient Rome but also of the Hohenstaufens. The *augustalis* and its half piece demonstrate the enduring vitality of Rome's legacy well into the Middle Ags. French kings of the Anjou family succeeded Frederick I on the throne of Sicily until 1282, when on Easter Monday at the hour of Vespers, the people of Palermo rebelled and massacred the French. The Sicilians' freedom was brief; the Spanish saved them from French vengeance but established their own rule over the island.

In Naples, where the French dynasty of Anjou ruled until 1504, a delicate coin was minted both in gold and in silver since 1278. The coins were known

134. The denar of King Odalricus (1012-37) of Bohemia displays the naive but very imaginative artistry of medieval Bohemian coin engraving. 20 mm.

135. During the Middle Ages Hungary issued
many small silver coins such as the attractive
pieces of King Bela II (1131-41) and Bela IV
(1235-70); the gold ducat, struck in great abun-
dance from rich mines, expanded in usage beyond its national borders. Largest: 22 mm.

as the *saluto d'oro* and *saluto d'argento,* respectively, and depicted the Salutation of the Virgin Mary. In 1304 a middle-sized silver coin called a
gigliato was issued. The enthroned figure of Charles II appears on one side
and a cross and four lilies on the other. These coins, although certainly influenced by the traditions of French monetary art, also reflect the high artistic
standards of Italy, then at the threshold of the Renaissance.

Coins of Spain

The medieval coinage of Spain reflects the political situation of the times. A
considerable part of southern Spain was in the hands of the Arabs, and the
Christian kingdoms of the north — Leon, Castile, and Aragon — were under-
standably preoccupied with ousting the infidels. The influence of Charlemagne's coinage continued for a long time in Spain and is reflected in the
minting of small silver *dineros* in Castile and Aragon. A memory of the Berber
conquerors, the Almoravides, lived on in the name *morabitini,* given to a gold
coin inspired by the Islamic *dinar* and minted by the kings of Castile late in the

107

12th century. These coins, of Moorish design, were inscribed with a profession of the Christian faith written in Arabic.

From late in the 13th century onward a great many gold coins were issued by the kings of Castile and Leon. The graceful design of the *dobla* displayed the blazons of Castile and Leon: a castle with three towers and a lion rampant. The *dobla* was issued with great frequency and in multiple denominations. Two of the most magnificent coins of the Middle Ages are a 10-*dobla* piece issued by Pedro the Cruel (1350-1368) that bears his profile, and a 60-*enrique* piece (the name is that of the monarch who issued the coin, Henry IV). This massive gold coin weighed 229 grams and shows Henry enthroned; it is a masterwork of Spanish Gothic.

Castile and Aragon were united in 1469 through the marriage of Isabella of Castile to Ferdinand II of Aragon. The crowned images of the two monarchs grace the gold coins minted in celebration of their greatest victory: the conquest in 1492 of Granada, the last Moorish stronghold in Spain. In honor of the event a new gold unit, created during the coinage reform of 1497, was named the *excelente de la Granada*. The gold *excelente* of 3.52 grams was issued in various multiples; the double *excelente*, minted with the wealth of gold bullion seized in the New World, became one of the most common gold coins in the world. It was struck in Seville and at other mints in Spain and in the Spanish Netherlands; although it bears the names and likenesses of Ferdinand and Isabella, it was minted again and again long after their deaths.

The same currency reform also produced multiples of the silver coin, the *real,* so that two-*real,* four-*real,* and eight-*real* pieces were minted. These attractive silver coins bore, in addition to the Spanish arms, a yoke, the blazon of Ferdinand, and a bundle of arrows, Isabella's symbol. The *real* and its multiples were destined to be among the most long-lived of all Spanish coins and entered the lore of pirate treasures.

Coins of Eastern Europe and the Balkans

The monetary history of eastern and southeastern Europe during the Middle Ages reveals the ties that bound the west to the east. Bohemia, Poland, Hungary, Bulgaria, and Serbia were crossroads where not only the money of neighboring Germany, but English, French, Italian, Byzantine, and even Arab money was known and exchanged. Here, more than anywhere in Europe, coins served as the heralds of Christendom.

In Bohemia, while the *denar,* or silver *penny,* became smaller in diameter during the late 11th and 12th centuries, it gained in artistic refinement. A variety of motifs bears witness to the beliefs of the times. An angel carries a child, wild beasts are hunted, and groups of as many as five individuals are displayed on coins less than half an inch in diameter. In 1300 King Wenceslaus II of Bohemia introduced a new silver coin, the *groat,* inspired by the French *gros tournois.* This Prague *groat,* as it was called, was destined to become one of the most popular coins of the Middle Ages; it bore a crown, surrounded by a triple circle of inscription, and the blazon of Bohemia, a lion rampant.

Poland's coinage originated in the 10th century with the striking of silver *denars* modeled on a German coin, the Regensburg *penny.* A series of thin

136. The minuscule silver kopecks and dengas (15th and 16th centuries) from Novgorod and Pskov in medieval Russia display an interesting variety of themes: man and beast, facing head, and especially prince on horseback. First: 16 mm.

137. The figure of Christ on a Byzantine electrum nomisma of the 12th century was repeated on groats struck by Venice (grosso matapan of Giovanni Dandolo, 1280-89) and on those struck in Serbia (Stephan Dragutin, 1272-1316). First left: 35 mm., last right: 20 mm.

coins, *bracteates,* die-marked on one face only were struck during the reign of Mieszko III (1173-1202). One group of these displays allegorical figures identified with such inscriptions in Latin as "Faith" and "Charity." Others, struck between 1181 and 1202, bear inscriptions in Hebrew letters that record the king's name and in some cases the name of the Jewish minter. Evidently Jewish financiers had supported Mieszko against his rebellious subjects, and he had granted them in return the right to be the royal minters.

Hungarian coins of the period exhibit certain distinctive features. Some of their diminutive coins during the 11th and 12th centuries, especially under King Bela II (1131-1141), are jewel-like in their neat, clearly defined modeling of highly abstract designs; for example, a royal head becomes a triangle, and its features are rendered as dots and lines. The Hungarians struck many coins during the 12th and 13th centuries that were die-marked on one face only. The style, although primitive, is exquisite; the enthroned figure of Bela IV (1235-1270) is a good example.

Italian influences entered Hungary together with the Angevin kings, and the Hungarian *groat,* first minted in 1329, copies not the Prague *groat* but the Neapolitan *grosso.* Hungary's earliest gold coinage copied Florentine designs, but within a few decades the figure of Hungary's canonized king, St. Ladislaw, and the Hungarian coat of arms replaced Saint John the Baptist and the Florentine lily on the Hungarian *florin.* With the monetary reform undertaken by Hungary's great king, Matthias Corvinus (1458-1490), the image of the Madonna and Child became a permanent feature of the nation's coinage for centuries.

Russian money changed, in the fourteenth century, from bars of silver to small silver coins, called *denga,* a Tartar name. Images used on *dengas* were varied and quite exotic: centaurs, dragons, birds, lions, archers, and mounted princes. *Dengas* are often designated as "wire money," because the silver was rolled into a wire-shaped roll and then cut to proper weight before being flattened and struck out.

Despite Russia's spiritual leadership among the southern Slavs, the Bulgars and Serbians turned toward Byzantium and Venice for inspiration. The silver *groats* of the Bulgarian king, Czar Asen II (1218-1241), show the debt to Byzantium. They display a standing figure of Asen, together with the image of St. Demetrius and an enthroned Christ. The Serbian *groat,* copying the Venetian *matapan,* has a change only in the inscription; this names their own St. Stephen instead of St. Mark, the patron saint of Venice.

The bimetallic system of the late Middle Ages gradually emerged in response to the vibrant commercial needs of modernity. □

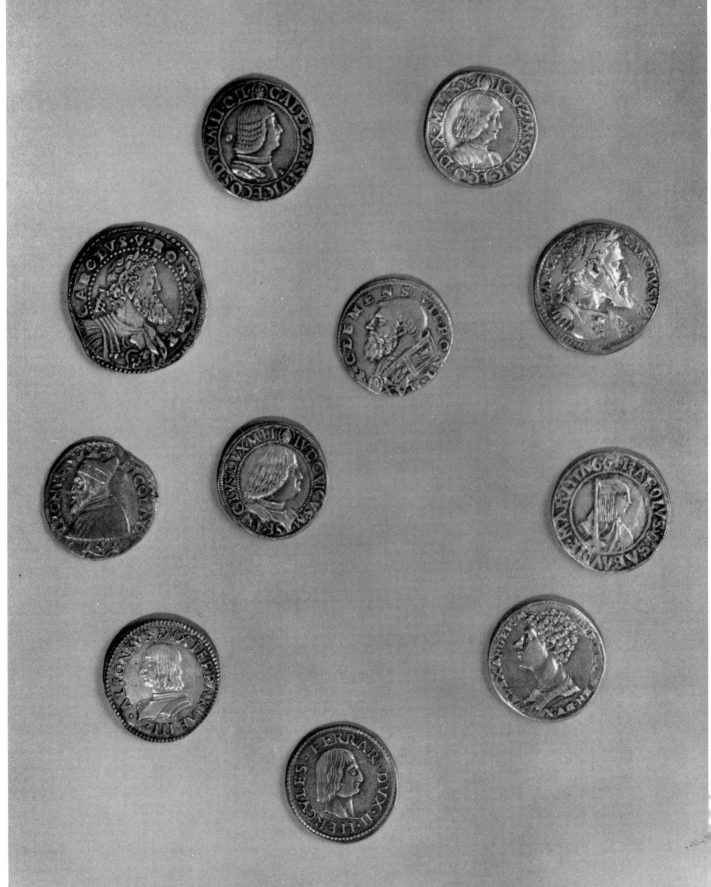

V: COINS FROM THE RENAISSANCE TO MODERN TIMES

New hope and self-reliance stimulated man's creative powers.

Culture and art thrive on money. The bustling trade of such Italian cities as Genoa, Venice, Siena, and Florence brought great wealth into the land from the time of the Crusades. Opulence created desire to enjoy a richer life, providing the impulse to change from the limiting medieval style of life. An exciting optimism replaced a fearful and penitent mentality. New hope and self-reliance stimulated man's creative powers.

The innovative spirit of the Renaissance, an era of the "rebirth" of classical learning and experience in Europe, is first evident in the mid-14th century, when men such as Dante and Petrarch flourished, and becomes virtually all-pervasive during the 15th century. The various states of Italy were in the forefront of this movement to emancipate men's minds. It was a busy period of search and discovery; scholars drew upon old manuscripts, ancient monuments, and even antique coins in pursuit of every possible vestige of classical life and wisdom. A traveler such as Marco Polo visited new lands and rediscovered remote civilizations, immensely widening the spiritual horizon of the western world. Curiosity required that everything be explored; even man himself proved to be an interesting subject. One consequence in the arts was that portraiture gained in importance; now it was intended to present the physical likeness of a real human being, not some abstract symbol of an idea or institution.

These elements of fresh thought were echoed in the Italian coinages of the period. Venice, "la Serenissima," was the rich and powerful mistress of the seas; its caravels sailed far and wide, extending a commercial empire even to the coasts of the Black Sea. The French diplomat and historian Philippe de Commines described Venice in 1495 as "the most triumphant city that I have ever seen . . . governed with the greatest wisdom, and serving God with the most solemnity." Two decades earlier, in 1472, Venice had issued a silver coin that weighed 6.52 grams and was called, in honor of the Doge Nicolo Tron (1417-1474), the *lira tron*. The *lira* carries on one side Tron's profile; he is seen wearing the characteristic pointed headdress of a doge, the *corno ducale*. The Lion of St. Mark appears on the reverse. But, as a chronicler of the time stated, ". . . tyrants put themselves on coins and not the heads of republics," and the *lira tron* was therefore discontinued. Venice, moreover, held to this principle; during the remainder of its long and rich numismatic history no further portraits appeared on Venetian coins.

A similar policy was followed by the rulers of Genoa and of Florence. Other Italian princes and *condottieri*, who had often fought their way to power, did not share this republican attitude. They welcomed the portrait coin as a means of publicity. The popularity of larger silver coins at this time gave artists a better opportunity to develop their designs; and soon these new coins, called *testoni, testa* being the Italian word for "head," because of the portraits that appeared on them, became the favorites. The silver *testoni* spread to Portugal, to France, and to Switzerland where, known respectively as *tostaos, testons,* or *Dicken*, they were also very popular.

Among the first to mint *testoni* were the Sforzas of Milan, and the first

◁139. *Renaissance princes: Galeazzo Maria Sforza (1444-76) of Milan and his son Giangaleazzo (1469-94); Charles V (1516-67) by Leone Leoni for Milan; Duke Charles I of Savoy (1482-90); Alessandro de'Medici of Florence (1510-37) by Benvenuto Cellini; the Dukes Ercole (1431-1505) and Alfonso I d'Este 1486-1534) of Ferrara; the Venetian Doge Nicolo Tron (1471-73); Charles V on a coin of Naples; in the center Ludovico Maria Sforza of Milan (1451-1508) by Caradosso, and Pope Clement VII (1523-34) by Benvenuto Cellini. First upper: 27 mm.*

Sforza to appear on a coin was Francesco (1450-1466) who in the best tradition of the *condottieri* occupied the Duchy of Milan by force in 1450. A very expressive, lifelike rendering of the aged duke graced one face of a gold coin he minted; the reverse showed a medieval knight in armor, galloping, his sword drawn. His son, Galeazzo Maria, embraced his father's practice, and the son's profile appears on Milan's first *testoni,* issued soon after 1474. Galeazzo's features reveal the dissolute character of a man whose cruel reign was ended by his assassination. The widow of Galeazzo ruled as regent for her son. The delicate profile of the youth appears on what are among the most charming portrait coins of the Renaissance; his childlike face appears framed by long locks on some coins; on others he is wearing a round bonnet over shoulder-length hair, contrasting with the energetic and inspired features of his uncle, Ludovico Maria, called "il Moro." The latter's coin portrait is by the hand of a family artist, a gem engraver and goldsmith named Cristofano Foppa, called "Caradosso." The artist probably found his inspiration in the designs of Leonardo da Vinci, who spent his most productive years at the brilliant court of Ludovico il Moro. In 1499 this Sforza prince lost his throne to Louis XII of France and spent his remaining years a prisoner in that foreign land. For over ten years the coins of Milan were issued in the name of the new master, the king of France. Thus began a long series of coins struck in the name of foreign rulers, from Charles V to Emperor Francis Joseph of Austria.

Another outstanding center of the arts was the Duchy of Ferrara, ruled by the Este family. On the coins of Ferrara can be found figures of both classical inspiration and of a religious character. The noble features of Prince Alfonso, husband of the famous Lucrezia Borgia, show the remarkable quality of these Este family portraits. Rivaling the splendor of Ferrara was Mantua under the Gonzagas. On a *grosso,* or *groat,* of the early 15th century, we see an allegorical view of medieval Mantua with the tabernacle that contained the city's most cherished Christian relic: fragments of a sponge that had, according to tradition, been drenched with the blood of Christ. The powerful coin portraits of the princes of Mantua, as well as the fine compositions for the reverses, were influenced by the great painters and sculptors residing at Mantua, es-

141. The half-Guldiner, 1484, and the Guldiner, 1486, the first dollar-size coin ever struck, were both issued by the Archduke Sigismund of Tyrol, the "Rich in Coin", whose wealth became proverbial. First coin: 35 mm., second coin: 41 mm.

142. Minting by hand in Tyrol as shown in a book from Schwaz, 1556.

143. Leonardo da Vinci's (1452-1519) invention and designs for striking coins with a drop-hammer mechanism used recently by IBM to reconstruct a workable model.

pecially Andrea Mantegna and Giulio Romano. The Mantuan goldsmith, Gian Battista Cavalli, later moved to the Hapsburg court at Hall in the Tyrol, thereby contributing to the expansion of Renaissance art north of the Alps.

Rome had shared very little in the intellectual life of the other Italian principalities in the early 15th century. But Sixtus IV (1471-1484), was a great builder, restorer, and patron of the arts; his name is perpetuated in the Sistine Chapel. Proud of his public works, Sixtus issued silver coins with the inscription *publicae utilitati*, "for the people's use." The silver *groats* and double *groats* of Sixtus bear a very impressive portrait of the pontiff — the first Pope whose likeness appeared on the coinage of Rome. Tragic events shook the Church during the brief pontificate of Clement VII (1523-1534) whose portrait coin was engraved by Benvenuto Cellini, the famous Florentine goldsmith and sculptor. Cellini's rival, the gifted artist Leone Leoni (1509-1590) served Charles V, when the emperor introduced the Milanese "scudo d'argento," one of the earliest *dollar*-sized coins to appear in Italy. The *testons* of Charles V were among the most imposing of Leoni's coin creations.

From the monetary viewpoint the real division between the Middle Ages and modern times happened north of the Alps in Hapsburg Tyrol, a region that grew increasingly important as the trade route between Italy and Germany. The Archduke Sigismund, who ruled from 1439 to 1496, started the prac-

144. A show-taler of 1506 used by Emperor Maximilian I to commemorate his wedding in 1479 to Mary of Burgundy who died in 1482. 42 mm.

tice of recoining Hungarian and Italian gold *ducats* into *Guldens* of his own. He moved his mint in 1476 from Meran to Hall, on the River Inn, to be closer to the large deposits of silver recently discovered in that area. Sigismund had in his service a Venetian minter, Antonio de Caballis, known in the Tyrol as Anthonis von Ross. Based on his experience with the Venetian *lira tron,* von Ross wanted to replace gold coinage with large silver coins of the same value. Following his minter's advice, Sigismund struck in 1484 silver *Halbguldiner,* which weighed 15.92 grams. Two years later the *Guldiner* was minted, which was also called an *Uncialis* because it weighed about one ounce. This coin, the first *dollar*-sized silver coin ever struck, was very attractive. The archduke is portrayed on one side in full regalia, and on the other he is seen mounted and dressed in knight's armor. It was said that the archduke, happy and proud to see his image so displayed, had a pail filled with these silver pieces so that he could dip his hands into them. His wealth became proverbial and he was nicknamed *der Munzreiche* ("the rich in coins"). The large silver *guldiners* were intended to replace the gold *gulden,* but the population in general preferred gold. As a result the *guldiners* remained showpieces for many years, principally used as gifts.

During the rule of another Hapsburg as Holy Roman Emperor, Maximilian I (1493-1519), one such showpiece was struck in Hall in 1506 in commemoration of the wedding of the then Prince Maximilian to Princess Mary of Burgundy in 1479. The coin was not struck until years after the young bride had died following a fall from a horse; indeed, by then Maximilian had remarried. The Hapsburg emperor ordered a copy made of an earlier medal, engraved by a famous Renaissance sculptor, Giovanni Candida, at a time when, as prince, he and his bride resided at the Burgundian court. The youthful charm of the young couple, had been masterfully captured by Candida and was also beautifully rendered in the flat relief of the coin. This superb silver piece inaugurated a rich series of Hapsburg *talers.*

How did a large silver coin, known originally as a *guldiner,* come to be called a *taler* or *talar, tallero, daalder,* and, eventually, *dollar?* The name originated in a far-off region in the Erzgebirge of Bohemia where, in 1516, in an   116 area called Joachimsthal, that is, "the valley of St. Joachim," enormous deposits of silver were discovered. The rich lode belonged to the counts of Schlick who, in 1520, were granted by the king of Bohemia the right to use their silver to mint large *Groschen*, or *Guldiners*. The coins bore the image of St. Joachim, the patron of the region. In a period of eight short years, more than 2 million of these coins were struck from the silver of Joachimsthal. Such a wealth of coinage naturally soon began to circulate in neighboring areas, where the coins were known by the name of their place of origin, *Joachimsthalers*. Eventually only the last part of the word, *thaler (taler)*, was used and, with this simplified spelling it became generally accepted as a name for any large silver coin.

The *taler's* growth in popularity is certainly related to the fact that large quantities of silver were available at this time. Some bullion came from the New World, but much of the silver came from German, Hungarian, and Bohemian mines. Saxony was one of the countries richest in silver. The large output of the mines at Schneeberg and Schreckenberg late in the 15th century inspired the Prince Elector Frederick III in 1500 to mint a *Guldiner* like Archduke Sigismund's. In fact, a craftsman from the mint at Hall cut the dies for this first large Saxon silver piece. A contemporary described it as an "Annaberg thick *Pfennig* with three faces and long hair." He was referring to the portraits of the prince elector, his brother John, and his cousin, Albert, all wearing *Klappmutzen* (a cap with a cut brim) which gave the coin its popular name, the *Klappmutzentaler*.

Frederick III, called the Wise, was one of the most illustrious princes in Ger-

145. *The fine portraits of the Prince Elector Frederick III, the Wise (1486-1526) of Saxony engraved by Nuremberg masters and shown on some of his coins were copied on a modern three-mark piece of 1917 from Saxony. First coin upper left: 43 mm.*

man history — a sponsor of Martin Luther and supporter of the Reformation, patron of the arts, and a ruler who showed a real concern for the minting of his coins. In his service were some of the great artists of the period: the painter Lucas Cranach and two Nuremberg goldsmiths and die cutters, Hans Krug and Hans Kraft. A *taler* minted in 1507, showing Frederick in a tight-fitting wire cap, was struck with dies made by Hans Krug. It may have been Frederick who inspired other artists of the time to take an interest in the design or manufacture of coins; for example, the design for a Palatinate *taler* of 1522 came from Albrecht Dürer's hand. Finely designed *talers* were also produced by Swiss cities and in the German city of Cologne.

In the first decade of the 16th century the archbishops of Salzburg used the wealth of their own silver mines to mint *talers*. The first, called a *Ruben-taler*, or "turnip *taler*," bore the image of that vegetable, which was the blazon of Archbishop Leonard von Keutschach. Later, show *talers*, such as the double-*taler* struck by an art-loving bishop, Matthäus Lang (1519-1540) depicting St. Radiana attacked by wolves, are among the finest German coins. Charles V hoped to unify the greatly diversified monetary systems adopted by various princes throughout his vast empire. In 1521 he established the silver *Guldiner* and its six subdivisions as imperial coins. This monetary ordinance was indispensable to the future development of coinages in modern Europe. The *taler* continued to circulate widely throughout Europe, its expansion due in part to the technical progress which replaced striking by hand with machines.

146. The departure of St. Ursula, a British princess, martyred by the Huns near Cologne and venerated by that city, is depicted on this two-*taler* piece of Cologne (about 1512). 45 mm.

147. Beautiful talers were produced by the art-loving archbishops of Salzburg: the portrait of Matthaus Lang (1522) by the famous Augsburg artist Hans Schwartz; and a tower surrounded by storms symbolizing firmness in adversity of Wolfgang Th. von Raitenau (1594). First coin: 40 mm.

118

The turn of the 16th century saw an intermingling of French and Italian influences. By 1500 the French military grip on Milan was firm, and Italy was deprived of one of its richest regions. In return, however, Italian culture conquered the French, as Italian art treasures and artists appeared at the French court. The effect of the influx was apparent in the French coinage. Louis XII of France, while he was Duke of Milan, circulated silver *testons* that bore his portrait. In 1513, toward the end of his reign, a *teston* bearing his likeness was also circulated in France. The French *teston* was elegant enough, but it lacked the fine portrait quality of his Italian coinage.

Francis I (1515-1547), the brilliant ruler, welcomed to his court such Italian artists as the Florentine painter Andrea del Sarto, Leonardo da Vinci, and Benvenuto Cellini. His political ambitions were reflected in his many portrait coins. A long series of *testons* and half-*testons* show Francis at various stages in his life: young and clean-shaven, and middle-aged and bearded, wearing cuirass and crown. The salamander, the blazon of Francis, is a symbol that appears on many of the coins issued during his reign. Under Francis's successor, Henry II (1547-1559), a gold coin called an *Henri d'or* was minted. Chivalry, though on the wane, could claim this king as its champion — he died of wounds received in a tournament. At the same time the influence of Italian humanism was evident in Henry's coinage. This is scarcely surprising; Henry's wife was Catherine de Medici, daughter of Lorenzo the Magnificent. For example, one of Henry's coin designs was purely classical in inspiration. Copied after a coin of Imperial Rome, it represented France as the ancient province of Gaul.

It was at this same time that new methods of minting were being explored. The popularity of large *taler*-sized coins had posed production problems, and experiments in mechanization were already under way in Germany. The French were very much interested in any system that might simultaneously speed the rate of coin production and reduce the cost. French experts studied the water-driven machines undergoing development by Max Schwab of Augsburg. Schwab's machines first rolled strips of metal to an even thickness, then punched out the blank planchets, and finally struck the die impressions

148. *The first dollar-sized coins: the Guldiner of 1486 of Archduke Sigismund of Tyrol; a Joachimstaler struck by the Counts of Schlick in Bohemia in the 1520s. The first English crown struck in 1551 by Edward VI. Top coin: 40 mm.*

149. Portrait of the aging King Henry VIII of England as he appeared on his groats struck from 1544 to 1547. 24 mm.

onto the blanks. An ingenious worker in iron, Aubin Olivier, added to Schwab's system an invention of his own. This was a kind of split collar that held the blank planchets as the dies struck them and not only assured a perfectly round rim but allowed the rim to be marked with lettering or milling.

The French set up Schwab's new machines in Paris, in the gardens called *des Etuves*. They were considered a fascinating innovation, and Henry's successor, young King Charles IX (1560-1574), was said to enjoy personally striking coins by such means. The mint workers did not share the king's enthusiasm, however, and mechanized coining was bitterly opposed. Finally, using the excuse that the new method was too costly, the authorities in 1585 restored the old manual minting methods. Only medals and special issues (and, later, copper coins) were produced by the water-powered screw presses at the *Monnaie du Moulin,* or "watermill mint."

In England during this period the coinage experienced significant changes. Henry VII (1485-1509), the first Tudor king, accumulated vast fortunes for England. His coinage constituted a transition between the money of the Middle Ages and the money of modern times. Henry issued a large gold coin, the *sovereign,* in 1489; it was equal in value to 20 silver *shillings* and weighed 15.55 grams. The finest gold coin then minted in all Europe, the *sovereign* showed on the obverse a likeness of the king; on the reverse appeared the Tudor rose, superimposed on a shield. In addition to medieval coinages such as this, the king had minted toward the end of his reign a silver *teston* and a *groat.* Both coins bore a profile of the crowned king engraved by a German artist, Alexander Brugsal, in the manner of other Renaissance coin portraits.

For the first 16 years that his successor, Henry VIII (1509-1547) ruled, the English coinage remained unchanged; the portrait of Henry VII continued to appear, and only a modified inscription indicated that a new ruler held

150. A quarter-gulden piece stamped, in 1574 by the city of Leiden under seige by the Spaniards, on cardboard taken from old church book-bindings. 31 mm.

151. The delicately engraved coat of arms of Holland on a rider or ducaton struck in gold in 1687. 41 mm.

England's throne. The coinage reform of 1526 by Henry VIII was aimed at lowering the amount of gold in the *sovereign* in order to bring the coin closer in gold content to that of many of the foreign gold coins that flooded England. Some of Henry's silver *groats* and half-*groats* bore the initials of the archbishops of Canterbury, of York, and of Durham, who still enjoyed the traditional privilege of striking coins for the crown. The initials "TW" and "TC," found on some of the coins, represented, respectively, Thomas Cardinal Wolsey, erstwhile Archbishop of York, and Lord Chancellor to Henry VIII; and Thomas Cranmer, Archbishop of Canterbury. On the reverse of some of his coins Wolsey added a small symbol — a cardinal's hat. His action was considered illegal, and even treasonous; when Wolsey fell into disgrace and was stripped of all offices and honors, this minting figured in the bill of indictment brought against him. As Shakespeare wrote, in *Henry VIII*: ". . . out of mere ambition you have caused Your holy hat to be stamped on the king's coin." Wolsey escaped trial, because he died while en route to London to face his accusers. Cranmer was condemned for heresy during the rule of Queen Mary, the Catholic or Bloody Mary, and was burned at the stake.

His treasury depleted, Henry VIII pursued a policy of debasing the coinage, and his silver coins were ultimately an alloy that contained only one-third silver by weight. From 1544 onward coins carried a bearded portrait of Henry which resembles pictures in contemporary woodcuts of the king. His ponderous head, seen full face and bearing the crown, appeared on the last silver *groats* minted during Henry's reign. The image duplicates a fuller figure of Henry, enthroned, that appeared on the gold sovereigns of the same years. Both coins were much reduced in fineness and in weight.

The unfortunate son of Henry VIII and Jane Seymour, Edward VI, a mere boy of 10 at his father's death, ruled only briefly but nonetheless left behind an extensive numismatic record. The delicate features of the young monarch, who died at age 16, graced many of his silver coins: his crowned profile appeared on the *shilling*, as the *teston* was known by then; his image, full face, was on a new *sixpence*, or half-*shilling*; and his figure on horseback was on England's new *crown*, a large silver coin that weighed 31.014 grams. This last-mentioned coin was the first English coin to carry a date; it was struck during the last three years (1551-1553) of Edward's reign. Edward's silver crown, which represented one of several attempts to restore the English coinage to earlier standards of weight and fineness, was England's first dollar-sized coin, counterpart to the *taler* issues of other powers.

Coins of the Lowlands

In the Low Countries, which had been rich in coinages since early in the Middle Ages, Antwerp now rose to become one of Europe's richest and most active financial centers. In 1460, for example, Antwerp opened Europe's first stock exchange. In this region both the wealthy princes of Burgundy and the Holy Roman Emperor, Charles V, produced fine coins. Charles and Philip II beggared the imperial treasury, directing the bulk of the silver taken from the New World into the Netherlands where pay for the troops and other war expenses absorbed enormous wealth.

In 1568 began a long and bitter war of independence that pitted the Protestants and patriots of the Low Countries against the Holy Roman Empire as exemplified by Philip, who ruled not only in the Netherlands but also in Spain. The period that followed, marked by fierce battles between Netherlands patriots and Spanish troops of Philip under such famous leaders as the Duke of Alva, Don Juan of Austria, and Duke Alessandro Farnese, produced a fascinating numismatic record. The patriots' coins appeared in a variety of metals — gold, silver, tin, and lead — and forms — round, square, and single-faced. They were minted under conditions of extreme hardship and often made from melted-down statues or church treasure. These coins speak of the desperate resistance made by many cities under siege; names such as Haarlem, Middelburg, Groningen, Amsterdam, Campen, and Maestrich can be found on them. Many of the cities followed the example of Leiden, which withstood a long Spanish siege. The people of Leiden struck coins in silver and in copper and even impressed their dies on cardboard taken from the bindings of old church records, proudly proclaiming *pugno pro patria*, "I fight for my fatherland," and displaying a lion rampant, holding a pole topped by a liberty cap. The inscriptions on the coins of Campen read: *extremum subsidium*, "the ultimate help." The coins of Maestrich humbly prayed *protege, Domine, populum tuum propter nominis tui gloriam*, "Protect your people, O Lord, for the glory of your name," but defiantly displayed a hand grasping a sword.

The northern provinces of the Netherlands were the first to gain independence. They promptly minted interesting new coins; one of these, the silver *leeuwendaalder*, or "lion *daalder*," which bore the image of a lion rampant, became a popular coin in international trade. It was used extensively in the American colonies, where it was called the "dog *dollar*."

The dignified image of William I of Orange, the power behind the independence movement and the first *stathouder* of the seven independent northern provinces (Holland, Zeeland, Utrecht, Gelderland, Overijssel, Friesland, and Groningen), took the place of Philip's likeness on the gold *ducats* and silver *daalders* of the united provinces. After William's assassination by a religious fanatic, an unexpected figure appeared on Dutch silver coins. This was Robert Dudley, Earl of Leicester, the longtime favorite of Elizabeth I of England and one of the most colorful figures at the Elizabethan court. Leicester com-

152. Religion continued to be a favorite subject in the Baroque period: the baptism in the River Jordan (Tuscany, 1684); pilgrims at the Holy Door in St. Peter's and Pope surrounded by Cardinals (Papal Rome, 1675, 1696); Virgin and Child (Genoa, 1682); St. Anthony (Paderborn, 1685); St. John preaching, St. Peter helping the lame, a religious quotation and a view of the Campidoglio with figures symbolizing the arts (Papal Rome, 1699, 1677, 1685, 1706). First top: 45 mm.

manded an English expedition to the Low Countries and was there elected governor general. During his brief stay an attempt was made to unify the coinage of the seven provinces, and the earl's laurel-wreathed image appeared on a silver *real*. A circle composed of the shields of the seven provinces surrounding a bundle of arrows, the emblem of the new union, completed the design. Leicester's rule in the Netherlands was a fleeting interlude, but the gold *ducat* minted at that time and showing the figure of a knight holding a bundle of arrows became one of the most long-lived of all Dutch coins. It was still struck as a trade coin until recent times and grew to be among the most popular of all gold coins in international trade.

From the Baroque to Modern Times

From the enlightened realism of the Renaissance we reach the exuberant period of the Baroque. Countries and vast territories were devastated by wars fomented by religious intolerance or by dynastic rivalries.

The great wealth of precious metals shipped to Europe from the New World diminished from a torrent to a trickle in the 17th century. It had reached its climax in the last decade of the 1500s when each year saw the importation of gold and silver worth 10 million or more *pesos*. In the mints of Europe, portraits of each nation's rulers remained the principal coin motif. Although many artists of renown were called upon to immortalize their princes, the emphasis began to shift in a way that reflected the spirit of the times. Character and personality seemed to diminish, overshadowed by a display of surface decorum. High ruffs, fine armor, festoons of honors and decorations, elaborate hair styles — all these external trappings were dominant on many coins. As in the other arts, in coinage, too, the Baroque prevailed. Nevertheless, at least in Italy, the old standards were still preserved. Although Italy had long since passed its financial zenith, numerous superb gold and silver coins were produced by various princely houses.

Coins of the Italian Lands

Unus non sufficit (mundus) — "One (world) does not suffice" — with these haughty words, King Charles II of Naples inscribed a *piastra* in 1684 to boast of the Hapsburg pride in ruling over two "worlds." Large gold and silver coins struck by Venice and Genoa proclaim the enduring power and wealth of these maritime republics. Parallel with its superb gold issues, Venice struck a great variety of beautiful *dollar*-sized silver coins. *Oselle,* a remarkable series of silver presentation pieces, were distributed by the doge on the first day of the new year. Their name explains that they replaced earlier gifts of birds — "*ucelli.*" One osella provides a view of the center of Venice showing the Piazzetta and the Palace of the Doges.

In Florence the Medici princes embellished their *piastra,* the large silver coin, with an outstanding image of St. John the Baptist. The dukes of Mantua picked zodiacal signs and even a large hound, the pride of their hunting parties, for their coins. One of the most graceful coins, the so-called *pezza della rosa* — "the coin with a rose" — came from Leghorn, the Tuscan harbor. Its motto *gratia obvia ultio quesita* — "my grace is given naturally, my

153. Sumptuous strikings of heavy gold coins often served as presentation pieces. The two 100-ducats struck in Poland, 1621, and in Prague, 1629, as well as the 50-zecchini piece of Venice (c. 1779-1789) can be compared in size and weight to a regular Venetian zecchino of 1694-1700 or to one of the smallest gold coins, a 1/32 ducat of Regensburg (c. 1700). First upper left: 70 mm.

154. *View of* Piazza San Marco *and the palace of the Doges in Venice on a painting by Antonio Canaletto (about 1731) and on an osella struck in 1684 by the Doge Marcantonio Giustinian. Coin: 36 mm.*

punishment is provoked," was quoted from the ancient writer Seneca by Prince Ferdinand II to explain his basic philosophy.

The Popes excelled all other rulers in coin aesthetics during the Baroque period. Painters and sculptors had gravitated toward Rome even in late Renaissance times. The men who held Peter's chair in the late 16th century and during the 17th century continued the established tradition in lavish style. Giovanni Bernini, a gifted sculptor and architect, advised the pope to install more efficient hydraulic presses for his mint. From the time of Urban VIII (1623-1644) to that of Clement XII (1730-1740), the popes issued such gold coins as *scudi d'oro* and even *quadruple* that weighed as much as 13 grams. The papal silver coinage was rich in *scudi, dollar*-sized coins, and smaller *testons*. A varied and rich iconography, conceived in lavish and lively Baroque style, celebrated the popes' remarkable efforts to embellish Rome and its surroundings and publicize the spiritual life of the church. Gaspare Mola designed the group of coins that bore on its large silver *scudi* the strong profile of Urban VIII, the stalwart defender of orthodoxy under whom Galileo was tried and condemned by the Inquisition.

During the pontificate of Clement X (1670-1676), a Bavarian engraver, Alberto Hamerani, established an artistic dynasty which served 13 popes in the course of five successive generations. Alberto engraved a silver *scudo* in 1672 that displayed a view of the harbor of Civitavecchia which had been rebuilt by Clement X. Pope Innocent XI (1676-1689) used the silver sent to Rome (in reaction to the Turkish seige of Vienna) to mint *testones* in 1677 that showed Peter helping the lame; their inscription read *Quod habeo tibi do,* or "What I have I give to you." Both this graceful engraving and the scene with Christ on a stormy sea were the works of Giovanni Hamerani, one of Alberto's sons

126

155. "It rules or rather serves", is the motto on this testone depicting a table with coins struck in 1703 by Pope Clement XI. 32 mm.

156. Pezza della rosa – "the coin of the rose" struck by Cosimo III de' Medici in 1718 for the Tuscan harbor of Leghorn. 43 mm.

157. Hunting dog of the Gonzaga princes on a silver ducatone of Mantua, 1627. 44 mm.

158. Rome at the time of the Popes: Piranesi's ▷ view of Piazza Navona (mid 1700s), and two silver half-scudi of Pope Clement X depicting the harbor of Ripetta in the center of Rome, 1706, and the Pantheon of Agrippa, 1711. Coins: 36 & 38 mm.

and the most talented member of the family.

The French artist Ferdinand Saint-Urbain was one of the most renowned engravers of his day. He settled in Rome in 1683 and worked for 13 years at the papal mint. His composition on a 1699 scudo, showing the Hebrews in the desert collecting manna, commemorated the reduction of the wheat tax effected by Pope Innocent XII (1691-1700), often called the "father of the poor."

Clement XI (1700-1721) restored the Pantheon and other Roman buildings and ordered the minting of several coins noting his accomplishments. Scenes include the Ripetta Harbor on the River Tiber; the Pantheon itself; the fountain and obelisk restored by the Pope in the Pantheon square; and the bridge built in 1712 over the Rio Maggiore near Civita Castellana. All these coins were the work of a third member of the Hamerani family, Ermenegildo.

Clement XII, though a great patron of the arts — his love for antiquities led to the founding of the Capitoline Museum and the papal "Coin Cabinet," — did little to continue the tradition of excellence in the papal mint. Clement's coinage lacked artistic inspiration. See, for example, the allegorical depiction of the Church as a female figure floating on a cloud, designed by still another Hamerani, Ottone, in mid-18th century. Essentially a stereotype, the motif continued to be used on papal coins for almost a century. Coin portraits of the popes, while outstanding artistic achievements, could not compare with the fine and forceful renditions of earlier days. By the end of the 18th century, the art of papal coinage continued though without distinction.

Coins of France

In France changes in the coinage took place during the rule of Louis XIII (1610-1643). A very gifted engraver, Jean Varin of Liège, joined the Paris mint in 1629. A decade later Varin cut the dies for a new gold coin, called the louis d'or. Weighing 6.75 grams, it was valued at 10 silver livres and bore a simple bust of Louis in the classical style. In 1641, France at last followed the example of the other nations of Europe and produced a dollar-sized silver

159. Series of coins struck during the seventy-three year reign of Louis XIV of France showing the king as he changed from a five year-old boy to an old man. First coin: 34 mm.

coin, the so-called *louis d'argent,* or *ecu blanc,* which bore the same bust of Louis XIII.

Louis XIV (1643-1715) succeeded his father when he was a child of five and reigned for 73 years. Known in history as the "Sun King," he presided over a golden age of arts and letters which, oddly enough, was scarcely reflected in the royal coinage. Louis was a passionate numismatic scholar, and a painting shows the young king listening to a lecture on coins by Varin. For all that, however, his mintings fall far short of good art. The best that can be said is that the coins comprise a kind of portrait gallery that presents the king's image almost year by year from early youth to old age. The portraits are dignified, but they reflect aloofness rather than the charm and warmth of a real personality.

The nation's finances were strained by the Sun King's wars and other expenditures. The disastrous course of affairs continued under Louis XV when the monetary schemes of John Law brought the finances of France to a catastrophic point in 1721 (see Chapter VIII). These panics notwithstanding, one of the nation's silver *ecus* — the so-called "wreath *ecu*" minted under Louis XV and under his successor, Louis XVI — became one of the coins most widely circulated in international trade; large numbers of them were to be found in the American colonies.

The storming of the Bastille in 1789 is regarded as a prelude to a new, democratic period when royal power seemingly ended. Yet two years later, in 1791, the image of Louis XVI continued to appear on the new silver coinage, the *ecu constitutionnel,* and it was not until 1793 that Louis lost his head. The new *ecu,* a masterly composition by Augustin Dupré, one of the most talented engravers of France, featured, on the reverse, a new allegorical male figure representing Law and Freedom. The copper *sou* of 1791 was even more explicit; the Phrygian liberty cap was accompanied by an inscription — *La Nation, la Loi, le Roi* — that left the monarchy plainly in third place.

The year 1795 brought France not only a new coinage but a new monetary system, the decimal system, which was to have far-reaching effects on the monetary systems of the world. The *franc* was now divisible into 10 *decimes* and the *decime* into 10 *centimes.* Dupré's genius continued to create inspiring symbols for the new era. He engraved a handsome allegorical figure for copper coins of the Republic, modeled after Madame Récamier, a famous beauty, who was depicted wearing the Phrygian liberty cap. For the silver five-*franc* piece Dupré designed a scene showing Hercules standing between the allegorical figures of Justice and Liberty. It was this five-*franc* piece that became the basic unit of the new monetary system.

But Revolutionary imagery was short-lived. By 1803 the allegorical figures had vanished, and a simple, bare head of the First Consul, Napoleon Bonaparte, appeared on French gold and silver coins. After his coronation in 1804, the title of emperor appeared together with Napoleon's image on the obverse, but the reverse still spoke of the Republic. The anomaly was not corrected until 1809.

Gold, which was almost unused by the Republic, was widely circulated under Napoleon. Forty-*franc* and 20-*franc* gold pieces were struck in large quantities by mints throughout France and those in other cities now subjugated: Rome, Turin, Genoa, and Utrecht. The 20-*franc* piece was soon called a *Napoleon*, and this name is still widely applied to 20-*franc* gold coins by many.

After the fall of Napoleon and the restoration of the French monarchy under Louis XVIII, France passed through two revolutions — in 1830 and 1848 — only to see Louis Napoleon secure the same supreme power his uncle had held. During the intervening half-century, only royal portraits had appeared on French coins. Napoleon III, to prove the nation's great wealth in gold, promptly introduced two new gold coins, the large 50- and 100-*franc* pieces.

The monetary reforms of Revolutionary and Napoleonic France were eventually adopted by other European states: by Belgium in 1832, by Switzerland in 1850, and by Italy in 1862. This development led to the founding of the "Latin Union" under the direction of France in 1865. The Union recognized as its basic unit a silver franc weighing five grams and a gold 20-*franc* piece weighing 6.45 grams. In the next few years Rumania, Spain, and Greece adjusted their coinages to the system, and it remained virtually unchanged until 1916.

The disasters of the Franco-Prussian War put an end to the rule of Napoleon III, leaving France in confusion and Paris in the hands of the Commune. While fighting raged in the streets of Paris, Citizen Camélinat, the official in charge of the mint, busily minted coins for the use of his comrades. The Revolutionary coin design engraved in 1795 by Dupré and displaying Hercules, Justice, and Liberty was revived on a new five-*franc* piece; the silver used for the minting of the coins was obtained from the vaults of the Banque de France, from imperial silver vessels seized in the Tuileries, and from other art objects found in the apartments of Empress Eugénie. Identical with earlier French issues, the Commune coins could be distinguished only by a small symbol — a trident — selected by the director of the mint. Speed of production was essential, so that only a few of the coins showed a change in border inscription. Of the 600,000 pieces struck, the bulk still carried the earlier motto: *Dieu protege la France,* or "God guards France," an ironic statement for a supposedly atheistic commune. Most of the coins were later recalled and melted down.

160. *Well-balanced design and neat engraving distinguished Spanish coinage: eight-real pieces struck by Charles I (1516-55) with the names of Ferdinand and Isabella; by Philip II (1555-98); Philip IV (1636); and Philip V (1731). First coin top: 40 mm.*

Coins of England

In 1603 James VI of Scotland succeeded Elizabeth and ascended the throne as James I of England. The union of Scotland and England, very much on the king's mind, was emphasized in his coinage. The inscription *Tueatur unita Deus,* or "God protect the union," appeared on the *crown* (a gold coin), and a text from Ezekiel, *Faciam eos in gentem unam,* or "I will make them one nation," on a new gold coin, valued at 20 *shillings,* that was popularly called a *unite.* Indications of value appeared for the first time on English gold coins during James's reign. The gold *laurel* was marked with the Roman numeral XX to indicate a value of 20 *shillings;* the *spur ryal* bore the numeral XV, and the angel, the numeral X, to indicate their values of 15 and 10 *shillings,* respectively. Silver coins struck from metal obtained from mines in Wales showed ostrich plumes, the blazon of the Prince of Wales, in addition to the other royal symbols.

During the eventful reign of Charles I (1625-1649), a French die-sinker, Nicolas Briot, moved to London and was employed at the Tower mint. From his hands came a number of fine portrait busts and mounted figures of the king. Among Charles's many issues, the so-called "Declaration" coinage merits special attention. The large gold triple *unites* and the heavy silver pound and half-pound pieces struck at Shrewsbury and Oxford during the civil war, under-

161. *The gold "fine" sovereign (1558-1561) was one of England's most beautiful coins; the enthroned figure represents Queen Elizabeth I holding scepter and orb; on the reverse the royal arms are surrounded by the petals of a rose. 43 mm.*

162. *Times of war and peace on the coinage* ▷ *of Charles I (1625-49) of England: gold unit or sceptre and silver 60 shillings struck for Scotland, about 1637, with the fine engraving of N. Briot. The war forced the king to issue the gold triple unite, struck in Oxford and Shrewsbury, 1642-43, displaying Charles' famous proclamation and the heavy silver pound of Shrewsbury, 1642, with the king riding over a pile of scattered weapons. First coin upper left: 37 mm.*

lined the king's basic concessions made at Wellington, September 19, 1642: "the religion of the Protestants, the laws of England, the liberty of Parliament." This period of war left an interesting number of "necessity" issues produced in towns and castles under siege. Briot tried to introduce mechanization — in the form of the screw press — at the mint, but his attempts, although approved by the king, did not succeed. It was not until the Restoration brought the monarchy back to England in the person of Charles II (1660-1685) that mechanization triumphed. The first coins of Charles's reign were struck as before, with the hammer, but beginning in 1662 the entire English minting came to be "milled coinage," that is, struck by machine. During the reign of Charles II a new gold unit, valued at 20 *shillings* was issued. It came to be known as the *guinea,* because the bullion from which it was minted was brought from Guinea by the Africa Company. The series included five-*guinea,* two-*guinea,* one-*guinea,* and half-*guinea* coins, and it continued in issue under subsequent British rulers until 1816.

During Charles II's time a fascinating dispute took place between two of his mint engravers, Thomas Simon and John Roettier brought over from Amster-

dam. Since Charles favored Roettier, Simon expressed his disappointment by creating one of the most accomplished portrait coins of modern times. This so-called "petition *crown*" had inscribed on it, in miniscule letters on the edge, "Thomas Simon most humbly prays Your Majesty to compare this his tryal [sic] piece with the Dutch and if more truly drawn & embossed more gracefuly order'd [sic] and more accurately engraved to relieve him." One year later Simon died in the terrible plague of 1665.

It now became the English habit to mark coins with symbols indicating the origin of their metal in the same way that ostrich plumes had earlier signified Welsh silver. An elephant or a castle indicated gold or silver from the Africa Company; a rose, silver from the west of England. Other memorials also appeared. Gold and silver coins minted in 1702 and 1703 carried the word "VIGO" under the bust of Queen Anne, implying that they had been struck from bullion taken from the Spanish treasure fleet burned at Vigo Bay in October, 1702. The word "LIMA" similarly appeared on coins of 1745 and 1746, indicating that the bullion had been seized in South America by Admiral Anson during his voyage around the world (1740-1744).

The coins of Mary, Queen of Scots (1542-1567), are especially picturesque.   132

163. Prospector with divining rod and a cross section of a mine on a large three-taler piece of 1681 from Brunswick-New Luneburg, Germany. 72 mm.

164. Many interesting square-shaped silver Klippe pieces were issued by John George II and other Saxon princes for shooting matches arranged at the court of Dresden in commemoration of happy events: (from left to right) the birth of the crown-prince in 1699; a festival in honor of the princess-consort, 1676; and the wedding of a daughter in 1662. Middle coin: 65 mm.

165. The death of a prince was often commemorated on coins: so-called "butterfly taler" struck on the occasion of the death of Frederick Augustus I of Saxony (1694-1733); and a taler struck 1699 by Prince Augustus of Saxe-Weissenfels in memory of his wife Anna Maria. First left: 44 mm.

Religious quotations such as *Ecce ancilla Domini* — "behold the maiden of the Lord," or *Quae Deus conjunxit nemo separet* — "what God hath joined together let no man put asunder," were added to coins struck only two years prior to her husband Darnley's murder.

Beset by financial and monetary problems in the aftermath of a long series of wars, England instituted a currency reform in 1816. The bimetallic system was abandoned in favor of a gold standard, and silver and copper were reduced to the status of subsidiary coinages. Benedetto Pistrucci, a talented Italian gem engraver and medallist, had moved to London in 1814. As a suitable subject for the reverse of the new coinage, he suggested St. George and the dragon and executed a sample design on a jasper cameo. The master of the mint approved, and Pistrucci proceeded to cut the dies for the new reverse against heavy criticism. His masterpiece has remained the nation's favorite coin design for more than 150 years.

Queen Victoria's graceful, young, profile head, the work of the mint's chief engraver, William Wyon, saw use on English gold and silver coins for many years. In 1846 Wyon produced an unusual coin: a one-*crown* piece showing Victoria in medieval costume and inscribed with lettering in the Gothic style.

Soon known as the "Gothic *crown*," the coin was struck again in 1847 and 1853 but was never put into circulation.

Coins of Germanic Lands

It was a German prince — Julius, Duke of Brunswick — who, late in the 16th century, conceived the theory of a monetary reserve. The need to prevent the silver that flowed in torrents from his mines in the Harz Mountains from disturbing his duchy's financial balance, as the import of metals from the New World was doing elsewhere, forced his idea into practice. Technical advances in minting allowed Julius to strike very large silver coins — multiple *talers,* of various sizes, some equivalent in weight to 10 *talers* or even 12. The larger coins weighed as much as 354 grams, or close to 14 ounces. The prince's subjects were compelled to purchase these multiple *talers* in amounts proportional to their wealth, but they could not circulate the coins, which were meant only to be stored. Each holder was required to produce the big silver pieces on demand and to exchange them for regular coins whenever the necessity arose. In this way Julius succeeded in establishing a silver reserve, readily available in times of need, while simultaneously preventing an inflation of the currency. The multiple *talers* of Brunswick were struck for 100 years. They were called *Loeser,* or "redeemable coins," because

166. The talers of the Baroque period present a fascinating gallery of costumes and hair-fashions: Klappmutzen or caps with a cut brim (upper left) and a fur-collared coat of the 1500s; high collars as well as delicate lace-trimmings and lace veils, and a bell-shaped farthingale of the 1600s seen on coins of Saxony, the Holy Roman Empire, Wurttemberg and Sweden. First upper left: 41 mm.

167. *The wealth and power of the Holy Roman Empire were expressed in many broad or thick multiple silver* talers *and gold* ducats; *double show-*taler, *1509 of Maximilian I; thick 5-*talers *of 1651; double-*taler *of 1675 and a 10-*ducat *piece of 1703. First coin left: 53 mm.*

of their inscription: *Genannt Braunschweigische Julius Loeser,"* that is, "Called the redeemable [coins of] Julius of Brunswick."

During the 17th century the Brunswick *Loeser* developed into showpieces, devoted to representing the rulers' life histories, and the pattern established by the dukes of Brunswick was copied by a number of other German princes. At many courts silver *talers* and gold *ducats* of both the 17th and the 18th centuries gained new importance as commemorative coins, marking such events as royal births, coronations, weddings, and funerals.

In 1618 the outbreak of the Thirty Years' War was followed by great speculation in money and runaway inflation. Within a year the price of a bushel of wheat in the German lands rose from four to 55 *talers*. Agents all over Europe bought up good coins in order to melt, debase, and remint the metal. Mints sprang up everywhere, and the German lands were flooded with worthless coins. "The new money was almost pure copper, only blanched and rendered white," a contemporary description stated. "[The whiteness] lasted only about eight days; then [the coins] turned fire-red. Boilers, pipes, troughs, and whatever else was of copper were dismounted, brought to the mint, and transformed into money . . . wherever a church had a baptismal font of

135

168. Martin Luther's life on coins: Luther's portrait by Lucas Cranach (1525); his bust on a show-taler of Eisleben, 1661; together with Huss on a taler of Magdeburg, 1617; a portrait of his wife Catharina von Bora on a show-taler of Gotha, 1717; and a view of Wittenberg, 1717. The box-taler, 1730, depicting the Augsburg Confession held in 1530 and hand-painted inclusions illustrating religious scenes. First coin upper left: 45 mm.

169. Citizens walking within the walls of the beautiful Bavarian city of Augsburg. Its medieval cathedral and Rathaus are depicted on this 1672 taler struck in the name of Emperor Leopold I. 50 mm.

170. This attractive show-taler struck in 1713 by Constantine Brancoveanu, Prince of Walachia (1689-1714) furnished incriminating proof in his trial at Constantinople. 44 mm.

copper it had to go to the mint . . . no saints could help; it was sold by those who had been baptized in it."

The economy could not return to prewar conditions at the end of the Thirty Years' War. Silver had grown too dear, and the *taler* lost its importance as a main circulating coin. Rulers continued to strike *talers,* but some fulfilled a different function, that of the showpiece or gift. Coin portraits of many heroes and villains of those eventful times often appear, for example: Eusebius Wallenstein, one of the leading generals of the Thirty Years' War; Rudolph II, the learned ruler of the Holy Roman Empire, who encouraged alchemists to transmute base metal into gold at his court in Prague. The coinages of the Holy Roman Empire, although simple in their basic design, were limited to fine portraits and elaborate coats of arms. In some of their superb gold coins — often struck in multiples of five, ten, and even up to one hundred *ducats* — the wealth and power of this vast empire were revealed.

In the Germanic lands, Protestant princes celebrated the first and second centennials of the Reformation as well as the Augsburg Confession of 1530. Luther's portrait, however, appeared only on rare occasions. In 1717 the city of Gotha depicted Luther and his wife Catherine Bora on a show-*taler.*

Very picturesque elements of German and Swiss *taler* iconography, from the 1600s on, were representations of cities which guide us along gabled houses through old city gates into Augsburg, and Frankfurt, or over bridges into Basel, Zurich, and Lucerne.

A great German sculptor and medallist, Karl Voigt, was appointed to the Munich mint in 1829 by the Bavarian monarch, Louis I, an outstanding admirer of the arts. Under the patronage of Louis, Voigt created a series of coins called the "history *talers.*" These coins were mostly the size of a *taler* or a double-*taler,* with, on the reverse, a succession of scenes commemorating family events during Louis's reign, or representing monuments or newly created orders and decorations. Gold *ducats,* struck from metal washed from the Danube, the Rhine, the Isar, and the Inn, carried charming views

171. Copper rubles struck in 1770 and 1771 at the Sestoretsk arms works. Catherine II hoped that these coins, weighing over two pounds, would redeem paper notes in circulation. 77 mm.

172. *Two centuries of Russian coinage:* Jefimok or counterstamped taler of Saxony of 1655; beard-token, 1705, paid as tax for growing a beard under Peter the Great's rule; a square copper grivna, 1726; a fine portrait ruble of Peter the Great, 1719; and a 1½ ruble, 1836, of Nicholas I depicting the Tsarina and the imperial children. First coin left: 45 mm.

of the old medieval city of Speyer on the Rhine, and of Munich with its famous cathedral, the Frauenkirche, on the Isar.

Germany did not achieve national monetary unity until 1871, following the Franco-Prussian War, when a gold standard and a uniform coinage were introduced. Until then no fewer than 67 different kinds of money, often including obsolete and obsolescent coins, had circulated in the German lands. In general, neither the artistic rendition nor the historic content of these silver pieces was especially noteworthy; they did not compare in quality with earlier German issues.

During the rule of Wilhelm II (1888-1918), Germany minted coins both for home use and for its overseas colonies. Some of the colonial coins, such as the 1916 gold 15-*rupee* piece for circulation in German East Africa, are of unusual interest. The coin shows an elephant with Mount Kilimanjaro in the background. Another issue, in both gold and silver, bears a bird-of-paradise; the coins were meant for circulation in German New Guinea in 1895 and are held to be among the most beautiful pieces in modern coinage.

173. Queen Mary of Romania in her coronation costume on a 1922 gold fifty lei piece,
designed by P. Dammann. 40 mm.

Other European Coins

One of the oddest kinds of money ever known in Europe was made and
circulated in Sweden during the rule of Queen Christina. She succeeded her
father, Gustavus II Adolphus, the "Lion of the North" and hero of the
Protestant cause during the Thirty Years' War, after his death in battle in
1632. In an effort to make use of the nation's large copper reserves, Christina
in 1644 authorized the issuance of *platmynt*, or "plate money," made of
copper to take the place of silver coins. The plates were rectangular, and
some were of enormous dimensions. The largest, a 10-*daler* piece, weighed
19.7 kilograms, or more than 43 pounds. The plates were produced in mints
situated near copper-mining towns such as Avesta. Although scarcely practical, they were minted in various denominations, from one-and-a-half *dalers*
to 10 *dalers,* until 1776.

During the same era, a Swedish financier came to the aid of Charles XII
(1697-1718), the king whose military endeavors against Peter the Great had
exhausted Sweden's economy. Baron Georg Heinrich von Görtz was em-
powered by Charles in 1715 to take extraordinary financial measures. The
method he adopted — the issuance of a fiduciary currency with a low intrinsic value — was exactly opposite to the copperplate policy of Christina.
Görtz introduced token copper coins, quickly named "Görtz *dalers,*" bearing
mythological and allegorical figures, which were to be redeemable in gold
and silver after the war. Charles's sudden death in 1718 left all in disarray.
More than 20 million promissory copper coins were in circulation and now
seemed worthless. Görtz was condemned to death and beheaded, a martyr

175. Napoleon and members of his family; portrait of Bonaparte by A. J. Gros; Napoleon as emperor of France shown with bare (1804) and with laureate head (1812) and as King of Italy (1810); his brother-in-law, Joachim Murat, King of Naples (1813); his brother Louis, King of Holland (1808); and his brother Jerome, King of Westphalia (1810). First coin: 38 mm.

174. Emblematic Roman eagle commemorating the Revolution of 1799 by the citizens of the Eternal City: "Day which compensates for so many years of sorrow". 43 mm.

who paid with his life for introducing the kind of currency that is now accepted throughout the world.

Coins contributed greatly to the martyr-death in 1714 of a Walachian Prince ruling one of the Danubian principalities under the suzerainty of the Turks. The wealthy Prince, Constantine Brancoveanu (1689-1714), had struck large silver pieces showing him in his lush, national costume with plumes fastened to his fur cap. After making secret liaisons with the Russians and the Austrians, he was captured by the Turks and brought for trial to Constantinople. There he and his sons were beheaded. His coins had figured as proof of his treasonous striving for independence!

Starting in 1700 Peter the Great introduced a westernized coinage in Russia. A portrait of the czar, engraved by diesinkers brought from abroad, adorned the obverse of the silver coins, which were proof of Peter's great success in securing a place for Russia among the great powers of Europe. It seems hardly conceivable that, 20 years earlier, the same ruler had issued "beard tokens" that showed the wearer of a beard to be one who had paid the tax levied on such a privilege.

During the 19th century the Russian coinage system was bimetallic, and the

176. Queen Victoria of England represented as Queen Una from the Elizabethan fairy book by Edmund Spenser, guiding the British lion. This rare pattern five-pound piece of 1839 by William Wyon never became an official coin. 38 mm.

178. Striking design of a Canadian goose selected by Canada for its Centennial celebration in 1967. 36 mm.

ruble remained the basic unit. The gold 10-ruble and five-ruble pieces and lesser silver coins of the early 1800's were heraldic in design and graceful in appearance. A Russian experiment in the late 1820s attempted to utilize new and rich platinum strikes in the Urals. Three-ruble, six-ruble, and 12-ruble coins were minted from platinum for a number of years, until increasing popular distrust and a reduced output of the metal combined to put an end to this unusual coinage in 1845. The final years of Romanoff rule were marked by the minting of a series of silver rubles in the 1900s commemorating the memory of the czars Alexander II and Alexander III, the centennial of the French defeat in 1812, the bicentennial of Peter the Great's victory at Gangut in 1714, and even the 300th anniversary of Romanoff rule. Few could guess that, when the bust of Nicholas II was coupled with that of Michael, the first Romanoff czar, on a commemorative ruble in 1913, the coins would show the beginning and end of that dynasty, extinguished barely four years later

177. Wax model on brass for the "lion of Judah" prepared for Ethiopian coinage by F. X. Pawlik, the engraver of the Austrian mint; and the accepted design for the talari coin (1899) by Jules C. Chaplain of the Paris mint. Coin 40 mm.

179. The simple and graceful design of a menorah by Myriam Caroly on an Israeli 1958 five pound piece. 34 mm.

at Ekaterinburg.

For more than a century now, all over Europe as elsewhere in the world, paper money has carried the main load of providing a monetary medium, and coins, seldom any longer minted in precious metals, have been largely relegated the task of serving as small change. Nonetheless, coin iconography still has a mission to fulfill. The Menorah by Miriam Caroly that graces one Israeli coin, although highly modernistic in design, may be didactic, in that it expresses an old and venerated religious tradition. By the same token, the accomplished grace of the new allegorical figure of Italia by Giampaoli conjures up memories of the Renaissance, Italy's chief period of artistic greatness. But we must ask ourselves what else other than pleasure — pure aesthetic pleasure — could have caused the Irish to display on their coins of the 1920s and 1930s a whole menagerie of animals: a woodcock, a sow with piglets, a rabbit, and a horse. ☐

181. First coins in the New World, silver four-, two- and one-real pieces struck in Mexico (1536-1542) in the name of Charles I of Spain and his mother Johanna. Largest: 33 mm.

VI: COINS OF THE NEW WORLD: FROM COLUMBUS TO KENNEDY

"I can tell you of a land where people eat and drink from golden dishes, where gold is as cheap to them as iron is to you. . . ."

Balboa's description of the New World was inaccurate though enticing. For over 450 years men have sailed westward from Europe to discover and possess mythical treasures. Gold, silver and precious gems were indeed found in the Western Hemisphere. But the real treasure evolved from the land. People who came from all parts of the globe, seeking El Dorado, found instead man's most valuable need, opportunity. And opportunity wedded to natural resources, inventiveness and hard work created the greatest economic achievement of mankind. Of the daring men who first sailed uncharted oceans in frail ships, some were motivated by curiosity, some by religion, some by nationalism, — but all were tempted by the lure of money.

The Search for El Dorado

In 1536 less than 50 years after Columbus set foot on the relative wilderness of America, a Spanish mint in Mexico City struck the first coins to be made in the New World. They were silver, and the initial issue included one-, two-, and three-*real* pieces and half- and quarter-*reales* (this last coin being called a *cuartilla*). Both the *cuartilla* and the three-*real* piece were soon discontinued as impractical, and in 1538 a four-*real* piece was added to the array. That same year, the Spanish monarch, Charles I (1516-1556), issued a decree prohibiting the coinage of gold and copper in his New World dominions. In fact copper coins were badly needed in daily transactions, and in their absence the Indians simply turned to the pre-Conquest practice of using cocoa beans in trade. The exchange was set at 140 beans for one *real*. The cocoa bean continued circulating in New Spain for many years.

182. A 1739 gold eight-escudo coin struck at Lima, Peru. 30 mm.

The first New World *real* weighed 3.43 grams, with multiples and fractions of corresponding weights. The coins were issued in the names of Charles and his invalid mother, Joanna, the ill-fated daughter of Ferdinand and Isabella. The inscription indicated that the royal mother and son were monarchs of both Spain and the Indies. On the obverse appeared the crowned and quartered shield of Spain, with lions and castles representing the kingdoms of Leon and Castile, as well as a pomegranate, the emblem of Granada. The initial "M" with a small "o" above, indicated that Mexico was the issuing mint; other single letters on the coins identified various mintmasters. The device on the reverse had been specially designed for Charles. Two crowned pillars symbolized the Pillars of Hercules, once deemed the western limit of the Old World. A bold inscription — *Plus ultra,* or "farther beyond" — witnessed to Charles's pride in the Spanish conquest of the New World.

In 1531 Francisco Pizarro invaded the Inca Empire in South America and added a new dominion to the Spanish crown. Following the murder of the Inca ruler, Atahualpa, immeasurable treasure fell into the hands of the conquistadores. In 1542 Charles granted the Viceroyalty of Peru authority over all Spanish South America.

183. Portraits of Spanish kings depicted on their Spanish-American coinages (from left to right): Philip V, Ferdinand VI, Charles III, Charles IV and Ferdinand VII, the last to rule in the colonies. First left: 36 mm.

The Viceroyalty of Peru was extremely rich in gold and silver and was a logical site for a new mint. In August, 1565 Charles's successor, Philip II, decreed the creation of a mint in Lima. As in Mexico, the minting of gold and copper coins was expressly forbidden. The silver coins struck at Lima between 1568 and 1570 displayed the name of Philip II and the mint initial but otherwise they bore the same designs as the coinage issued in Mexico in the names of Charles and Joanna. The Lima coins are quite rare today. The minting included denominations from a quarter-*real* up to an eight-*real* piece. The latter, a large, *dollar*-sized coin that weighed approximately 27 grams, was eventually to be issued by every mint in the Spanish colonial empire. It became one of the most widely circulated and generally accepted coins of the modern world, being used not only in the two Americas but also in the Near East and Far East. In the United States, *pieces-of-eight* were among the most popular of coins and enjoyed the status of legal tender there until 1857.

After a few years the minting operation in Peru was formally transferred from Lima to Potosí in the heart of the mining region in what is present-day Bolivia. Standing at an altitude of 13,700 feet, Potosí is one of the highest cities in the world. The Cerro Potosí, a peak that rises a thousand feet or so above the city, yielded an immense wealth of silver. Between the founding of the mint there in the 16th century and the end of Spanish rule in 1825, the silver coins struck in Potosí are estimated to have had an aggregate value of eight billion *reals.* This figure ignores the value of the gold coins minted there after 1777. The city's wealth became proverbial, and the Spanish expression *vale un Potosi,* that is, "worth a Potosí," is still used to describe a rich person.

In 1570 a new coin design was introduced by Philip II, and dies bearing the design arrived in Potosí in 1572, in time for the mint's first strikings. The Spanish shield on the obverse of the coin carried the blazons of the Hapsburg land holdings in Spain, Italy, and the Low Countries. On the reverse, in place of the Pillars of Hercules, there appeared a cross and, in its quarters, the emblems of the old Spanish crown — castles and lions. The mint at Potosí struck coins of this design until 1773.

A letter from Madrid in 1583 reports to the great Fugger banking house in Augsburg: "The fleet from Spanish India, praise be to God, arrived upon the 148

184. *Spanish-American coinage varied little in design from mint to mint; an initial or monogram distinguished them (from left to right): Potosi, Guatemala, Santiago de Chile, Santa Fe de Bogota, Popayan and Mexico. First left: 38 mm.*

185. *"The poor and the rich will be lending us the much needed funds with which to carry on," were the hopes of Don Jose Morelos (1765-1815) who struck these coins in copper and silver (1811-1814) to finance his revolution in Mexico. First: 36 mm.*

13th day of this month without mishap. It carries a shipment of about fifteen millions. It is said that they unloaded and left a million in Havana, because the ships were too heavily laden. This is a pretty penny, which will give new life to commerce."

Sometimes the fleet encountered fierce and pitiless enemies. In July, 1715 an armada of ten Spanish ships left Havana on a sunny day with a treasure worth about fourteen million *pesos* and never arrived in Seville. Men and treasures were lost in a terrible hurricane which smashed the ships against reefs on the Florida coast seven days after they left Havana. Almost 250 years later, a diving expedition recovered old treasures which eluded the salvage operations of contemporaries. Gold in coins and ingots, fragments of china, jewels, lumps of newly minted *pieces-of-eight* encrusted with coral, gold *doubloons* of fine design destined for the royal treasury, were discovered, providing us with a glance at the immense riches which found their way to Europe. This wealth in coins came from mints scattered over Central and South America.

For the mints in Spanish America the year 1675 was an important one. On February 25 a royal order from Spain at last permitted the striking of gold coins overseas. The mint in Mexico was the first to produce gold coins, and Lima was next. The unit was the *escudo*, a gold coin weighing 3.38 grams, with multiples of two, four, and eight *escudos*. These were called *doblon de a dos, doblon de a cuatro,* and *doblon de a ocho,* respectively. The largest, the eight-*escudo* piece, was also called an *onza*.

The monetary reform of June, 1728, revolutionized the coinage of Spanish America. Philip V decreed a new gold and silver coinage struck by machine. It was at this time that the famous "pillar *dollar*" was created. Its design presented the old motif of the Pillars of Hercules combined with two hemispheres. The most characteristic name given to the pillar *dollars* was the *real fuerte columnario, fuerte* indicating that the coin was made of purer silver. This design was first minted in Mexico in 1732.

The silver coinage of Spanish America underwent further changes in 1771 and 1772 when Charles III replaced the pillar design with his own portrait bust. This design, only the portraits changing with the passing of each ruler, remained in use until the final days of Spanish rule in the New World. Nor was the end long in coming. Early in the 19th century the people of Spain rose in arms against Napoleon. At the same time in New Spain a popular uprising began against the centuries-old oppression of the Spanish crown. In September, 1810 under the leadership of a priest, Don Miguel Hidalgo y Costilla (1753-1811), the Mexicans began what was to prove a long and bloody struggle for social reform and political independence.

One of the richest mining centers in New Spain, Guanajuato, was seized by the insurgents, and barely a month after the uprising began, Hidalgo's men started a mint there to provide the money so badly needed to support the war. Hidalgo himself furnished the plans and specifications, and workers were recruited, some of them counterfeiters serving sentences in the Guanajuato jail. The excellently copied silver *pieces-of-eight* from Guanajuato could not be distinguished from those produced at the royal mint. When Guanajuato was recaptured scarcely two months after the uprising had begun, the loyalists marveled at the excellence of the insurgents' mint and moved the machinery to Mexico City for use in the mint there.

186. The high peaks of the Andes with the Llullaillaco Volcano in Chile and the Sierra Madre in Guatemala are depicted on national gold coins of the 1820s. First left: 37 mm.

187. Eight escudos, 1828. The radiant sun symbolized newly gained freedom from Spanish rule in the Province of Rio de la Plata (Argentina). 36 mm.

188. An imaginary portrait of Manco Capac, one of the last Inca kings on a gold fifty-soles piece of Peru, 1931. 34 mm.

Hidalgo was captured and shot in July of the following year, but the fight was continued by another priest, Don José María Morelos y Pavón (1765-1815), who became an outstanding military leader. Like Hidalgo, Morelos was aware that, to succeed, a revolution needs money, and he promptly produced a coinage of his own that bore his name. "This coinage," he wrote, "is to be considered as a promissory note by which the National Treasury obligates itself to pay in gold or silver the value indicated on each piece."

Morelos was captured and shot in December, 1815, but the revolution was not crushed. Six years later the insurgent commander Augustín de Iturbide entered Mexico City in triumph, and Spanish rule came to an end. For less than a year Mexico became an empire when General Iturbide had himself crowned emperor in July, 1823, taking the name of Augustín I. Gold and silver coins were minted in 1822 and 1823 bearing the likeness of the new ruler on the obverse. After ruling for eight months General Iturbide was forced to abdicate; his attempt to regain the throne in 1824 ended in his execution before a firing squad.

After the Iturbide episode Mexico was organized as a republic; the republican coinage expressed the strong feelings that inspired the nation. A sunburst surrounding a liberty cap inscribed with the word *Libertad* graced the reverse of the silver coinage. On the gold coinage appeared the Constitution and a pole topped by a liberty cap, together with the inscription *Libertad en la ley,* or "Liberty under the law." The obverse of both gold and silver coins showed the eagle and cactus iconography first introduced by Iturbide. According to Aztec legend, Huitzilopochtli, the god of war, advised the wandering Aztecs to settle down wherever they came upon an eagle with a snake in its beak, perched on a cactus. The Aztecs spied the omen on a rocky islet in the waters of Lake Texcoco and built their capital city, Tenochtitlán, on the spot. The device was presented in two different versions on the first coins of the republic. One showed the eagle in profile, whereas the other showed the eagle full face. The first design, called the "hooked-neck eagle" by collectors, was minted for only a limited time and is now a highly sought-after numismatic rarity.

The young republic was overthrown by French intervention and, under the guns of Napoleon III's troops, the Archduke Maximilian of Austria was installed as emperor of Mexico. He was to reign for only three years (1864-1867) and his short-lived rule left Mexico with one heritage, at least. The decimal monetary system, of which Maximilian's one-*peso* and 50-*centavo* coins formed a part, remained in use after the ill-fated emperor died before a firing squad in June, 1867. The restored republic maintained the Aztec eagle on the obverse of its coins.

Modern Mexican coinage presents a wide array of designs. Commemorating the 100th anniversary of Hidalgo's revolution in 1910, the Mexicans minted an impressive silver *peso,* nicknamed the "caballito," or "hobby horse," because the figure of Victory on the reverse of the coin is shown on horseback. The early 1900s saw Mexico pass through a period when there was open battle between conservative and revolutionary forces. Such names as Pancho Villa (1877-1923) and Emiliano Zapata (1877-1919) echo the times when various groups of revolutionaries often issued their own money.

Silver for the rebels' coins was often obtained by confiscating bullion at the mines. This was so for one of the first issues of *pesos* and 50-*centavo* pieces struck in October, 1913 by Villa's *Fuerzas Constitucionalistas* in Chihuahua. The most interesting of the revolutionary coins were the *pesos* struck in an Indian village in the state of Durango; they bore the inscription *Muera Huerta*, or "Death to Huerta," the conservative general who then held the office of president. Huerta was so enraged that he ordered the death penalty for anyone who was found possessing these coins. During the revolution, the governor of Oaxaca, the pureblood Indian, José Inez Davila, issued silver and gold coins bearing the portrait of President Juarez.

Contemporary Mexican coinage is a gallery of famous historical personalities, and the revolution against Spain, with its heroes, comprises one main theme. On the 200th anniversary of Hidalgo's birth, for example, a five-*peso* coin was minted that showed the church in Dolores where the insurgent priest had given the inflammatory sermon that triggered the uprising against the crown. Nor has the pre-Spanish period been forgotten. A gold 20-*peso* coin shows the Aztec calendar, a copper 20-*centavo* piece shows the Temple of the Sun, and a silver five-*peso* piece bears the portrait of Cuauhtémoc (1495-1525), the last of the Aztec rulers. Such tributes to the brave enemies of the Spanish conquistadores are evidence of the sense of continuity between past and present that the coinage of Mexico so well conveys.

The independence movement that began in Mexico spread like a brush fire through the rest of the Spanish New World, and insurgent forces arose in many parts of Central and South America. Among the patriots in the Spanish colonies, a score of exceptional leaders came to prominence. Simón Bolívar (1783-1830), called *El Libertador*, his lieutenant, Antonio José de Súcre (1795-1830), and José San Martin (1778-1850) are but three of the many who fought for and won independence. As was to be expected, the new states at once coined new currencies, although the old Spanish denominations — the *escudo, peso,* and *real* — were usually retained. New names for coins were introduced in a few countries; in Peru and Bolivia, for example, the new *sueldo* was equal to a *real* in value, and the new *boliviano* was equal to a *peso*. The latter new name, of course, honored Simón Bolívar who, as "the Liberator," was South America's greatest hero. Not only has the *boliviano* remained in use both in Bolivia and in Venezuela up to the present, but

Bolívar's portrait has also appeared on the coins of many other Latin American nations.

Over the years the nations of South America converted from the old Spanish denominations to the more practical decimal system. The change began in Colombia in 1847. In general, this system is followed throughout South America today, although the peso may be variously called a *sucre*, a *boliviano*, or a *sol*.

The ferment within the Spanish colonies was not unknown in the great Portuguese enclave in South America, Brazil. Nonetheless, Brazil's monetary history seems rather uneventful in comparison. The vast territory suffered periodically from a shortage of coins. Gold and silver coins from Portugal, Spanish *pieces-of-eight*, and even quantities of gold dust circulated, but even so the Brazilians were forced to rely mainly on barter in their commerce. Then Pedro II in 1688 authorized the establishment of mints in Brazil, an action that helped to ease the situation. Meanwhile, counterstamps were used on the gold and silver coins flowing into Brazil from the Lima and Potosí mints across the Andes. The counterstamps either showed the actual value of the Spanish coins in *reis* or arbitrarily increased the value of the coins in order to keep up with the inflation across the sea in Portugal. *Reis* is the plural of the Portuguese word *real*, or "royal," a name given to a Portuguese coin. The coin was far less valuable than the Spanish *real*, however, and a 1,000-*real* unit, the *milreis*, was eventually established. At the same time, large Portuguese gold coins — *dobras*, *meia dobras*, and *escudos* (1,600-*reis* pieces) — also circulated in Brazil and the United States.

When the new mints in Brazil started issuing national coinage, beautiful coins were struck in Rio de Janeiro, in Bahia, in Pernambuco, and in Villa Rica in the rich mining region of Minas Gerães. The gold coins bore a graceful cross enclosed by the familiar words *In hoc signo vinces*. This image was combined with the arms of Portugal. Large letters at the angles of the cross indicated

190. Coinages of Mexican revolutionaries: "Reforms, Liberty, Justice and Law" proclaimed by Emiliano Zapata on a two-peso piece, 1914; the portrait of the Governor Benito P. Juarez, of Indian parentage, on a 60-peso coin issued by the state of Oaxaca; and a 50-centavo struck by Porfirio Diaz in 1913 in Chihuahua. First left: 39 mm.

which mint had struck the coin. The silver coins bore a globe superimposed on a similar cross, enclosed by the words *Subque signo nata stabit*, or "the land born under [this] sign will prosper."

The year 1822 marked the beginning of the independent empire of Brazil, first under the rule of Pedro I (1822-1831) and then under his son, Pedro II (1831-1889), who resigned the throne when the republic was proclaimed in 1889. Both emperors issued coins of their own; the gold coins of Pedro II, in 10-*milreis* and 20-*milreis* denominations, bore a notable portrait of the emperor in court costume, wearing a typically Baroque high ruff.

153 In 1900 in commemoration of the 400th anniversary of its discovery, Brazil

issued one of the largest silver coins of modern times — a 4,000-*reis* piece depicting Pedro Cabral, the discoveror of Brazil, setting foot in the new land.

In Brazil's gold mining districts before 1808, only gold dust or gold bars were permitted, and no gold coins could circulate. Mine owners brought the gold dust to a foundry for casting, and one-fifth of the dust was set aside for the crown. The rest of the metal was melted down and cast in the form of a bar. Many of the bars have survived; they bear the names of such well-known mining areas as Serro Frio, Rio das Mortes, Villa Rica, and Mato Grosso.

After 1839 the United Provinces broke up into the independent states of Guatemala, Costa Rica, Honduras, El Salvadore, and Nicaragua. Some of these states soon initiated their own coinage, but others did so only after decades had passed. The new denominations and the coin iconography in many respects were similar to those of South America. In the 1920s Guatemala introduced a coinage with a new unit, the *quetzal*. The name is that of a strikingly beautiful and rare bird of the high mountain forests of Central America that is the national bird of Guatemala.

On its gold coins minted in 1850 Costa Rica proudly exhibited the figure of an Indian. Toward the end of the 19th century, however, the nation dedicated its coinage to Columbus instead. In 1897 a new gold unit — the *colon*, named after Columbus — was introduced. Gold coins in multiples of *colons* carried the great discoverer's profile.

After its separation from Columbia in 1903, Panama honored another famous Spaniard, Vasco Nuñez de Balboa (1475-1517), who first colonized the area in 1510. Balboa's portrait has appeared on Panama's coins ever since. One of them, a two-and-one-half *centimo* piece, small in diameter but thick, was soon nicknamed the "Panama pill." In 1930 Panama followed the example of many other states in Latin America by giving its monetary unit the name of its national hero: the *balboa*.

191. Brazilian bars from the rich gold-producing district of Minas Gerais, 1727 and from the mining area of Rio das Mortes, 1817. Coin: 39 mm.

Were the unusual to be a coin-lover's principal interest, no area could better satisfy him than the West Indies. These islands, including some of the first places that Columbus visited, attracted a long succession of conquerors. Between 1492 and 1504 Spanish rule was extended to include Santo Domingo and Cuba (both discovered on Columbus's first voyage), Puerto Rico and Jamaica (on his second voyage), and Trinidad (on his third voyage). The English set foot later in Barbados, Grenada, St. Lucia, Tobago, and some of the Leeward Islands; the French settled Guadeloupe and Martinique; the Dutch, Curaçao; the Danes, St. Thomas in the Virgin Islands; and the Swedes, St. Barthélemy in the Leewards. Only a few of these island territories were granted the privilege of producing their own coinage. The practice followed by France was typical. In 1731 and 1732 two silver coins — a 12-*sol* and a six-*sol* — were minted in France. Bearing the image of Louis XV, the coins were shipped off for use in the *Isles du Vent*, the French possessions in the Leeward Islands.

The British held the most extensive possessions in the Caribbean, but they issued special coinages only occasionally. In 1609 Sir George Somers, bound for Virginia, was shipwrecked on one of the islands of the Bermuda group. The group was then renamed in his honor Somers's Islands. In 1615 the "Company of the City of London for the Plantation of the Somers's Islands" 154

192. Pedro Alvares Cabral, commemorated by Brazil in 1900, shown setting foot on the newly discovered land four hundred years earlier. 50 mm.

was granted royal authority to issue coins for its people, and a series of brass coins, carrying the image of a boar, was minted; the four coins were valued from two to 12 *pence*. The "hog money," as the coinage was soon nicknamed, is generally considered to be the first special coinage made on behalf of any British territory in the New World.

Barbados, another British possession, received an interesting coin late in the 18th century: the "pineapple *penny*." The copper coin was struck in London in 1788 on behalf of a wealthy plantation owner, Sir Philip Gibbs. The design of the obverse showed the head of a Negro with a feather coronet and, on the reverse, a pineapple. In 1792 another penny, as well as a half-penny, showing King George III playing the role of Neptune, trident in hand and mounted on a chariot drawn by two sea horses, was also struck for Gibbs's use in Barbados.

155   Still, the imports were never plentiful enough to meet the British islands'

need for cash and especially for small change. To remedy this lack, silver coins — *pieces-of-eight* and lesser values — were cut into halves, quarters, and even eighths; the last-named fractions were usually called *bitts*. One *bitt,* corresponding to one Spanish *real,* was in general equivalent to nine English *pence.* These fractional coins were often authenticated by overstamping. In St. Kitts, for example, they were stamped with the letter "S." In Dominica Spanish silver coins were circulated after a heart-shaped hole was cut in the center; the purpose of the strange mutilation was to keep the pierced coinage, now reduced in actual value, from leaving the island.

In Nevis, an island notorious as the main slave market in the West Indies, only small, worn silver coins circulated. They were counterstamped both with the name of the island and with a numeral expressing the value of the coin in units known as *dogs.* One *dog* was equal to one-and-one-half *pence,* and coins valued at four, six, seven, and nine *dogs* were circulated. Copper coins, stamped only with the island's name, were valued at one *dog* and were nicknamed "black *dogs.*"

In most instances the various gold coins that circulated were valued by their weight and were often kept wrapped in a paper marked with the coin's weight and value. In Grenada late in the 18th century gold coin values were based on minimum weights; if a coin was found to be underweight, it was brought up to the necessary minimum weight by inserting a gold plug that often bore a counterstamp. Portuguese gold coins were often plugged with inserts of debased gold alloy; when the authorities detected such a deception they did not hesitate to "unplug" the coin.

Meanwhile the English colonists on the North American mainland, destined to rise in revolt long before insurrection swept the Spanish colonies to the south, were also suffering similar pains.

194. Cecil Calvert, the Second Lord Baltimore (1605-1675) depicted on a silver shilling struck by him for the Colony of Maryland in 1658. 25 mm.

195. Figure of an Indian on a Massachusetts 1789 cent. 29 mm.

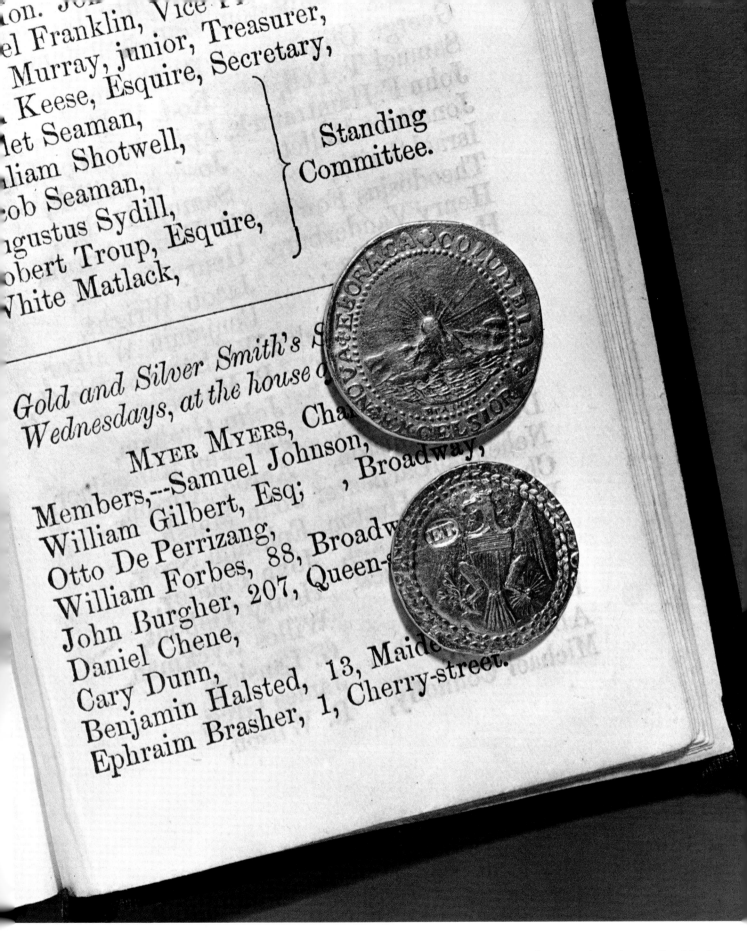

on. JO...
el Franklin, Vice P...
Murray, junior, Treasurer,
Keese, Esquire, Secretary,
let Seaman,
liam Shotwell,
ob Seaman,
gustus Sydill,
obert Troup, Esquire,
Vhite Matlack,

} Standing
Committee.

Gold and Silver Smith's S...
Wednesdays, at the house...

MYER MYERS, Cha...
Members,--Samuel Johnson,...
William Gilbert, Esq; ..., Broadway,
Otto De Perrizang,
William Forbes, 88, Broadw...
John Burgher, 207, Queen-s...
Daniel Chene,
Cary Dunn,
Benjamin Halsted, 13, Maide...
Ephraim Brasher, 1, Cherry-street.

196. Ephraim Brasher, who was listed in the New York directory of 1787 as a member of the Silver-Smiths' Society produced these two gold strikings in 1787, valued at one doubloon and half-doubloon, as examples of his ability as minter. Larger: 30 mm.

Coins of the United States

"Now when a buyer comes to ask for a commodity," wrote a Bostonian in 1695, "sometimes before the merchant answers that he has it, he sais [sic], 'Is your pay ready?' Perhaps the chap replies, 'Yes.' 'What do you pay in?' sais the merchant. The buyer having answered, then the price is set; as suppose he wants a six d [penny] knife, in pay [provisions] it is 12d, in pay as money eight d; and in hard money [silver coin] its own value six d. It seems a very intricate way of trade."

Various national groups brought some coins with them from the old country including the French silver *ecus*, the Dutch *daalders* and *doits*, the Portuguese *moidores* and *johannes* or *joes*, and the Spanish gold *doubloons* and *pistoles*. The sad fact was, however, that they had very little money to circulate. The English colonists did most of their reckoning in *pounds, shillings, and pence*. Supplies from Europe were badly needed, and for these imports they often had to pay in coin. Yet the plight of the American colonists left London unmoved, for at that time a great scarcity of silver coin existed in England because of the flow of bullion to the new territories in India. Finally, in the spring of 1652, the General Court of Massachusetts set up a mint, which was authorized to strike silver *shillings, sixpence*, and *threepence*. John Hull, a silversmith, and a friend, Robert Ganderson, were in charge of the mint, which operated in Hull's home in Boston. The first issues bore the monogram "NE" on one side and the value of the coin on the other.

Within six months the design was discontinued because extensive clipping

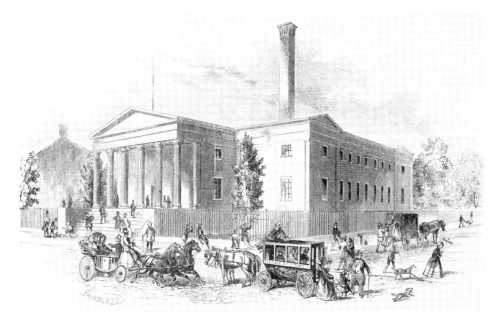

197. *Exterior view of the United States Mint.*

was mutilating and thus debasing the coins. New regulations were issued in October: henceforth the coins would possess an inscribed border so no clipping could be done. It depicted a tree on one side, and carried the date of minting and the value on the other. The first tree to appear on the Massachusetts coins was a willow. Eight years later the design was changed to an oak, and this was followed several years later by a pine tree. The Massachusetts coinage was intended for local use only, and its low silver content — 22.5 per cent below that of English coins — was aimed at keeping it at home.

The example of Massachusetts was soon followed by Maryland, where a 158

198. Five dollars, 1822, one of the great rarities in the United States series. 25 mm.

group of leading colonists convinced the Lord Proprietor, the second Lord Baltimore, that coins would foster trade far more than the barter of tobacco leaves or such commodities as shot and powder. In 1659 silver *shillings*, *sixpence*, and *groats* were struck in London and sent to Lord Baltimore's brother, Philip Calvert, Secretary of State in the colony. With these coins the Baroque style characteristic of English coins of the period briefly found a place in the American colonies. A finely engraved profile head of Lord Baltimore and his coat of arms appeared on these coins. Some time later, a fourth coin — a copper *denarius*, which today is exceedingly rare — was added to the

Maryland series.

A medley of pieces produced in England for various occasions found their way into the colonies. Copper tokens marked two greater English scourges: the plague of 1665 and the London fire of 1666. Toward the end of the 1600s these token designs were used in the New World. But the inscription "Preserve London" was changed to read: "Preserve New England" or "Carolina and the Lord Protector."

In the early 1700s William Wood, an English metal worker, was granted a royal patent to strike coins for Ireland and the American Colonies. Beautifully designed coins represented the king's portrait and, in addition, a rose or the figure of Hibernia (for Ireland). The cheap alloy called "bath metal," consisting of copper and zinc with a small addition of silver was the reason for their rejection in the colonies as well as in Ireland.

In the 1730s Samuel Higley of Granby, Connecticut, undertook to manufacture his own money. Higley had received a physician's diploma from Yale, but he seemed more interested in metallurgy than in medicine and smelted iron ore to produce the first American steel. He bought a copper mine at Simsbury, Connecticut, and founded a private mint. It is said that he liked to pay his tavern reckoning with his own coins — *threepence* pieces made of pure copper, with a design showing a deer, three hammers, each with a crown, and the date 1737. When his coins were found to be underweight, Higley added an inscription that read "Value me as you please — I am good

199. The mint engraver Christian Gobrecht (1785-1844) developed his famous seated Liberty design from a painting by Thomas Sully; consecutive drawings, on mica for engraving on metal; an original brass die and a lead stamping show his various steps in producing the pattern dollars of 1836-39. Dollar (right): 39 mm.

200. Christian Gobrecht used a design of an eagle by Titian Peale to produce a large model in bronze which was then reduced and tried out for a pattern half-dollar. But the pattern dollars of 1836-1839 show a different design. Dollar (right) 39 mm.

copper.'' England sanctioned the striking of official coins for the State of Virginia just before the Revolutionary War. The coins were produced in London in 1773 but distribution was delayed for a year. By then, people sensed the impending war and immediately hoarded these coins.

The outbreak of the American Revolution faced the colonies with the serious problem of financing the conflict. Congress was not able to raise taxes or impose any other levies; in desperation, it authorized paper money (see Chapter VIII). The *Continentals* issued by Congress and sundry paper issues put out by the various colonies drove specie into hiding. The Congress adopted the Spanish milled silver *dollar* as the metallic unit ostensibly backing its paper money. Simultaneously, plans were made to issue a federal coin — the first dollar-sized coin — and as early as 1776 trial pieces had been struck in brass, pewter, and silver. The coin design, done with the help of Elisha Gallaudet, a New York engraver, was inspired by the Continental paper notes and echoed the philosophy of Benjamin Franklin. The word *Fugio,* or "I flee," appears beside a radiant sun that lights a sundial. The reminder "Mind your business" appears on the obverse, while 13 interlinked rings, symbolic of the 13 united colonies, surround a central inscription — "American Congress — We are one" — on the reverse. A lack of bullion, however, prevented Congress from minting any of the coins, although in February, 1777, a resolution for the establishment of a mint was adopted.

161 The rebel colonies' financial situation improved considerably after the alli-

ance with France of 1778. Large quantities of French silver and gold came into circulation. Holland contributed $3 million, and Spain sent specie from Havana. England, too, contributed; many a rebel farmer and merchant eventually pocketed the coins paid to the British forces in America.

The Articles of Confederation, adopted in November, 1777 and fully ratified in 1781, gave Congress only the right to regulate the alloy and value of coins, while reserving the right of coining to the member colonies. Vermont was the first to undertake large-scale minting of copper coins. Reuben Harmon, Jr., was granted a coinage license, and, though his mint at Rupert was rather primitive, its first coins (struck in 1785) were acceptable in quality. The design incorporated the Green Mountains and a plow as symbols of liberty and peaceful husbandry.

Connecticut soon outdid all others in sheer quantity of production. Between 1785 and 1788 its mints produced some 29,000 pounds of *coppers*. On one side appeared the bust of a figure in armor that could have been mistaken for a British monarch. On the other side was a seated, quite distorted allegorical Liberty figure that owed its inspiration to the figure of Britannia. To avoid confusion, the inscription read "Independence and Liberty." It was on these New Jersey *coppers* that the motto *E pluribus unum*, or "From many, one," first appeared. Between 1786 and 1788, Massachusetts produced a well-designed copper coinage that displayed an Indian with bow and arrow and an eagle holding arrows and laurels in its talons. Massachusetts was the first state to designate its copper coins as *cents* and half-*cents*, the *cent* being equivalent in value to one-hundredth of a Spanish silver *dollar*. The usage is evidence that the decimal system was being given serious consideration in the United States before its adoption in France in 1795.

A Manhattan goldsmith, Ephraim Brasher, whiled away the time in 1787 as he awaited state authorization to coin copper by producing two kinds of gold pieces valued at 16 and eight *dollars*, respectively. The gold pieces bore a primitive but attractive eagle design and showed the sea, and the sun shining over a mountaintop. The coins were stamped with Brasher's initials, "EB," and became known as the "Brasher *doubloon*" and "Brasher half-*doubloon*." They are among the most valuable coins of the American past, and they have a unique place in the literature of American treasure lore.

One major problem facing the newly united colonies was how to prepare a national coinage that could be freely exchangeable with the various coins

162

203. John Little Moffat, an assayer from New York, issued gold ingots in San Francisco (1849-1853) marked with his name; a 20-dollar piece issued in 1853 by the San Francisco Assay Office bore his name written on the coronet of the Liberty head. Large coin: 34 mm.

already in circulation. As one example of the problem, the most widely accepted foreign coin in America, the Spanish *dollar*, was accepted at different valuations in different places. In 1782 Robert Morris, a New York financier, not only recommended establishing a national mint but suggested that the decimal system of values, a major and fundamental innovation, be introduced. "It was desirable," he wrote, "that money should be increased in the

205. Miners bringing gold dust to a bank in ▷ Denver City, Colorado, c. 1866.

204. An ore crusher shown on a gold five-dollar piece (1861), struck by John Parsons & Company in Colorado, near the Tarryall mines. 27 mm.

decimal ratio, because by that means all calculations . . . are rendered much more simple and accurate, and, of course, more within the power of the great mass of people." If Robert Morris had his way, Americans would be counting today in *marks*, *quints*, and *cents*, a *mark* being formed of one thousand units. Thomas Jefferson rejected this proposal as "too laborious." He proposed instead that the Spanish *dollar* be the basic unit, stating that ". . . the *dollar* is a known coin, and the most familiar of all to the minds of the people. It is already adopted from South to North, has identified our currency, and therefore happily offers itself as a unit already introduced." He recommended that the value of the *dollar* be defined in terms of a ratio of 15 to one between its silver content and the equivalent in gold. Jefferson thus set the stage for a national bimetallic currency; with a decimal system which was a new and revolutionary idea.

Jefferson asked that the coinage contain a gold piece, valued at 10 *dollars*, two silver pieces, a *dollar* and one-tenth of a *dollar* (the *disme*, or *dime*, a word derived from the French *dixieme*, or "tenth"), and a hundredth of a *dollar*, or *cent*, to be struck in copper. Unfortunately, all these proposals remained only proposals for many years. A committee of representatives from each state debated various points at length, yet, though the lack of a national mint and coinage weighed heavily on the new country, no decisions were made. Even Washington complained, "a man must travel with a pair of scales in his pocket or run the risk of receiving gold at one-fourth less." In September, 1786 Congress once more authorized the establishment of a mint, but the first regular minting did not take place until 1793.

Under the influence of the first Secretary of the Treasury, Alexander Hamilton, the Congress in April, 1792 established a system of coin denominations,

206. An 1858 Indian-head penny and James B. Longacre's wax model for this coin. Coin: 19 mm.

207. In 1852 an attempt was made to increase the diameter of the gold one-dollar piece. This led to unsuccessful experiments using a coin struck with dies for the dime, and perforating it in order to reduce it to the required weight. 18 mm.

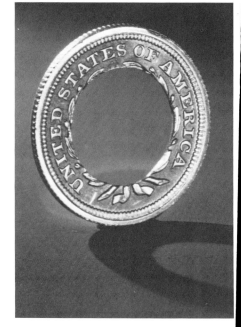

values, and weights that was to stand unchanged for nearly two centuries. The Coinage Act listed 10 different coin values: 10-*dollar* gold pieces, called *eagles,* after the device they bore, and two other gold coins, a five-*dollar* and a two-and-a-half *dollar* piece. In addition to the silver *dollar* there were silver half and quarter-*dollars, dimes,* and half *dimes;* two copper pieces, a *cent* and a half *cent,* completed the group. Initially the two *coppers* were supposed to contain metal enough to equal their face value, which would have made them rather large coins. Hamilton agreed to a reduction in weight but insisted that their value be maintained by the addition of silver. Congress in 1793, however, ordered the weight of the copper *cent* reduced, and reduced it even further in 1795 because of a copper shortage. The action was denounced by many persons as "legal robbery."

Philadelphia was selected as the site of the first United States Mint, and David Rittenhouse of Pennsylvania, an eminent scientist and active political figure during the Revolution, was named its first director. The plain brick structure was modestly equipped; horses provided the necessary power and hand-operated presses were used to stamp the coins. Jefferson, under whose jurisdiction as Secretary of State the mint fell, wanted to bring one of Europe's best engravers and minting experts, Jean-Pierre Droz of Switzerland, to Philadelphia. The plan miscarried, however, and Rittenhouse, with Henry Voigt as a coiner, proceeded to make the necessary engines and dies. In October, 1792 George Washington supplied the mint with some silver, and 1,500 half *dimes* were struck and used by the President as presentation pieces for friends and distinguished foreign visitors. The mint's first regular issues — copper *cents* and half *cents* — left the mint in 1793.

In the first years the mint operated under difficult conditions. Bullion was not easy to obtain; copper often could be had only in the form of scrap metal or donations of household utensils, and the mint's first copper purchase was a mere six pounds. Fortunately, a good supply of silver was at hand in the form of foreign coins. In 1794, for example, the Bank of Maryland sent to the mint *ecus* valued at $80,000. In contrast to this, the first gold bullion, provided by a Boston merchant, did not reach the mint until 1795 and sufficed for the striking of only 744 half *eagles.* Half *dimes,* half *dollars,* and *dollars* were first issued in 1794; *dimes* and quarter *dollars,* in 1796. Lengthy debates took place about the use of George Washington's portrait on the coins. But sad memories connected with portraits of English monarchs on past coinages helped defeat the bill. Liberty, the goddess of freedom, was selected instead and this figure dominated United States coinages for almost two hundred years. The artistic quality of these early coins was remarkable, even though it was 1794 before the mint could employ a full-time engraver, Robert Scot by name. John Adams declared that he knew "of no coins of gold better executed than our *eagles,* nor of silver than our *dollars.*"

Soon after the Coinage Act of 1792, the price of gold rose on the world market. In consequence, the gold coins produced by the United States Mint were worth more as bullion than their face value. Inevitably, the coins disappeared from circulation, being either hoarded or shipped abroad; by 1821 it was estimated that six million *dollars* worth of gold had vanished. The fine new silver *dollars,* too, began to disappear as speculators shipped them to the West Indies and exchanged them for Spanish *dollars* that were old

208. The motto "In God We Trust" appeared during the difficult years of the Civil War; it changed from "Our Trust is in God" as seen on a drawing for a double-eagle by J. Longacre to "God Our Trust" on a pattern half-dollar 1862 (upper right), and a pattern 2-cents, 1863 (lower left) to "In God We Trust" as seen on the pattern 20-dollars, 1865 (upper left) and a 2-cent piece, 1865 (lower right). First upper left: 35 mm.

209. Attempts of the United States Treasury in the 1860s and 1870s to create an internationally exchangeable coinage with denominations expressed in foreign currencies. The most famous is the 4-dollar gold piece of 1879 (lower right) called "stella" from the star design on the reverse side. Large bronze: 35 mm.

and worn but contained a greater weight of silver. In 1806 James Madison, then Secretary of State, ordered the director of the mint to see ". . . that all the silver to be coined at the mint shall be of small denominations, so that the value of the largest pieces shall not exceed half a *dollar*." Simultaneously, the striking of gold *eagles* was suspended. It was more than a generation later before gold *eagles* and silver *dollars* reappeared in circulation.

Because of the scarcity of coins, paper money rapidly came into use. Silver *dollars* or half *dollars* were deposited as security for the paper money issued by various banks, but by the War of 1812 the new nation had reached another low point in monetary policy; inflation was completely out of control and specie had vanished from circulation. In the 1820s gold was found in North Carolina and Georgia, and a boom — actually America's first gold rush — rapidly developed. By 1830 a private minter, Templeton Reid, in Gainesville, Georgia, was issuing 10-*dollar*, five-*dollar,* and two-and-a-half *dollar* gold coins inscribed with his name and the identification as "Georgia Gold." The next year another private minter, the Bechtler family was established in North Carolina; they produced a variety of gold coins marked with their names. The Bechtlers struck the first one-*dollar* pieces in the United States.

To make use of the large quantities of gold being mined in the south, a law of 1835 directed the establishment of three new mints: at Dahlonega, Georgia, and Charlotte, North Carolina, where only gold coins were struck, and at New Orleans, Louisiana, where both gold and silver coins were produced. The dies

210. In 1877, following requests from California for large gold coins, the United States Mint had two trial pieces prepared for a 50-dollar coin designed by William Barber. One year earlier George T. Morgan worked on sketches for a 100-dollar piece. Coin: 51 mm.

for the regional mints were manufactured at the Philadelphia mint, and the local issuances bore the mint marks "D," "C," and "O," respectively.

Between 1836 and 1839 patterns for a new silver *dollar* were prepared by Christian Gobrecht, engraver at the Philadelphia mint. His famous seated Liberty and a majestic flying eagle were developed from designs by Thomas Sully and Titian Peale, and the first strikings were released in 1840.

In 1848 James Marshall discovered a small gold nugget while digging foundations for John Sutter's sawmill on the American River in California. The discovery started the most famous gold rush in history. Samples of California gold dust and nuggets were sent by Governor Mason to the Secretary of War in Washington who forwarded them to the director of the mint with a request for a special minting. With the gold the mint struck a limited number of quarter *eagles*; in addition to the usual design and the date 1848, the coins bore the minute letters "CAL" on the obverse. In California untold riches changed hands constantly. But there were practically no coins. Gold dust became the usual means of payment. A series of private strikings began in 1849 known under the name of "pioneer gold." Most pieces tried to imitate the design of official United States gold coinage. Other pieces were shaped in the form of bars. There were also round and octagonal fifty *dollar* pieces referred to as "slugs." Late in 1853 a United States branch mint was established in San Francisco and began to produce official gold and silver coins. The gold rush in other states and territories, like Oregon (1849) and

211. Coin designs which were never accepted. Liberty heads designed by William Barber, Joseph A. Bailly and George T. Morgan in the 1870s and 1880s which were rejected for official coinage. Center top: 38 mm.

Colorado (1860), produced few but interesting private gold pieces. Among the most interesting are the gold coins of the Mormons of Utah, executed under the direction of their leader, Brigham Young.

What the California strikes meant to the nation is easily summarized. From a level of less than a million *dollars* in 1847, United States gold production jumped to more than 50 million *dollars* in 1850. The minting of gold coins increased proportionately: from four million in 1846 to 37 million in 1850. The United States lived with an overabundance of gold coins; as a member of Congress put it, "Gold is the only standard of value by which all property is now measured; it is virtually the only currency of the country." One consequence was the issuance of the largest and most prestigious gold coin, a 20-*dollar* gold piece, or "double *eagle*," and a small one-*dollar* gold piece. Designed by James B. Longacre, both coins became very popular; the gold *dollar* coin, which after 1854 displayed Liberty wearing a feather headdress in Indian fashion, helped to compensate for the scarcity of silver dollars which, for a time after 1840, were rarely minted.

An important step in the direction of a fiduciary coinage, that is, one with an intrinsic metal value lower than the coin's nominal value, was the law enacted in February, 1853, by which the silver contents of the half *dollar,* quarter-*dollar, dime,* and half *dime* were reduced by about 7 per cent. The act, moreover, declared that such coins could be struck only from bullion purchased by the mint; such a requirement prevented any coinage of privately owned silver; it was the first time that the government had denied its citizens the right of free coinage. Although in theory a bimetallic system was still upheld, the act moved the nation farther along the road to a single gold standard. A few years later, when it seemed that the scarcity of silver coins had come to an end, Congress, in the Coinage Act of February, 1857, declared that foreign coins no longer were legal tender. The action brought to an end the circulation of the Spanish *dollar* and its fractions after more than two centuries of circulation as the most reliable coin the American people had known. Congress also created a silver three-*cent* piece or *trime.* This smallest of all United States coins (weighing only 0.80 grams) was a   168 momentous step taken by Congress since it created a subsidiary or fiduciary coin, where the value exceeded its intrinsic content. Simultaneously, the unpopular half *cent* was abolished, and the copper *cent* was replaced by a smaller copper-nickel *cent*. Production of the large copper *cent* had proved very costly because of the high price of copper. As early as 1837, Lewis Feuchtwanger of New York wanted the mint to adopt a small *cent* of his own design, made of German silver (an alloy of copper, nickel, and zinc). Not until 20 years later, however, did a copper-nickel alloy find acceptance by the mint; an attractive coin bearing a flying eagle designed by James B. Longacre was adopted in 1857. The nickel alloy made coins more resistant to wear and at the same time increased their intrinsic value; the holders of small Spanish and Mexican silver coins gladly exchanged them for the Longacre *pennies*.

During the Civil War large quantities of privately minted copper tokens were used and in order to stem their flood the mint initiated the striking of a bronze *cent* (that is, an alloy of copper, tin, and zinc) which carried the Indian-head design produced by J. B. Longacre, that was first used in 1858. The law of 1864 that introduced the bronze *cent* also authorized a two-*cent* piece, which was the first United States coin to bear the motto "In God We Trust." The motto was proposed during the difficult months of the Civil War by a Pennsylvania clergyman, the Reverend M. R. Watkinson of Ridleyville.

At the end of the war seventeen different coin types were in circulation. Only in 1873 were some denominations abolished, thus consolidating the coinages in use. The Coinage Act of February, 1873 was a further step in the nation's shift from a bimetallic to a gold standard. A new silver *dollar* — the "commercial" or "trade" *dollar*, with a higher content of fine silver — was introduced. It was intended primarily to replace the Mexican silver *dollar* in Far Eastern trade. The mint produced several designs for the new *dollar*, and the model finally chosen was an attractive composition by William Barber that showed a seated Liberty, extending an olive branch and surrounded by sheaves of grain as a symbol of bounty. The regular *dollar*, although known as America's most unpopular coin, was reissued in 1878 with a new design by the mint engraver, George T. Morgan.

As early as 1866 the United States showed an interest in the unified international coinage system advocated by France. Coin patterns prepared by the Mint in the 1860s and 1870s reflect these plans and show values in *dollars* as well as the corresponding amounts in *sterling, marks, kronen, gulden*, and *francs*. An unusual coin, a four-*dollar* piece with the poetic name "stella," is an example of this abortive scheme.

The closing years of the 19th century saw the first issues of United States commemorative coins. For the 400th anniversary of the discovery of America, celebrated nationally at the 1892 Columbian Exposition in Chicago, half-*dollar* and quarter-*dollar* pieces were struck in honor of Christopher Columbus and his patroness, Isabella of Spain. Again, in 1915 in connection with the Panama Pacific Exposition, not only was a commemorative silver half *dollar* struck but also an impressive series of gold one-*dollar*, two-and-a-half-*dollar*, and 50-*dollar* pieces were issued.

In 1905 President Theodore Roosevelt undertook to improve the aesthetics

212. From the middle of the 19th century, some United States coin designs tried to pay tribute to the American Indian by adorning the head of Liberty with a feather bonnet. Later, in 1907, Bela Lyon Pratt created a real Indian head for the quarter and half eagle, followed in 1913 by the impressive, composite portrait of an Indian chief designed by James E. Fraser for the nickel. First upper left: 20 mm.

of the United States gold coinage. Impressed by the beauty of ancient Greek coins — he reputedly carried an Athenian *tetradrachm* as a pocket piece — Roosevelt approached the most accomplished sculptor of the United States, Augustus Saint-Gaudens, and asked him to produce a new design for the *eagle* and the double-*eagle.* The sculptor's striding Liberty, intended for the double-*eagle,* was a unique and difficult composition, rendering a figure in motion, seen from the front against a complex background. The mint raised serious objections against the high relief of Saint-Gaudens' design, insisting that too many strikings would be necessary to bring up the relief. In the process of lowering the design, the beauty of the sculptor's concept was destroyed. Roosevelt's plan for the *eagle* was equally a failure. Saint-Gaudens produced a stately profiled head of Liberty, but at the suggestion of the President an Indian feather bonnet was added that produced a hopelessly incongruous effect.

Roosevelt's concept, at least, had its later triumphs. The eminent sculptor Victor D. Brenner was commissioned to produce the dignified portrait of Lincoln that appeared on a new *cent* introduced in 1909, the 100th anniversary of Lincoln's birth. In 1913 the head of an Indian and of a bison, the work of James E. Fraser, were chosen as distinctive American motifs for a new five-*cent* piece. In 1961 for the first time in the history of the United States coinage, separate designs were prepared for various silver coins. Adolph Weinman created the designs for the half *dollar* and the *dime,* and Hermon McNeil designed the quarter-*dollar.* Between 1904 and 1921 no silver *dollars* were minted.

After Lincoln's bust appeared on *pennies* to mark the centennial of his birth, George Washington was similarly commemorated on his bicentennial in 1932. The bust that appeared on the quarter-*dollar* minted that year was designed by John Flanagan. In 1938 Thomas Jefferson was similarly honored on a new *nickel* that bore his portrait and a view of Monticello, his Virginia home. In 1946, less than a year after the death of Franklin D. Roosevelt, a new *dime,* with a portrait of the President by John R. Sinnock, was released. In 1948, a Franklin half *dollar* was issued. To this gallery of famous Americans the past decade has added two more: the Kennedy half *dollar,* designed by Gilroy Roberts and Frank Gasparro in 1964 and the Eisenhower *dollar* in 1971, also by Gasparro.

The two pieces were, and still are, hoarded as souvenirs and for investment. The Kennedy half *dollar* in particular has broken all records for popularity. Hundreds of millions of these coins are being privately held at home and abroad. Not even a drastic reduction in silver content — first to a "clad" coin with only 40 per cent of silver in 1965 and then in 1971 to a clad cupronickel piece — has diminished the coin's popularity. □

213. Flying eagle on an experimental striking of a double-eagle 1907, designed by the famous sculptor Augustus Saint-Gaudens at the request of President Theodore Roosevelt who hoped to create a more aesthetically pleasing coinage. 34 mm.

214. Half-dollar with portrait of President John F. Kennedy by Gilroy Roberts. 30 mm.

VII| NEAR AND FAR EAST

VII: COINS OF THE NEAR AND FAR EAST: FROM THE BLACK SEA TO THE PACIFIC.

There is no God but Allah . . . No God but Vishnu . . . No God but Genghis Khan . . . No God but Money.

To the east of the Byzantine frontier beginning in A.D. 226 a new dynasty — the Sasanian — occupied the Persian throne for almost 400 years. The Sasanian kings warred with their neighbors to the east and west, but it was a new nation — the Turks — that at last sealed their fate. In 633, the year of the coronation of King Yazdegerd III, the Turks under Omar crossed the border of the Sasanian Empire, and less than eight years later that empire had ceased to exist. Yazdegerd was assassinated, and his descendants ended their days as refugees at the Chinese imperial court, half a world away from Ctesiphon.

Before its fall, the Sasanian court at Ctesiphon was among the most brilliant the world has ever known. Chosroes I (531-579), an able general, received tribute from Byzantium; a great administrator and a patron of literature and the arts, Chosroes enjoyed a reputation as an enlightened and tolerant philosopher-king that extended far beyond the borders of the empire. His grandson, Chosroes II (590-628), conquered Jerusalem and is said to have carried off the true Cross. The Sassanians brought about a revival of the Zoroastrian religion, with its cult of tending an "eternal" fire in honor of Ormuzd (Ahuramazda), the All-Father from whom, according to Zoroastrian doctrine, the world emanates. A rock relief at Naqsh-i Rustem depicts Ormazd presenting one early Sassanian king — Shapur I — with his ring of sovereignty.

The 29 Sasanian kings are well recorded in their national coinage. The bust of each successive ruler, together with his name and title, appeared on the obverse of all his coins; the reverse represented the Zoroastrian "fire altar." Most Sasanian coins were silver; only a few gold coins and even fewer coppe coins were minted. The principal coin was a silver *drachm* weighing approximately four grams. Probably as a reflection of the Greco-Roman tradition of coin portraiture, and perhaps even with the help of artists educated in that tradition, the busts of the first Sasanian rulers were realistically rendered. Indeed, the coins issued by Shapur I, the son of the founder of the dynasty, Ardashir I, are perhaps the finest in the entire series. With time the representation of the ruler became stereotyped in form, devoid of personality, and, in fact, without any resemblance to reality. Instead, the symbol of royalty — the crown — became the significant iconographic element on the coins. According to Sasanian tradition each king had his own special crown, quite unlike the crowns of his predecessors. The high-domed tiara of one ruler would be replaced by his successor with a close-fitting Persian cap with ear flaps, perhaps decorated with wings, an eagle's head with a pearl on its beak, a boar's head, horns, a crescent moon, or some other symbol. In the end the crowns became so ornate and heavy that they could not possibly be worn. Chosroes II's crown reputedly weighed 170 pounds; it hung from the ceiling of the throne room suspended by a golden chain.

On the coins we see a globe above the crown; this was the *korymbos*, a

◁ 216. *The Sasanian King Shapur II (309-379) at the royal hunt shown on a silver plate; and portrait of King Varahran II (275-283) and his family on a silver drachm; fire altar with attendants on a drachm of Varahran I (276-293) and an imitation of a Sasanian drachm by the Arabs (about A.D. 670). First coin upper left: 27 mm.*

217. *"There is no God but God, Mohammed is the Prophet of God" – this Muslim profession of faith is delicately inscribed in the center of this silver dirhem struck in A.D. 954/55 by Sallarid princes in the Caspian Sea area.*

large ball of hair, wrapped in silk, that each king wore. The king was always depicted as a bearded man, and often the tip of the royal beard was tied with a ribbon. As the Sasanian empire declined, its coinage deteriorated to wafer-thin silver disks but "survived" in the coinages of other peoples.

Coins of Islam

On June 15, 622, only a generation before the Turks brought down the last Sasanian ruler, an obscure philosopher-warrior left the Arabian city of Mecca to seek the security of Medina: a new place where he might spread his new creed. Under the electrifying leadership of Mohammed, the people of Arabia soon rose to be a fearsome power. In a few brief years after Mohammed's death in 632 Damascus, Jerusalem, Ctesiphon, and Alexandria had fallen to the conquering Arabs; nothing seemed to withstand them.

The new power united under one administration and one language parts of the world possessing very different prior histories; it was essential that Islam come to terms with these cultures and traditions. The Arab conquerors' general policy of making the best use of local traditions was reflected in their coinage. The Moslem governors of the conquered Sasanian provinces continued to issue silver *drachms* similar to those struck by the last Sassanian kings, adding only an Arabic inscription that stated the new governor's name. Arab-Sasanian coins of this kind circulated in the eastern parts of the conquered realm for almost two centuries.

The establishment of the Umayyad dynasty in 661 with Damascus as the capital, marked the beginning of the Arab empire's greatest period of power and glory. New conquests extended the Arab domain from the borders of India on the east to northern Africa on the west, and farther into Spain. Under the Caliph Abd-al-Malik (685-705), the new world power finally decided to introduce its own coinage. Since the Byzantine gold *solidus* had been the pillar of the entire economy in the Mediterranean area, the Moslems minted a gold coin of the same weight: the *dinar*. The unit was divisible, as the *solidus* had been, into one-half and one-third *dinars*. At first struck only in Damascus, these gold coins were later issued by mints in many other cities: Baghdad, Misr in Egypt, Córdoba in Spain, and elsewhere. To round out the coinage, the caliphate also minted a silver *dirhem* and a copper *fulus* or *fals*, a name derived from the Roman *follis*. These first mintings set a pattern that was followed by almost all subsequent Islamic coinages.

176

219. The role of the horse in the life of the wandering peoples of Eastern Asia as depicted in their coins: galloping hunter and horseman on silver and bronze coins of the Seljuks of Rum (7th century A.D.); and a horse and its filly on a bronze coin of the Muslim Begtimurids (12th century A.D.) in present-day South-Eastern Turkey. 22, 32 & 23 mm.

220. The so-called "horoscope dirhem" which the Sultan of the Seljuks of Rum, Kay Khusro II (A.D. 1236-1245) dedicated to his beautiful Georgian wife carrying her zodiacal sign, "Sun in Leo". 24 & 23 mm.

221. The Urtukids used a unique array of images copied from ancient Greek, Roman and Byzantine coins on their copper pieces (12th century A.D.): a head copied after a Syrian king; a facing head with two Victories; a bust of Byzantine design facing another head similar to that of Emperor Nero; a niumbate angel. First upper left: 32 mm.

Because the religion of Islam forbade the representation of living creatures in art or architecture, the Moslem coin designers confined themselves to inscriptions professing their faith in Allah and in his prophet, Mohammed, and proclaiming the superiority of the creed of Islam over that of all other religions. Whereas formerly the rich, myth-filled iconography of the Greco-Roman tradition had appeared, the coins now bore purely ornamental designs: geometrical forms intertwined in graceful arabesques. The style of the inscriptions, especially those written in Kufic (the early Arabic calligraphy, with its decorative strokes and dots), fitted perfectly with a style or ornamentation that emphasized an infinity of decorative detail.

The Umayyad dynasty was replaced in 750 by a new line from Persia. The Abbasid caliphs (750-1258), who introduced Persian culture to the Arab empire, gave Islam some of its greatest decades of splendor and prosperity. New trade routes were opened and with them came wealth and cultural refinement. One of the most famous caliphs of this Islamic golden age was Harun al-Rashid (786-809). He was a patron of scholars and lawmakers; his fame reached western Europe, and he even exchanged gifts and embassies with Charlemagne.

In this great caliph's coinage vanity won over the moral rigidity of earlier days. From Harun's day onward the name and titles of successive Abbasid caliphs regularly appeared on the coins, in some cases together with the name of the heir apparent or that of the grand vizier. Soon, however, the glory of the Abbasids began to decline; the power of the caliphate passed into other hands, and the caliph became no more than a spiritual leader. Although the Abbasid dynasty lasted until the Mongol invasion of the Near East in 1258, its centralized power had ended centuries earlier.

The Umayyads continued to hold power in Spain even though the Abbasids had overthrown them in the east. Such cities as Córdoba, Granada, and Murcia were centers of Islamic splendor and literary fame. In these cities, as also in Málaga and Seville, were mints whence gold *dinars* and silver *dirhems* flowed into the treasuries of the Moorish caliphs of Spain. Many

179

of these coins have a special charm, with both faces covered with elegant Arabic calligraphy.

Egypt played an important role as an independent caliphate under the leadership of the Fatimids (968-1171), so-called because they were descendants of Mohammed's daughter, Fatima. Many coins, gold *dinars* in particular, were struck by the Fatimids in Cairo and in Mahdia. But this dynasty was soon overshadowed by one of the great figures of the medieval world: Saladin (Sultan of Egypt and Syria, 1173-1193). Saladin suppressed the Fatimids, bringing a new dynasty, that of the Ayyubids (1173-1250), to power. Gradually he included in his realm territories both in Egypt and in Syria, reaching from the Libyan Desert to Mesopotamia and the Persian Gulf, and from Aleppo to Nubia. Renowned for his bravery and wisdom, this Moslem leader engaged in a protracted struggle to recapture the Holy Land from the Crusaders; among his more notable adversaries were Philip II of France and Richard I, the Lion-Hearted, of England. Saladin's coinage, especially his gold and silver coins, copied those of the Fatimids in weight, size, and the general arrangement of the inscriptions. His copper coins, however, were quite unorthodox. Some showed a recumbent lion; others bore a turbaned human figure, seated cross-legged, holding an orb in one hand. Both images fall completely outside the usual range of Islamic coin design.

Coins of the Turkish and Persian Empires

In Baghdad the decline of the Abbasid caliphate was marked by an increase in the influence wielded by the Turkish bodyguards of the caliphs. During the ninth century these troops had gained a position like that of the Praetorian Guard in ancient Rome, and, as did that elite force, they aspired to even greater power. Meanwhile new waves of Turks continued to enter the Arabian realm from the steppes of Central Asia. The Seljuk Turks occupied much of Persia, Mesopotamia, and Syria in the 11th century. One of their leaders, Alp Arslan ("Courageous Lion"), conquered Georgia and Armenia and even took the Byzantine emperor, Romanus IV Diogenes, prisoner.

The Seljuks went on to conquer other parts of Asia Minor, where they established the Sultanate of Rum. The coins issued by this Turkish principality were exceptional in artistic quality and superior even to the products of the Byzantine Empire and many kingdoms of western Europe. One such coin shows a Turkish rider with a drawn bow, possibly a representation of one of the Turkish conquerors. Such human images were rarely seen on Moslem coins, and their appearance on the coins of Rum may have been more a result of the need to produce a coinage acceptable to the merchants of Asia Minor than a matter of religious indifference or heresy. One charming series of Rum silver pieces shows a shining sun and, below this, a stalking lion. Known as "horoscope *dirhems*," they were evidence of the regard that one Rum sultan felt for his wife, a beautiful Georgian woman. The sultan had wanted to place her image on his coins but was persuaded by his counselors to avoid such flouting of Islamic tradition. He compromised by putting her birth sign — the Sun in Leo — on the coins.

Early in the 13th century Asia witnessed one of the greatest movements of

224. The graceful figure of the four-armed Siva or Shiva — "the Destroyer" — on a gold coin struck by the Kushan King Huvishka during the second century A.D. 19 mm.

225. Well-designed coins displaying a bust wearing an unusual headgear consisting of wings and a buffalo-head were produced during the 6th and 7th centuries A.D. by some rulers of the Iranian Huns inhabitating areas in present-day Afghanistan. 27 & 30 mm.

226. An elephant on a gold pagoda struck by the Gajapati kings of Orissa, on the east coast of India during the 12th century. 14 mm.

227. *The Mogul Akbar the Great (1556-1606) of Hindustan introduced square as well as round silver rupees. Round: 22 mm.*

228. *Akbar used a formula called ilahi or "divine era", expressing a new reckoning starting with the first year of his reign.*

people that the world has ever known. The Mongols under Genghis Khan (1206-1227) began their sweep from the steppes of Central Asia eastward into China and westward into Turkestan, Afghanistan, and southern Russia. A successor to Genghis, his grandson Kublai Khan (1257-1294), brought all China under Mongol rule, and Kublai's brother, Hulagu (1256-1265), overran the Seljuks of Persia in 1256 and went on to establish the great empire of the Ilkhans, extending from western Asia to the shores of the Mediterranean. The Mongol military successes were striking, but in general the Ilkhan coinage did no more than conform to the existing Moslem style, and even lacked the elegance and beauty of its Arab prototypes.

The advancing Mongols had driven before them another group of Turks who, under the leadership of Osman I, (1290?-1326), established a western Asian dynasty of their own. Within decades the Osmanli (Ottoman) Turks reduced the Byzantine Empire to a territory little larger than the city of Constantinople and soon controlled an area that extended from the Euphrates in the east to the Danube in the west.

As noted earlier (see Chapter IV), May 29, 1453, marked the fall of the last Byzantine stronghold, Constantinople, into the hands of the Osmanli conqueror, Mohammed II. The fall of Constantinople, imperial successor to Byzantium, symbolized the closing of an era. Soon enough the Ottoman Empire held sway not only over Asia Minor but also over Egypt, Tripoli, Tunis, Algiers, and Morocco. If one compares the coins struck by this newest world power with those minted under Rome or Byzantium, one is shocked by the unimpressive character of the early Ottoman coinage. To be sure, the Turks were following the usual Moslem precepts so that only inscriptions were used as decorative devices, but even so one looks in vain for anything comparable to the grace and beauty of early Arab coins.

The first Ottoman currency consisted of small coins struck in silver and copper. They carried simple religious inscriptions and only later bore the name and title of the sultan at whose direction they were struck, the year of his reign, and the name of the mint. Not until the mid-15th century did the Ottomans strike their own gold coin: the *altun*. Minted in 1478 the *altun* was patterned after the most popular gold coin of these days, the Venetian *zecchino*. For this reason the name given to the Turkish *altun* in the west was the *sequin*.

By the 17th century the Turkish coinage had become almost identical in size and weight to the most commonly circulated coins of Europe. A large silver piece, the *piastre*, or *ghurush*, and a smaller silver coin, the *para*, were among the most popular denominations. Fine large silver coins — a double *ghurush* (equivalent to 80 *paras*), and a *yuzlik* (equivalent to 100 *paras*) — were minted, as was a gold coin, the *zer mabub*, weighing 2.6 grams.

In contrast to the simplicity of the Turkish coins, contemporary Persian coinages were quite sophisticated. The Persian *ashrafi*, a coin weighing 3.4 grams, was at first inscribed with Arabic legends and later with verses of Persian poetry that exhibited the refinement and grace of Persian calligraphy to good effect. The same delicate style can be noted in the heavier gold *mohur* of the early 1700s and was continued in the equally fine *toman*, a gold coin first introduced at the turn of the 19th century. Some of the multiple *tomans* struck by Nasr-ed-Din (1848-1896) are sumptuous pieces

229. The great Shah of Hindustan Jahangir, "Conqueror of the World" (1605-1627), and some of his gold mohurs and silver rupees with zodiacal signs. Under his successor, the possession of these coins carried the death penalty. 20 & 20 mm.

indeed. They departed from the Islamic tradition by depicting the figure of the ruler on his throne. The portrait of the ruler became a permanent feature of Persian and Iranian coins.

Coins of India

From the time of Alexander's momentous encounter with the civilizations of the Indian subcontinent, the tradition we know as Hellenistic was destined to linger in that remote land for centuries. Nonetheless, India had a history and tradition of its own. At a time quite possibly as remote as when the early Greeks first became acquainted with the art of coinage (see Chapter II), the Indians were already circulating small irregularly shaped pieces of punch-marked silver. As primitive as many of these ingots appear at first glance, a closer look at some of the linear designs that were punched into them reveals an amazingly varied and interesting symbolism. The designs range from simple outlines of animals — elephants, horses, cattle, or fish — to graceful, symbolic representations of mountains, rivers, or the sun. Toward the end of the first century A.D., powerful peoples from central Asia, the Kushans, established their kingdom in N.W. India, striking beautiful coins.

Late in the third century, the Gupta kings entered India from the north and created a powerful empire in northern India that extended from the Indus to the Ganges. The period of the Gupta dynasty, which endured into the sixth century, was one of the most glorious eras of Hindu civilization: a

230. Elephants caparisoned and decorated for a ceremony symbolized the royal power of Tipu Sahib, Sultan of Mysore, India, (1782-1799) who died fighting the British for the independence of his state. 31 and 24 mm.

231. Money in ancient China, from about 900 to 250 B.C., included tao or knife money, pu or spade money and the small I pi ch'ien or "ant nose" money. Longest knife: 185 mm.

golden age for the arts, literature, and philosophy. Quite naturally the Gupta coinage reflects this general trend, and indeed a splendid, vibrant, and sensuous art characterizes Gupta coin design. The Gupta mintings — mainly gold, with some silver and bronze — present a rich and varied spectrum. The charm of the Gupta coins is exemplified by a series of ornate but graceful images that acquaint the viewer with some of the divinities in the Hindu pantheon. Lakshmi, the goddess of beauty, is a sensuous Venus-like figure. We see her enthroned, or carried on the back of a lion, often holding her flower, the lotus. Others from this pantheon include the warrior god, Karttikeya, and the fearsome, destructive Siva riding his bull, Nandi. The White Huns or Hephtalites, were a nomadic people from northern Asia who passed into India from the 5th to the 7th centuries, producing several interesting coins and little else for posterity.

While northern India was continually subjected to invasion, central and southern India — the Deccan and Mysore — developed under more favorable conditions. The Romans, interested both in the spices (especially pepper) and the precious and semiprecious stones of southern India, maintained trade relations that brought large quantities of Roman gold and silver coins into the area. The Indians imitated Roman *aurei* and *denarii* and in due course began minting their own gold coins. Those struck in Orissa during the 12th century displayed a very elaborate design featuring an elephant. Another interesting gold coinage came from the kingdom of Vijayanagar, founded in southern India in 1336 as a bulwark against the Moslem invasions from the north. This kingdom's thick gold *pagodas* and half-*pagodas* bore inscriptions, which were written in the local tongue, and the images of deities from the Hindu pantheon. We find Siva seated with his consort Parvati, sensuous Lakshmi, and Vishnu, the "Preserver," who, with Brahma, the "Creator," and Siva, the "Destroyer," constitutes a Hindu triad.

While the kingdoms of central and southern India produced these picturesque coins, a Moslem dynasty, the Ghorid, established its rule over all northern India, founding the Sultanate of Delhi, and eventually extended it south into central India as well. The privileged position of the Moslems among their Hindu subjects was evident in all aspects of political and religious life and even found expression in their Moslem coinage. As noted earlier, Islamic precepts forbid the representation of living figures. The coinage issued at Delhi bore only inscriptions on both sides of the coins. The *Kalima,* or profession of faith ("there is no god but Allah and Mohammed is the Prophet of Allah"), formed a part of the coin inscription. The script was Arabic, but in some cases Sanskrit was also used. In addition the inscriptions included the name and title of the ruling sultan, the name of the mint, and the date of issue according to the Moslem reckoning. Trade relations with the rest of the Islamic world brought prosperity to India and made silver, hitherto quite scarce, much more available. Coins were soon struck in four metals — gold, silver, copper, and the copper-silver alloy known as "billon." Attempts were made to establish a stable relation between gold and silver. The principal units were a gold *dinara,* a silver *adli,* and a billon *tankah.*

In 1542 Delhi fell to a new conqueror, Sher Shah Suri, the Afghan. This warrior's most lasting achievement proved to be numismatic rather than military. He introduced a new silver coin, the *rupiya.* A broad silver piece

183

232. Silver ingots, known as sycee stamped with various indications of weight and value, were used throughout China's history. Rectangular piece: 53 mm.

that weighed 11.6 grams, it was a denomination destined to survive for centuries; although its value has diminished, even today the *rupee* is the basic monetary unit of the Republic of India.

New conquerors from the north soon cast their shadow over India. By the end of the 16th century the Mogul Empire was not only solidly established in northern India, but its leaders had seized 15 other provinces, which extended the rule into central India in the north and to Kabul and Kashmir in the northwest.

The Mogul rulers issued coins minted from gold, silver, and copper. A new gold coin was introduced: the *muhar*, weighing approximately 11 grams. It was exchangeable for nine silver *rupees*, and the *rupee* was valued at forty copper *dams*. The great Mogul ruler, Akbar, introduced other innovations. He had round and square coins struck on alternate months; square coins soon became a permanent feature of the Indian coinage. Akbar, a very tolerant man, ordered the *Kalima* omitted from Mogul coins as a gesture of tolerance toward other religions. He substituted a new, virtually non-denominational inscription: *Allahu Akbar Jalla Jalala* ("God is most great, eminent is His glory").

Akbar's son and successor, Jahangir (1605-1627), was interested in the arts and left his own imprint on the Mogul coinage. The gold and silver coins that he had struck in great quantities are distinguished by the elegant calligraphy of their inscriptions. Jahangir claimed to be a good Moslem, unlike his father, and restored the *Kalima* to his coinage, but as a man of letters he could not resist continuing to include in the coin inscriptions such poetic couplets as "By order of Shah Jahangir gold attained a hundred beauties when the name of Nur Jahan Badshah Beghum was placed on it." After the Shah's death, other coins bearing the zodiacal signs were ordered melted down. Those who continued to possess them believed they had talismanic powers but mere possession invoked the death penalty.

233. *The ancient symbol of the dragon and phoenix represented on Chinese silver dollars of the 1920s beside the image of an automobile; the sickel and hammer of the Communists; and Sun Yat-sen's portrait. His mausoleum at Nanking was not accepted for the official coinage designs. Dragon dollar: 39 mm.*

234. *Old and the new: Korean five-chon piece struck (1883) in the traditional way of Chinese cash; three-chon piece with enameled center; and two machine struck coins (1905), displaying the graceful hibiscus flower and the Phoenix bird. First coin upper left: 30 mm.*

235. *The bust of Emperor Kuang Hsu (1875-1900) on Chinese rupee of the early 1900s imitated the design of Queen Victoria's bust on a rupee of India. 31 mm.*

Coins of China

"With the opening of exchange between farmers, artisans, and merchants, there came into use money [in the form] of tortoise shells, cowrie shells, gold, the *ch'ien* spade, the knives, and the *pu* spade." Thus speaks a Chinese historian of the first century B.C. describing the earliest kinds of specie used in his country (see Chapter I). It is generally conceded that China preceded the West in the invention and use of money. By the end of the Chou dynasty (about 255 B.C.), however, such early precursors of conventional coinage as spade and knife money disappeared, and the round "cash-coin" became the common unit of exchange. According to tradition, the reins of state were next held by Shih Huang-ti (221-210), the "Yellow Emperor" and first ruler of the Ch'in dynasty. Not only is Shih credited with raising the Great Wall against China's barbarian enemies to the north, but he is said also to have introduced both a new system of weights and measures and a new coinage. Some round coins already existed near the end of the Chou dynasty. One of these was the *pao huo*, or "precious unit," a round coin with a square hole in its middle. The coin's roundness symbolized the heavens; its square hole, the earth. Shih put the new coinage on a sound basis and ordered the casting of a new coin, the *pan liang*, a copper piece weighing 15.5 grams.

The Chinese used copper almost exclusively for their coinage; gold was never a coining metal, and silver came into use for coins only in the 20th century. Gold and silver in ingot form were the metals used to effect large transactions; silver ingots were accepted as legal tender beginning in the 11th century. Shoe-shaped or boat-shaped silver ingots, known as *sycee*, came in various sizes and weighed as much as 100 *taels* (a *tael* is equal to approximately 30 grams). Copper cash-coins were frequently strung together on a cord, a string of 1,000 cash pieces being equal in value to one silver *tael*; early paper currency notes often depicted such strings of cash-coins.

The Ch'in dynasty was succeeded by the Han dynasty (202 B.C.-A.D. 9), a 200-year rule that saw greatly improved trade relations not only between China and Central Asia but also between China and the eastern outposts of the Greco-Roman world. The *pan liang* coinage of the previous dynasty was maintained, although the copper coins gradually weighed less. The annals state that, because the heavier coinage of the Ch'in dynasty was inconvenient, the "elm-leaf" cash issued by the Han dynasty was purposely made lighter.

After a tumultuous period China again became unified and prosperous under the Tang dynasty (618-907). The arts and literature flourished. New coins were cast, and a crosswise arrangement of the four characters on the obverse of each coin became customary. Two of these characters comprised the ruling emperor's special title, or *nien hao*; they appeared above and below the square hole on the obverse of the coin. Two more characters appeared to the left and right of the hole; the one on the left, *pao*, simply means "coin," while that on the right varied according to the kind of coin it adorned. At a later date the reverse of the coin also bore characters that indicated its value, the province where it had been issued, and, still later, the Manchu word for "coin."

Under the Sung dynasty (960-1280), continuous pressure exerted by the Mongols to the north forced withdrawal of the Sung capital to a coastal city south of the Yangtze River: Hangchow. Almost 1,000 different kinds of coins were issued by the beleaguered Sung dynasty. Many were cast in iron, alloyed with lead and tin, so that if they fell into Mongol hands they would be too soft and brittle to be made into weapons. In the end the Mongols under Genghis Khan's grandson, Kublai Khan, conquered all China, founding the Yüan dynasty (1280-1368).

Marco Polo, who spent almost 20 years at the court of Kublai Khan, makes mention of the "flying money," or paper currency, issued by Kublai [see CH. VIII]. The Mongols continued, however, to issue a metal coinage as before, although a shortage of metal meant that coins were scarce. The paper currency became badly inflated, and people in many parts of the empire returned to the practice of barter. Today the coins of the Yüan dynasty are rare.

In 1368 Mongol rule was succeeded by a Chinese dynasty, the Ming (1368-1644), and China entered a period of reconstruction, prosperity, and cultural revival. The capital was moved to Peking, which soon developed into one of the world's most beautiful cities. Some Ming coins of the late 16th century bear the inscription "currency of great tranquility." It is a fitting indication of the state of mind that prevailed during a dynasty that saw the currency restored to order and an end to the indiscriminate issuance of paper money.

In 1644 the last Ming emperor, menaced by invading Manchus from the northeast, killed himself. The Manchus ruled as the Ch'ing dynasty until the revolution in 1911. Copper cash-coins were issued up to the last days of the Ch'ing dynasty, and some of them carried Manchu inscriptions only. Endeavors to unify and modernize China's currency system culminated in 1889

236. A Japanese picture story showing complex manufacturing process used to produce large gold coins; seen above are obans and kobans from the 16th to the 19th century. First coin left: 90 x 147 mm.

237. The "modernized" coinage of the silver one yen and the gold twenty-yen pieces of Emperor Mutsuhito of Japan (1867-1912) bore beautiful designs of the imperial chrysanthemum, the radiant sun, and the imperial dragon. 39 & 35 mm.

186

in the opening of a modern mint at Canton. There silver coins of western type were struck in new denominations, the *dollar* and fractions thereof: 50-, 20- 10-, and five-*cent* pieces. Other mints in various provinces followed the example, and a fine series of so-called "dragon *dollars*" was produced under the last two Ch'ing emperors. On the obverse, in addition to Chinese and Manchu legends that identified the ruler, the coins bore a circular inscription in English. The reverse was dominated by the figure of a flying dragon, the imperial emblem. The dragon *dollars* struck during the last decades of Manchu rule were minted in a dozen or more provinces.

In 1911 the revolution broke out, and the first silver coins of the new republic carried the portrait of the revolutionary leader, Sun Yat-sen; the inscription on the reverse carried the words "Republic of China" in English and stated the value of the coin. In 1927, after Sun's death, attempts were made to produce a portrait dollar of particular splendor, and several European mints offered their services. One such portrait coin, produced by the Austrian mint in 1927, was a failure so far as Sun's likeness was concerned, but the reproduction on the reverse of that coin, of Sun's mausoleum at Nanking, with a setting sun in the background, is a remarkable example of coin sculpture. The model that was finally adopted in 1932 shows Sun Yat-sen's bust in profile on the obverse and, on the reverse, a Chinese junk at sea.

Coins of Japan

Whereas China has a comparatively long monetary history, Japan seems not to have substituted coinage for barter until the seventh century of the Christian era. Tradition holds that there were silver coins more than a hundred years earlier, during the reign of the Emperor Kenso (487), but the existence of such coins has never been corroborated.

Chinese copper cash-coins issued during the Tang dynasty found their way into Japan, and this kind of copper coin was evidently in general use by the end of the seventh century. Until 708, however, a copper shortage prevented minting in quantities. That year, in the reign of the Empress Genmyo, large deposits of silver and copper were discovered. At their new mint in the capital city of Nara, the Japanese used Chinese labor and followed Chinese designs to produce a large number of copper cash-coins. The Japanese, however, issued almost no silver coins and, of Japan's earliest gold coins — issued during the reign of the Emperor Junnin in 760 — only a single specimen has survived.

One interesting feature of the manufacture of Japanese copper coins is that they were cast in large, so-called "tree" molds. The "limbs" of a single tree mold might terminate in as many as 125 coin impressions, each a duplicate of the master die. After the molten copper was poured into the mold, it solidified into a treelike form with the single coins, like leaves on branches, ready to be broken off. The Japanese called these multiple castings *tane sen*, or "seed money."

For the next three centuries the history of Japanese coinage is one of gradual debasement until, with the people's confidence in their money at a low ebb, shortly after 958 the government ceased to issue money altogether. Another

238. Annamese gold coins with an interesting variety of symbols: the sun and the moon surrounded by five planets; the stormy sea; mountains; and three trees of longevity, as well as the imperial flying dragon (19th century). 45 & 43 mm.

239. The strange money of Siam: porcelain tokens used in gambling houses, and silver and gold ticals called "bullet money" ranging from a large eight-tical piece to a minuscule fraction of 1/32 tical (mid-19th century). First bullet coin upper left: 13 mm.

600 years were to pass before the government mints again went to work. Meanwhile, foreign coins became the medium of exchange. The import of Chinese coins in particular was promoted by a large number of Chinese refugees who fled to Japan after the Mongol conquest of China in the 13th century, and *eiraku sen*, as the Chinese coppers were called, were even accepted by the government in payment of taxes.

One of the feudal lords, or *daimyo*, named Oda Nobunaga, succeeded in unifying Japan in 1573. His successor went further and consolidated the nation's economy by monopolizing its gold and silver mines and issuing a uniform coinage. This feudal leader, Hideyoshi Toyotomi, began by casting the world's largest gold coin, the *oban*. A large oval coin, it weighed approximately 165 grams. Fractional *obans* were called *koban*. Some of Hideyoshi's gold and silver coinages were continued by his successor, Tokugawa Iyeyasu (1542-1616), who completed the monetary reform of Japan. A fixed relation was established between gold, silver, and copper. The standard unit of value was the gold *ryo*; it was equal in value to four gold *bu*, and the *bu* was equal to four gold *shu*. The gold coinage, heavily alloyed, preserved these relative values. The largest coin, the *oban*, was valued at 10 *ryo* and the *koban* was valued at one *ryo*. Smaller gold denominations included the *ichibuban*, valued at one *bu*, and the minuscule *isshuban*, valued at one *shu*. These gold coins were cast in the *Kinza*, or "gold mint," established by Iyeyasu at Tokyo, where he later set up the *Ginza*, or "silver mint." Silver was cast in the form of ingots such as the oval *cho-gin*, or "bean cake block," and the rectangular *mameita-gin*, or

240. Modern Siam used the elephant on coins of King Mongkut (1851-1868), and the three-headed elephant on silver ticals struck in the early 1900s. 31 & 30 mm.

241. *King Kalakaua (1874-1891) of Hawaii on a silver dollar of 1883 and his sister, Queen Liliuokalani (1891-1893), a gifted poetess and composer, on a pattern 20-dala gold piece of 1893, the year she was ousted. Coin left: 38 mm.*

"bean block." As they varied in size, the silver ingots were valued according to their weight. Copper coins were produced at a number of different mints. Early in the 17th century, seeking to avoid the necessity of cutting up silver pieces to make change, a merchant of Yamada started giving out receipts for silver; these *Yamada Hagahi* may rightly be considered Japan's first paper money. The merchant's innovation was soon widely imitated as feudal lords, town officials, and temple priests began to issue their own Following the overthrow of the shogunate and the restoration of imperial power in 1868, the vigorous, young Mutsuhito, the Meiji Emperor (1867-1912), included a complete revision of the Japanese currency among the "modernization" reforms that characterized the Meiji Restoration. The emperor's new coinage was "round in shape and decimal in denominations." A new unit, the yen (equal in value to $1 in United States currency), was created. Four gold coins were struck: a 20-yen, 10-yen, five-yen, and two-yen piece. There were five silver coins: a one-yen piece and four *sen* units — a 50, 20, 10, and a five-*sen* piece. Two copper units — the one-*sen* and the half-*sen* pieces — completed the issue. Beautiful coins with these denominations designed by Kano Natsuo, were struck at the Osaka mint, where the Japanese government set up the necessary mint machinery, purchased from the British mint at Hong Kong. The new coins, of course, comprised only a part of modern Japan's currency. Large quantities of paper money were also issued, and, as in most modern states, paper became the main instrument in facilitating trade and exchange in general.   □

VIII | PAPER MONEY

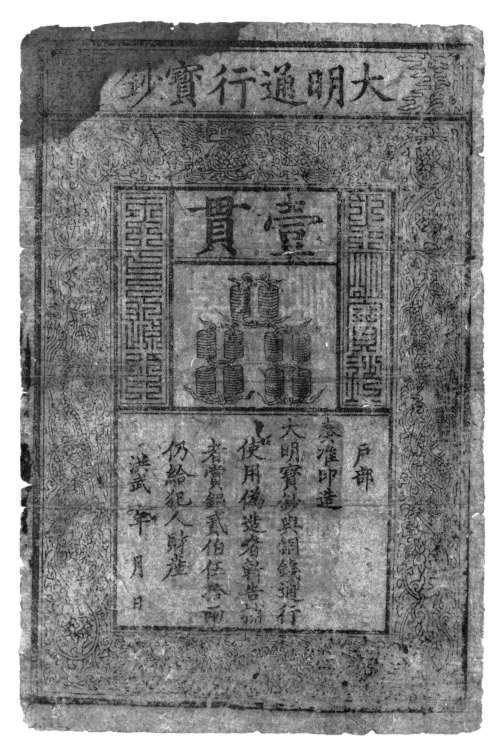

243. Note of one kwan or 1000 wen (cash) issued by the Chinese Emperor Hung-wu (A.D. 1368-1398), first emperor of the Ming dynasty. 225 x 333 mm.

VIII: PAPER MONEY: FROM CHAOS TO CONFIDENCE

Silk, leather, buckskin, and textiles — indeed any printable material —
has been used for centuries.

"In this city of Kanbalu [modern Peking]," wrote Marco Polo, "is the mint of the grand khan, who may truly be said to possess the secret of the alchemists, as he has the art of producing money by the following process . . . that thin inner rind which lies between the coarser bark and the wood of the [mulberry] tree . . . being steeped, and afterwards pounded in a mortar until reduced to a pulp, is made into paper. . . . When ready for use . . . it [is] cut into pieces of money of different sizes, nearly square, but somewhat longer than they are wide. Of these, the smallest pass for a *denier tournois* (see Chapter IV); the next size for a Venetian silver *groat*; others for two, five, and 10 *groats*; others for one, two, three, and as far as 10 *bezants* of gold.

"The coinage of this paper money is authenticated with as much form and ceremony as if it were actually of pure gold or silver; for to each note a number of officers, specially appointed, not only subscribe their names, but affix their signets also; and when this has been regularly done by the whole of them, the principal officer, deputed by his majesty, having dipped into vermilion the royal seal committed to his custody, stamps with it the piece of paper, so that the form of the seal tinged with the vermilion remains impressed upon it, by which it receives full authenticity as current money, and the act of counterfeiting it is punished as a capital offence."

This comprehensive 13th-century description of the Yüan dynasty's "flying money" is the earliest European description of a completely new economic concept: paper money. A generally accepted substitute for coins, Kublai Khan's paper notes could replace any metallic currency, could be converted in case of need into silver or gold, and, when damaged, could be replaced upon payment of a small premium. Many of these fundamental criteria of paper money have not changed in the 700 years since Marco Polo's day. The autocratic power that required the acceptance of paper notes in the 13th century has been replaced today by confidence, yet an amazing resemblance between the two systems still persists.

The mulberry paper notes described by Marco Polo were not the first paper money used in China. "Flying money" goes back to the T'ang dynasty (618-907). The T'ang notes were actually receipts for goods delivered by merchants to the state when a scarcity of coins made cash payments impossible. In the following centuries other Chinese dynasties also issued flying money. Often limited in circulation to a single city or province, the notes became more widely used in the early years of the Ming dynasty (1368-1644) that overthrew Mongol rule. Uncontrolled issue of paper led to depreciation, however, and despite many government attempts to control the value of paper money by decree, entire segments of the Chinese population suffered great financial losses. The situation described by a 14th-century source could find parallels in 18th-century France, in Germany during the 1920s, and in Hungary in the 1940s. "The cost of commodities soared upward and prices rose more than tenfold. Revolts broke out. What [money] was printed daily could not be counted."

Although the Ming dynasty repudiated paper money in the middle of the 15th century, the use of paper reached southeast Asia, and notes circulated in Burma, Annam, and Thailand. Both Persia in the 13th century and India in the 14th century attempted to follow the Chinese example by substituting paper for metallic currencies. Great hopes were attached to the venture and even poets sang its merits, but the Persian and Indian populations alike refused to accept the change and the efforts were soon ended.

A great outburst of European prosperity, beginning with the 14th century, created immense "money power" exercised by a few influential banking families such as the famous German Fuggers and the Medicis of Florence. These early bankers accepted deposits in money or goods, recorded them in their books, and gave receipts which were deemed negotiable securities and assumed, therefore, the functions of money.

The establishment of private banks in the 16th and 17th centuries was followed by a logical next step: the issuance of bank notes. The use of paper money in the western world thus had its beginnings in the initiative of bankers and not of governments. Midway through the 17th century Johan Palmstruck obtained permission from the Swedish crown to organize a bank in Stockholm. Because specie was in short supply, Palmstruck's *Stockholm Banco* in 1661 issued notes called *Kreditivsedlar,* or "credit notes." These notes are the earliest paper money issued in western Europe. The notes carried eight signatures and, to prevent counterfeiting, the paper was watermarked. The story has a sad ending. The bank could not redeem its notes. As a result of an investigation, Palmstruck was held responsible for certain substantial losses. After spending a long period in jail, he was freed only to die within a year, a poor and embittered man.

The Swedish failure was followed in a few decades by tumultuous happenings in France that further discredited paper money. John Law, a Scot, attempted to prop up the shaky finances of France after the death of Louis XIV. Law's plans won over the Regent, the Duke of Orleans, and in 1716 Law was granted the right to open a bank, the *Banque Generale.* It was funded by 12,000 shares, each having a substantial value of 500 *livres.*

The money issued by Law's bank had all the characteristics of a modern bank note. It was printed on special paper and guaranteed by the signatures of the bank's officers. But Law did not stop there. In 1717 he founded the *Compagnie d'Occident,* to exploit the territories of Louisiana and Canada. Many of the shares of the *Compagnie d'Occident* were transferred to Law's bank, and more paper money was issued, with the shares as security. The next year Law merged two older companies with interests in China and the East Indies to form the *Compagnie des Indes,* and repeated the process. Wild speculation ensued; for example, a bank share that had originally cost 500 *livres* was sold in December, 1719, for 12,500 *livres,* and the price of a share later rose to 18,000 *livres.* Frenchmen from all walks of life, and even foreigners who had come to Paris to get rich quickly, congregated at Law's headquarters to make or lose millions. In 1720, however, speculators started selling the bank shares. In order to stem the run, the bank began to buy up the shares and tried to fix the price. Royal decrees followed, prohibiting the private possession of jewels or coins in quantity, but the only result of these measures was the complete destruction of popular confidence in the bank

244. *Cosimo de' Medici (1389-1464), Florentine banker, portrait by Jacopo da Pontormo.*

245. *Jakob II Fugger (1459-1525), member of the powerful German bankers' family from Augsburg, in a portrait by Hans Holbein the Older.*

194

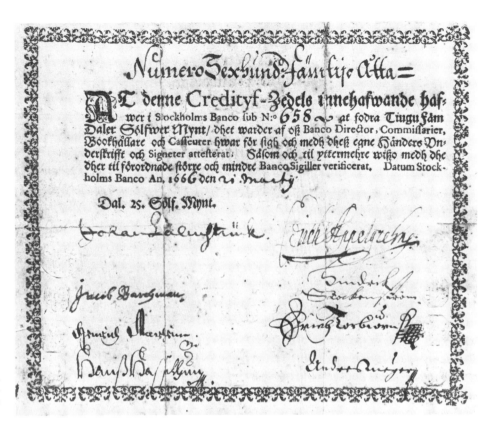

and its notes. The panic that followed toppled the whole system. By December, 1721 a 500-*livre* bank share had fallen in value to one *livre*. Law, once one of the wealthiest men in the world, fled France with only a few hundred *louis d'or* in his pockets. He died in Venice in 1729, poor and obscure.

The paper money of Palmstruck and Law was short-lived and left behind it only distrust. In one area, however, paper money worked its way in a more durable fashion into the economy of an entire nation. This was in the American colonies. Kept in complete financial dependency by the mother country, the colonists found cash hard to come by (see Chapter VI). It was imperative to find other media of exchange. In 1690 when Massachusetts incurred a debt of 50,000 *pounds* in the course of an ill-fated military expedition into Canada, the General Court of the Bay Colony decided to print "bills of credit" in the amount of 7,000 *pounds* because of the ". . . poverty and calamity of [the] country." The notes, in denominations upward from two *shillings* to 10 *pounds,* were printed from copper plates engraved by John Conny, a prominent silversmith of Boston. The colony's seal and the signatures of the issuing officials provided a guarantee of the notes' legality. Two years later the notes were declared legal tender for all kinds of payments.

Other colonies soon followed the example. In 1703 South Carolina authorized public credit notes to finance an expedition against St. Augustine in Spanish Florida. In 1709 Connecticut, a "colony of industrious husbandmen," issued a small number of paper credits. New York started using paper bills that same year, and New Jersey decided to finance an expedition against Canada with public bills of credit. In 1729 Benjamin Franklin, a strong supporter of paper money, expounded his views in an anonymous pamphlet entitled *A Modest Inquiry Into the Nature and Necessity of Paper Money.* Virginia, where "tobacco notes" soon circulated actively after being authorized in 1730, issued treasury notes in 1755 to cover the cost of General Braddock's expedition to Fort Duquesne.

In appearance, the paper money of the colonial period shows stylistic peculiarities that cannot be matched among the notes of other nations, whose paper money, with few exceptions, was then unadorned and rather plain. A wealth of delightful motifs can be found among the notes issued from 1690 to 1788 as each colony developed a style of its own, in many cases excelling the others in certain aspects of design. Fine border ornaments were characteristic of the New England colonies, whereas vignettes with emblems and mottoes were characteristic of Pennsylvania. Rich coats of arms appeared on New Jersey notes and graceful renderings of animals on the notes of Georgia and South Carolina. Many of the bills provide interesting examples of early woodcuts and engravings. The seal of Massachusetts that John Conny executed for the note issued in 1690 was the first copperplate engraving made in the colonies. Other Massachusetts notes, with such motifs as a "Sword in Hand" (1776) or a "Rising Sun" (1782), were designed by Paul Revere. The work of Thomas Coram of Charleston, South Carolina, depicting classical groups that include Hercules, Atlas, and Prometheus, is that of the trained artist. In the main, however, the notes were the work of anonymous craftsmen and offer an insight into the average colonial American's artistic and intellectual life.

As relations between the colonies and the crown turned from dissidence to open rebellion the Continental Congress perforce sanctioned issues of additional paper money (see Chapter VI). Having no power of taxation, the Congress charged its bills against the faith of the "Continent." At first intended only in anticipation of future taxes, the notes began to be used in exchange and came to be called "Continental currency," or "Continentals." As early as 1777, depreciation set in, and even after victory all the measures taken by the Congress could not stop the almost complete devaluation of the Continental

247. The enterprising financier, John Law (1671-1729) in a contemporary engraving.

248. Contemporary cartoon listing the many deceptive opportunities created by John Law.

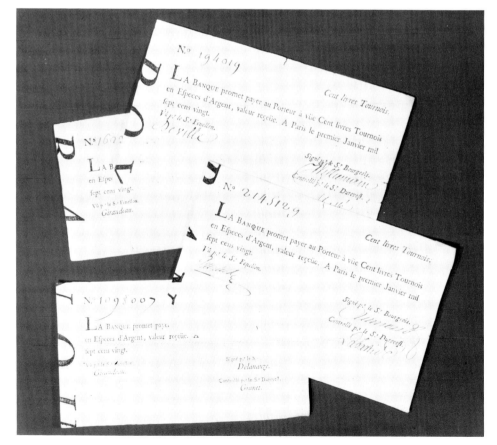

249. Notes for ten and one hundred livre tournois issued in 1720 by the Banque Royale under John Law's direction. Lower right: 16 x 114 mm.

bills. Meanwhile, each of the colonies issued new bills, in addition to those already circulating, to cover military expenses. Not until 1787 did the Constitution put an end to such issues by directing that no state "shall . . . emit bills of credit or make anything but gold or silver coin a tender in payments of debts." By then, however, the damage had been done and the phrase "not worth a Continental" became rooted in the language.

Impressed by the beneficial influence of the Bank of England on Great Britain's economy, the first United States Secretary of the Treasury, Alexander Hamilton, proposed the organization of a single, central, national bank, and in 1791 the Bank of the United States was granted a 20-year charter. The bank was authorized to issue notes that were legal tender, but its main importance lay in the restraint it imposed on state-authorized banks by refusing to accept the notes of any bank that did not have sufficient coverage. The first of these

250. Eagle supporting revolutionary emblems in central vignette embellishes this assignat for 400 livres issued in 1792 during the French Revolution. 190 x 113 mm.

banks had come into existence in 1784, when Massachusetts and New York gave state charters to private banks. A string of similar institutions began to appear in other states early in the 1800s, and a kind of mania ensued. As one commentator noted, "The whole country was bank crazy; any place where there was a church, a tavern, or a blacksmith shop was deemed a suitable place for setting up a bank."

Speculators found quick fortunes by setting up banks with little or no hard cash to cover the notes they issued. One such bank printed paper money worth more than half a million dollars, with a backing of only 86 dollars in specie. Often the same bags of specie moved from bank to bank just ahead of the state inspectors. When the mania reached its peak during the 1830s, the term "wildcat bank" was a mocking description of note issuers whose headquarters were somewhere in the unknown wilderness, and the term "saddlebag note" suggested the transient character of these fly-by-night institutions. The rise in the number of state banks in these years tells an eloquent story. Three such banks existed in 1790. By 1811 the number was 88, and by 1820 it was 307. In the 1830s the number reached 788, and the number of notes in circulation tripled in one decade. "Bank fever" reached its peak in 1835; in that one year more than 200 new banks were opened.

The short-lived prosperity came to a sudden end when, in 1836, Andrew Jackson, although himself in favor of the state-licensed banks, nonetheless

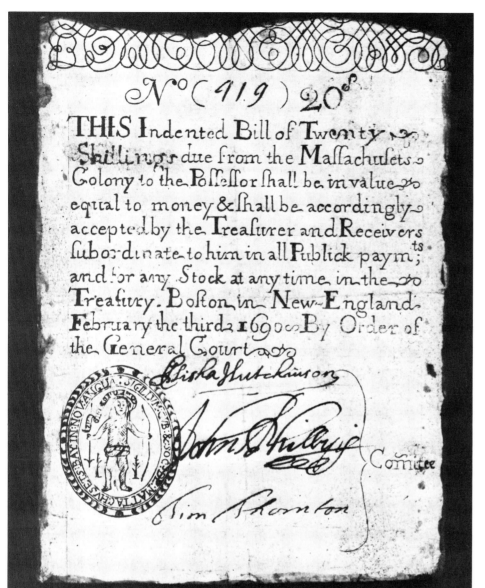

251. This twenty shilling-note printed in Boston in 1690 was among the first bills issued in the American Colonies. 105 x 143 mm.

252. Graceful vignettes adorning notes of Colonial Georgia. 83 x 71 mm.

253. A great wealth of delightful motifs: emblems with mottoes; coats of arms; drawings of interesting landmarks; and fine border ornaments found on the notes issued by the American States during the Revolutionary War. First lower left: 107 x 63 mm.

issued a "specie circular," requiring that payments for public lands be made in specie and not in bank notes. Shortly thereafter, the banks in New York suspended the redemption of their bank notes in specie, and the bottom fell out of state-licensed banks all around the nation. Specie vanished from circulation immediately. The coin shortage inspired the issue of notes of small denominations — promptly nicknamed "shinplasters" — to take the place of hoarded small change.

With the outbreak of the Civil War in 1861, the Federal Treasury was almost empty. Specie payments were promptly suspended, and Congress was forced to authorize the issue of paper money. The first Federal Treasury notes, authorized that same year, were "demand notes," giving the bearer the right to redeem them in specie "on demand." They were used as currency without, however, having any status as legal tender. These were the first "greenbacks," being printed with ink of another color than the usual black. They soon became the main currency of the North.

While the North thus developed a paper currency with a uniform national character, the South was engulfed in financial chaos. In addition to Confederate Treasury notes, various Confederate states, cities, and even individual citizens printed scrip. Inflation became rampant. Wrote one observer: "Before

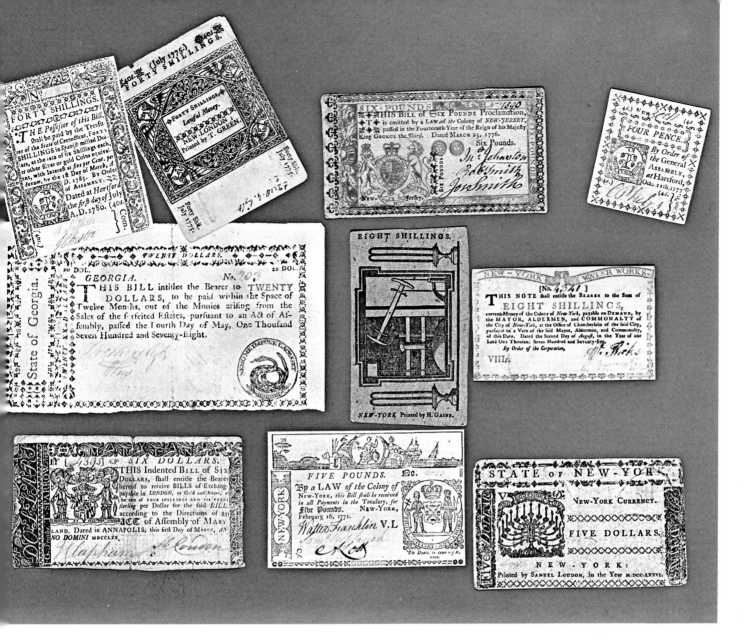

254. "Sword in hand", Paul Revere's design for a Massachusetts, Colonial note (1775). 76 x 102 mm.

the war . . . I went to market with . . . money in my pocket, and brought back my purchase in a basket; now I take the money in the basket, and bring the things home in my pocket." Confidence in Confederate money soon vanished, and before the end of the Civil War even Confederate troops were paid in kind or not at all.

Perhaps the most tragic instance of inflation in modern times was the monetary collapse of Germany after World War I. Germany entered the war as a major economic power and financed its war expenditures by means of public loans, but the costs of the effort ultimately exhausted the nation's resources, and as goods grew more scarce prices started to rise. The quantity of notes issued by the Reichsbank increased sevenfold during the war, and yet more notes continued to be printed and circulated.

Early in 1923 the United States *dollar* was worth 7,260 *marks;* before September the rate of exchange was millions to one; in October, billions to one; and in November, trillions to one. The rising rate of exchange was posted three times a day: morning, noon, and evening. Workers were paid their wages each morning, and everyone tried to finish shopping by noon in the certain knowledge that the money would be worth far less by evening. As one German commented, "Nobody stole money; it was worthless." Neither the

255. Many state bank notes in the United States display a kaleidoscope of colorful vignettes depicting scenes of a nation being transformed from a farming to an industrial society. Aver.: 170 x 75 mm.

256. The Second Bank of the United States in Philadelphia, c. 1820.

paper industry nor the printing presses could keep pace with the wild increases, and existing notes were overprinted with new values: million-*mark* notes, billion-*mark* notes, and even trillion-*mark* notes. Communities and private enterprises were encouraged to put out their own notes, and the consequent flood of paper was known under the generic name of *Notgeld,* or "money of necessity." At last, by means of drastic reform, the value of the *mark* was re-established. The *Rentenmark,* backed by land holdings, was issued at the rate of one new *mark* for a trillion inflation *marks.* Weary of the nightmare period of deprivation and insecurity, most Germans welcomed the reform, and public confidence was restored.

The German tragedy was not, however, the most enormous inflation the world has ever experienced. That record-breaking event took place in Hungary in 1946. The old unit of currency, the *pengo,* had by then become

257. Steel plate for the printing of $50 and $100 Confederate notes, 1861. 215 x 185 mm.

258. United States fractional currency: en-
cased postage stamps, 1862; a paste-up by the
U.S. Treasurer Francis E. Spinner showing his
proposed 50-cent postage-stamp-note; and a
bundle of twenty 50-cent notes of 1875 with
original paper strap. 50 cent notes: 113 mm.

259. Proof-sheet of twelve $100,000 gold cer-
tificates approved, December 17, 1934, for
printing. 330 x 440 mm.

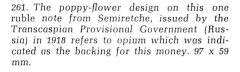
260. Basketfulls of German inflation notes, 1923, were needed to pay for goods and services. One billion: 145 x 88 mm.

unmanageable, and a new multiple unit — the *milpengo,* equal to a million *pengos* — was introduced. Within three months, the government was forced to introduce the *bilpengo,* equal to a billion *pengos,* in denominations ranging from 1,000 to 100 million *bilpengos.* Subsequently, still another unit — a billion *bilpengos* (in numerical notation, this is a one followed by 28 zeros) — was prepared. It was not issued, however, and on July 9, 1946, all Hungarian bank notes ceased to circulate. The last day of July, 1946 was also the last day of the world's greatest inflation. On August 1 a new unit — the *forint* — was introduced at the rate of one *forint* per four hundred million quadrillion *pengos* (a four followed by 23 zeros), and the inflation came to an end.

World War I produced a similarly tragic and confused situation in Russia. Inflation set in relatively soon and the volume of circulating paper money increased from millions to trillions. Insufficient notes were issued by the

261. The poppy-flower design on this one ruble note from Semiretche, issued by the Transcaspian Provisional Government (Russia) in 1918 refers to opium which was indicated as the backing for this money. 97 x 59 mm.

262. Cities under siege often had to produce their own money: Mayence held by the French in 1793; Khartoum (Sudan) in 1885; Langres in France in 1870; and Mafeking in South Africa in 1900. Mafeking: 160 x 120 mm.

Russian central government, many local groups printed their own scrip, and notes circulated, issued by the short-lived republics of Ukraine, Georgia, Armenia, Turkestan, and others.

263. Philippines "Victory" note 1944. 160 x 68 mm.

264. Special scrip issues used in a camp for Czech prisoners in Russia (1919), and German concentration camp notes (1943). Upper right: 140 x 96 mm.

The Romance of Paper Money

When faced with war, destruction, loss of property, or famine, man makes use of his full powers of survival. The issuance of war or emergency paper money shows this versatility of human inventiveness.

In 1574 when Spanish troops surrounded the Dutch city of Leiden, citizens tore up old church books, cut the bindings, and stamped small pieces of cardboard with their seal giving them legal power to circulate as lawful money. Notes written in Arabic and signed by the British Governor Charles George Gordon circulated in 1884 and 1885 when Khartoum in the Sudan lay under siege by the supporters of the fanatic Mahdi. Ten-peso Philippine notes with

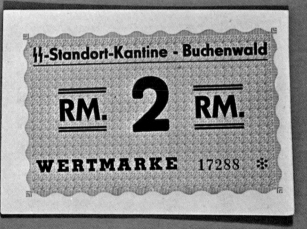

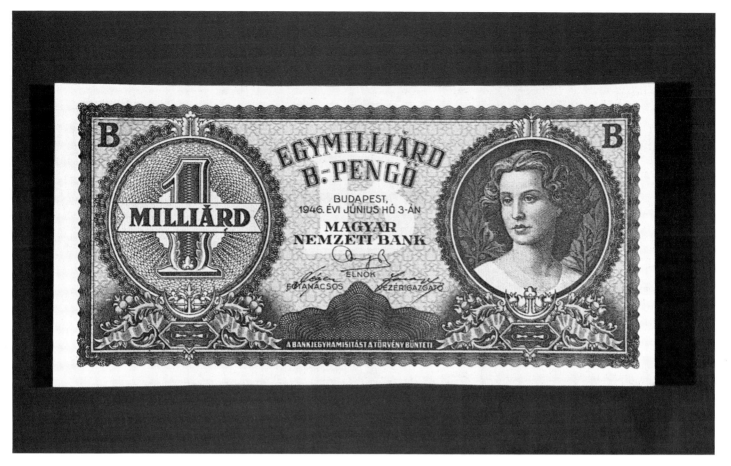

265. In 1946, during rampant inflation, Hungary issued a one billion bilpengo note. 175 x 84 mm.

267. Alaskan sealskin notes issued about 1820 by the Russian-American Company to remedy a coin shortage. Front note: 69 x 50 mm.

266. *Playing cards, calendar leaves, book-binder's paper, tickets, aluminium foil, leather and wood used for the manufacture of currency. Buckskin: 130 x 64 mm.*

the word "Victory" stamped in large black letters were issued for the first time on October 20, 1944, when General MacArthur established the Leyte Island beach head fulfilling his promise: "I Shall Return."

An immense variety of concentration camp and prisoner of war currencies exist dating from both great World Wars. A great rarity, for example, is a crudely designed World War I scrip note of one *ruble* issued for Czech prisoners in Russia. The notorious World War II German concentration camps of Buchenwald and Sachsenhausen had plain and simple notes used by their S.S. garrison. Oranienburg, a concentration camp north of Berlin, printed notes of a more complex design, some showing on the reverse the national emblems, the swastika and eagle flanked by two S.S. troopers standing guard in front of barbed wire. Of a similar sinister character were 1943 notes in values from one to 500 *kronen*, and signed by the Jewish elders of Theresienstadt, a small town north of Prague, which had been transformed into a concentration camp mostly for East European Jews. The notes were a receipt for work rendered inside the camp.

268. A 5000 ruble note, 1921, printed on silk in the Khorezm Republic in Uzbekistan, U.S.S.R. 145 x 117 mm.

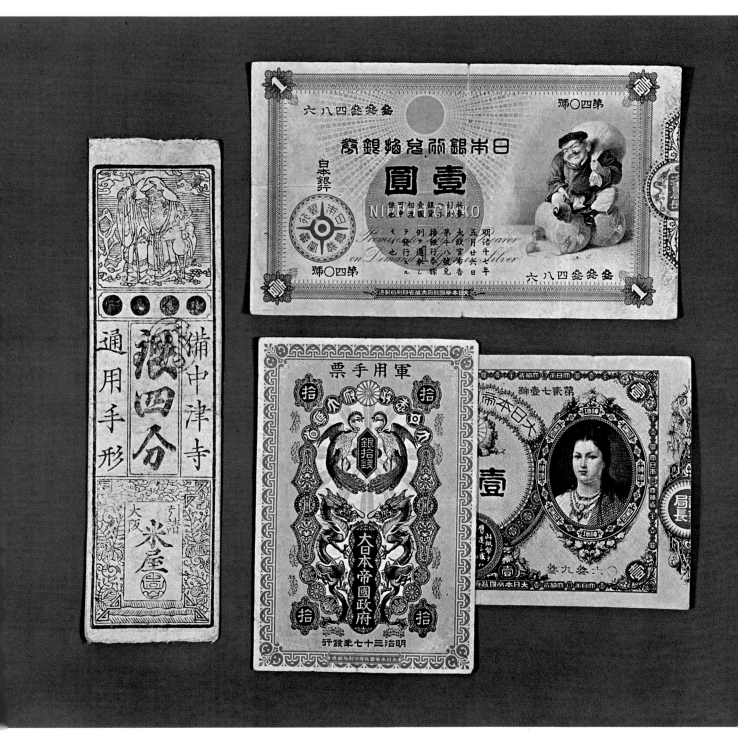

269. The delicate design on the Hansatsu or provincial notes. Colorful vignettes on national currency notes issued around the turn of the century reveal the exquisite beauty of Japanese paper money. First left: 42 x 155 mm.

Silk, leather, buckskin, and textiles — indeed any printable material — have been used for centuries as substitutes for paper money. Colorful and beautifully imprinted silk notes were issued in a Russian republic in 1921. A Chinese province under Communist control in 1933 produced legal tender on linen showing a closed fist surrounded by a star.

Alte Orlabrücke aus dem 16. Jahrhundert

Donautal Notgeld.

Rannariedl.

TIVOLI
Gut für
Gut für
50
Pf.
50
Pf.
die Bremer Stadtmusikanten
ZU·BREMEN·

IN DEM ARMEN RÖMSCHEN HEERE DIEN
TE AUCH ALS VOLONTÄRE SCAEVOLA EIN

RECHTSKANDIDAT DEN MAN SCHNÖD
GEFANGEN HAT WIE DIE ANDERN ALLE

75 Pf.

Notgeld Altona

Notgeld der Stadt Pößneck
FÜNF MILLIONEN MARK
zahlt die Stadthauptkasse in Pößneck
dem Einlieferer dieses Gutscheines.

Dieser Schein verliert
seine Gültigkeit vier Wochen
nach Bekanntmachung.

Pößneck d. 11. Aug. 1923
Der Gemeindevorsteher

50
Stadtgeld
der Stadt Altenburg
19 21
50
Pf.
Pf.

271. Modernistic, colorful designs are used on Netherlands' contemporary notes. 153 x 76 mm.

270. Wit and an almost romantic nostalgia exudes from the innumerable, colorful cartoonlike designs which enlivened the German and Austrian Notgeld or emergency issues of the 1920s. Lower right: 96 x 67 mm.

National artistic traditions often appear on paper money. Japanese provincial bank notes of the 18th and 19th centuries (Hansatsu) show delightful woodcut vignettes representing divinities and other mythical figures. From colonial times to the present, American craftsmanship has been a noteworthy feature of the iconographic evolution of paper money. Fine engraving work appeared on other paper currencies as well. Aesthetic considerations, while important, soon gave way to concerns about security and the need to maintain the integrity of legal scrip against counterfeiting. ☐

IX: COUNTERFEITERS AND COLLECTORS: THE ART OF COVETING

Nothing can replace the eye of the connoisseur.

Counterfeiting, the forgery of a legal circulating currency with the aim of receiving either goods or legal tender in exchange, is an old practice. Solon's legislation for Athens, early in the sixth century B.C., contains provisions against counterfeiting, as did the later laws of the Roman Empire. Clay molds for casting Roman coins have been found in Egypt and in parts of Europe beyond the Roman frontier; the inference that the molds were counterfeiters' equipment seems inescapable.

An illegal means of profiting that is not overt counterfeiting has been mentioned earlier. This is clipping, a careful trimming of metal from the edges of coins, a process that reduced the value of many coins during the Middle Ages and thereafter. The English Lord Protector, Oliver Cromwell, was only expressing the irritation of many before him when he had a Latin legend inscribed on the rims of many coins minted during his rule. It read: *Has nisi periturus mihi adimat nemo,* or "Let no one remove these [letters] from me under penalty of death."

Even the field of primitive media of exchange is not free of fraud. False dog teeth were manufactured in Berlin and counterfeit bronze *manillas* came from Birmingham.

The roster of counterfeiters is exceedingly long; many did it for profit, some to play tricks on well-known experts, others considered it a challenge to imitate in a perfect way the masterworks of ancient engravers.

Today, practically every collection of paper money includes notes with large overprints or perforations indicating that these notes are counterfeits. The scourge which has haunted every issuing authority since the earliest times, goes back in history as far as ancient China. When the first western paper money appeared in Sweden in 1661, counterfeiters soon went to work; and in France in the early 1700s counterfeiters did not shy away from faking John Law's short-lived issues. Colonial American notes carried (in vain) the warning: "Death to Counterfeit." But even hangings, the pillory, or public opprobrium seldom deterred criminals.

There are only two ways of discouraging counterfeiting: by making it dangerous or by making it so difficult that it becomes unattractive. One important element which challenges counterfeiting is the use of quality paper and printing. Special safety measures involving paper, inks, and printing secure a more foolproof method. Special inks have been developed, which are invisible under normal lights.

Benjamin Franklin applied an old method in paper money: the nature prints, known since Leonardo da Vinci's time, as a safety element. On the backs of paper bills, he imprinted various leafs, reproduced in type metal from plaster casts and used in lieu of engravings.

Nineteenth-century America provides one particularly colorful practitioner of the art. In 1882, when a Dutch immigrant settled in New Jersey to work as a sign painter, few persons would have guessed that the modest and unassuming stranger would eventually be known in police files as "Jim the Pen-

⊲ 273. A miser's dream.

275. The coin in Candida's hand can be identified easily as a bronze of the Roman Emperor Nero (A.D. 54-68).

man." At his farm in New Jersey, Emanuel Ninger produced fake United States notes by laboriously drawing them, using pen and brush. Ninger spent his handmade bank notes sparingly. In 1896, having made and passed some 40,000 *dollars* worth of notes, Ninger was unmasked when the ink on a counterfeit 50-*dollar* bill that he had placed on a damp bar counter started to run. Ninger's machine-method counterpart was one William Brockway, sometimes called the "king of counterfeiters." A skilled engraver, Brockway counterfeited bank notes by the thousands around the turn of the century and even made plates for the printing of fake United States bonds. Brockway served a number of terms in jail. Paroled at age 82, he died in 1920, having lived to be almost 100 years old.

Counterfeiting the money of an enemy state in the hope of undermining enemy finances has often been attempted. The largest and most successful counterfeiting operation of this kind ever perpetrated was mounted by Germany in World War II. Forged Bank of England notes were printed by the millions, enabling Germany to buy war supplies and the services of spies at

216

no real cost. The "mint" operated inside the Sachsenhausen concentration camp and used Jewish workers (whose lives were thereby saved) exclusively. Code-named "Operation Bernhard," after an S.S. Major, Bernhard Krüger, who directed the activity, the "mint" produced counterfeit English bank notes with a value of 135 million *pounds*.

The Numismatist: The Art of Collecting

The instinct that leads one to form a numismatic collection is probably only a refinement of the instinct that inflames hunters of all kinds. Thus it seems

276. Sumptuously decorated coin cabinet of King Louis XV of France.

277. A book printed in 1568 in Amsterdam, Holland, with drawings and descriptions of gold and silver coins from various European countries.

likely that the history of numismatics is as old as the history of money itself. Certainly, by the late Middle Ages when a desire for erudition was awakening, the coins of classical times proved to be wonderful and direct sources of information about the past. Even before the Renaissance period, Europe was rich in remarkable coin collections. In 15th-century Florence the great Cosimo de' Medici included Greek and Roman coins in his art collection, and his son Pietro and grandson Lorenzo the Magnificent added many coins to his assemblage. An inventory taken in 1465 lists 100 gold coins and 503 silver coins in the Medici cabinet; later, some 2,000 copper coins were added to the collection.

Across the Alps, the Hapsburgs had their own peculiar motives for collecting classical coins. They wanted to round out the family gallery of portraits of the various Holy Roman emperors by adding to them the emperors of Rome. Early documents indicate the presence of coin collections in Hapsburg hands as early as the 13th century; by the time of Emperor Maximilian I (1493-1519), the coin collection at the court in Vienna was a famous one.

217

In Augsburg during the 16th century, a wealthy German banker, Hans Jakob Fugger, owned, in addition to a famous library filled with precious manuscripts, a coin cabinet rich in ancient gold and silver pieces that the antiquarian Jacobus Strada of Mantua had bought for him, mostly in Italy. As time passed, however, coin collecting became increasingly a hobby of kings. The royal Bavarian collection grew substantially during the reign of Prince Maximilian I (1597-1651), the Elector of Bavaria. Eventually it became one of the outstanding coin cabinets in central Europe, even surpassing the collections of the Saxon princes in Dresden. In Brandenburg, the Prince Elector Joachim II (1535-1571) established the Berlin numismatic cabinet; it was later much enlarged by Frederick the Great.

The extreme seems to have been reached by the Emperor Charles VI, whose wife's portrait adorns the famous Maria Theresa *taler*. Charles carried his numismatic fervor so far that he would not be separated from his favorite coins even during military campaigns. Accordingly he had a portable coin case built, and it accompanied him to the battlefield.

280. Ancient methods of testing the silver content of coins. Roman Republican denarii with bankers' test-marks; the serrated edge guaranteed that the coin did not have a copper core. 18 & 19 mm.

281. Ancient clay moulds, found in Egypt, used for casting counterfeits of Roman coins; and similar, authentic coin of Emperor Maximinus (A.D. 309-313). Coin: 21 mm.

We can assume that the interest in coins which existed in colonial America did not differ greatly from similar interests in Europe. In New York, for example, the Tammany Society purchased coins in both 1793 and 1796; by 1811 its museum had some 300 ancient coins in its possession. Philadelphia was also a leading numismatic center.

The Numismatic and Antiquarian Society was founded in Philadelphia early in the 1800s, and soon a series of similar organizations sprang up elsewhere.

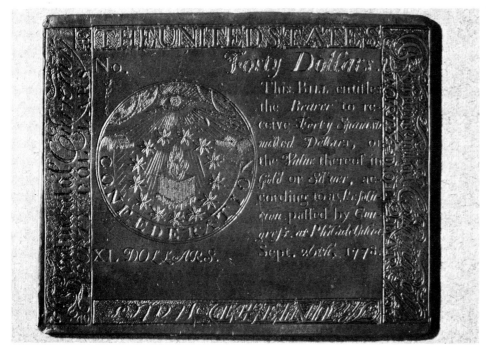

282. Copper plate used during the American Revolution by the British to counterfeit 40-dollar Continental currency notes of 1778 on their ship "Phoenix" stationed in the harbor of New York. 94 x 75 mm.

ADVERTISEMENT.
Persons, going into the other Colonies, may be supplied with any Number of counterfeited Congress Notes, for the Price of the Paper per Ream. They are so nearly and exactly executed, that there is no Risque in getting them off, it being almost impossible to discover, that they are not genuine. This has been proved by Bills to a very large Amount, which have already been successfully circulated. Enquire for Q. E. D. at the Coffee-House, from 11 P. M. to 4 A. M. during the present Month.

283. Advertisement of counterfeit Continental currency selling for the price of paper per ream. New York Gazette, 1777.

The Boston Numismatic Society was founded in 1860; the Rhode Island Numismatic Association (in Providence), in 1864. In Boston, the collection of William S. Appleton (1840-1903) was noted for its contents in both the classical and American field. A second Bostonian, Matthew A. Stickney (1805-1894), also accumulated a remarkable cabinet, emphasizing United States coins and medals. The New York group claimed among its leading collectors Charles I. Bushnell (1826-1883) who wrote a work on tokens. The principal Philadelphian numismatist of this period was Joseph J. Mickley (1799-1877), whose coin cabinet was famous for both quantity and quality.

A number of large and specialized collections were formed in the United States toward the close of the 19th century, and many rarities that came on the market in Europe found their way to America. The famous financier-philanthropist J. P. Morgan participated from New York in a famous auction sale held in Rome in 1907, bidding by cable against the European buyers. He unsuccessfully bid for a unique ancient Greek gold coin from Messine. His competitor, a leading Italian collector, set a record in its day by paying the highest price ever for a single coin.

Collections of nearly mythical value do not necessarily belong only to numismatists of the past. Recently, over a period of a scant 14 years, the president of a United States pharmaceutical firm, Josiah K. Lilly, Jr., assembled a cabinet of gold coins from all over the world that was worthy of a Croesus. The Lilly collection now belongs to the American people and is housed in the Smithsonian Institution. Even though almost royal means would be needed to build a similar collection today, the number of superb

284. A device against counterfeiting: nature prints or imprints of various leaves reproduced from plaster casts were first used on Colonial notes by Benjamin Franklin; 40-dollar note of the 1778 Continental Congress. 73 x 95 mm.

285. Emmanuel Ninger, known as "Jim the Penman," a master counterfeiter who designed his fake bills by hand. Photo: 64 x 131 mm.

collections presently in existence is surprisingly large. Moreover, owing in part to the instability of world finances, the number is steadily increasing.

One of the early guides for collectors, published in Paris by Père Louis Jobert in 1692, devoted an entire chapter to the pitfalls that counterfeit coins place in the path of the collector. Imitations of ancient coins began to circulate as long ago as Renaissance times, and any collector of ancient coins is familiar with the so-called "Paduans," a designation applied to large imitation Roman bronzes freely produced by reputable Italian sculptors of the period. The works of Giangiacomo Bonzagna of Parma (d. 1565) and of Giovanni Cavino of Padua (1499-1570) are the best known. Cavino worked under the direction of a local antiquarian, Alessandro Bassiano, and reproduced many "Roman" bronzes that show the unmistakable style of the Renaissance. The pieces were innocently intended to satisfy the Renaissance collectors' hunger for articles that reflected Roman history and culture. Today they are considered not Roman counterfeits but Renaissance medals that may occupy a place of honor in any collection.

Counterfeiting coins for collectors is nonetheless an activity that has brought the counterfeiters substantial riches and the collectors serious losses. The practice has plagued an otherwise "aristocratic" hobby for centuries and has steadily grown more skillful and more difficult to detect. The counterfeit coins can be cast in molds made from the original; they can be struck with fake dies, either cut freehand or copied from the original coins; they can be galvanoplastic copies or centrifuge casts. A skilled engraver can enhance the value of an original by altering the inscription, the date, or the symbols,

thereby transforming a common coin into a great rarity. Letters and numerals may be skillfully removed, metal "pushed" into place, and new inscriptions or dates re-engraved. Bronze coins can be made more valuable by the enhancing of the patina; the result of age and of special soil conditions, this decorative corrosion can be faked by the application of chemicals or even paint to the metal. One collector, examining a beautifully patined Roman bronze under a strong, hot lamp just before an auction, found his fingers stained green. Upon inquiring he learned that no one had ever previously questioned the coin's exquisite and "authentic" patina.

In the late 18th and the early 19th centuries, a master of the trade, Carl Wilhelm Becker, flourished. He counterfeited nearly 350 different antique coins and engraved freehand all the dies used to strike them. He minted his coins — mostly Greek, Roman, and medieval ones — with a sledgehammer, using genuine old coins as blanks. In order to "age" his strikings, he carried them in a box filled with iron shavings attached to the axle of his carriage. Some say that Becker advertised his coins for what they were, that is, copies. Nonetheless, his work deceived many experts, until photographs of the coins were published and detailed comparisons could be made. Another German, Nicolaus Seeländer of Erfurt, was so skilled in counterfeiting medieval coins and even inventing imaginary *bracteates* that a number of his creations were published as originals by the great expert on numismatics, G. L. Schlumberger.

288. The German master-counterfeiter, Carl Wilhelm Becker (1772-1836), cut dies by hand and struck his coins with a sledge-hammer. He copied this Roman aureus of Pompey the Great (left) and struck it in silver. The gold piece (right) is a Becker invention, representing Rudolph of Hapsburg (1218-1291).

Collectors and dealers alike try to protect themselves against counterfeiters and untrustworthy distributors. Today technical analyses can reveal the exact metallic content of a suspected coin and how it was produced. Methods range from examination with special microscopes to isotope techniques derived from nuclear physics. Certain complex tests can even demonstrate whether a coin was cast or struck. No matter how refined the technical analysis, however, it cannot replace the eye of a connoisseur, familiar with the styles and peculiarities of a series and the specific colors and lusters of ancient metals and patinas. It is to him, finally, that suspect coins may most readily reveal their secrets. □

289. This accomplished portrait of the Roman Emperor Marcus Aurelius (A.D. 161-180) was created during the Renaissance period when many classical coins were copied with great skill. These imitations, produced mostly by artists from Padua (Italy), were called "Paduans." 30 mm.

290. A modern counterfeiter used these dies in his workshop for manufacturing rare Greek, Roman, Byzantine and papal coins for collectors.

X | MEDALS

X: MEDALS: MAN'S QUEST FOR IMMORTALITY

The medal, without doubt, has fever. (Pierre Dehaye)

The very existence of medals reflects man's quest for immortality, or, at least, his hope of escaping oblivion. Although the medal, as such, is a creation of the Renaissance, the first stirrings of the concept that both events and personal exploits should be documented in some fashion go back to Greek and Roman times. Large coins, usually high multiples of the values struck for circulation as money, were issued in Greece and Rome on occasion to celebrate important events.

Medallions and the customs which created them faded during the Middle Ages. With the first stirrings of the Renaissance in Italy during the 1400s, however, scholars once again discovered the classical world, and both Greek and Roman coins and medallions were collected and their histories studied. The first significant re-creation of the ancient art from was inspired by the visit to Italy of John VIII Palaeologus, the Byzantine emperor who came in 1438 to participate in the Council of Ferrara (see Chapter IV). The imposing retinue of this next-to-last "Roman" emperor impressed the Veronese artist Pisanello to such a degree that he captured the event on a medallion with a portrait of John VIII on the obverse and a scene showing an abstract landscape on the reverse.

Pisanello, who designed at least 23 other medallions in the years that followed, thus established an art form that became the fashion at the courts of various Renaissance princes. Soon almost every princely family had one or more artists in residence. An immediate follower and possibly a pupil of Pisanello was Matteo di Pasti of Rimini and Verona; one of his best-known works is a portrait medal of Isotta da Rimini. In Florence, the stronghold of the Medicis and an artistic center, the medalist was Niccolo Spinelli, called *Il Fiorentino.* From his hands came medallion portraits of Cosimo de' Medici and of Cosimo's grandson, Lorenzo the Magnificent. One of the most picturesque medalists of the period was Leone Leoni of Arezzo. A contemporary of Michelangelo, Leoni was a gifted and sensitive artist and a master of the modeled surface. He was at the same time difficult, corrupt, and violent, and far from ignorant of perjury, theft, and even murder. A lifelong rivalry separated Leoni from his contemporary, Benvenuto Cellini, the famous goldsmith of Rome. For Michelangelo, however, Leoni had only admiration, and he produced a fine medallion portrait of the old sculptor. Some of Leoni's best-known works were portraits of the Holy Roman Emperor, Charles V (Charles I of Spain), and of the imperial household. Leoni traveled to Brussels to be with the emperor. He had rooms in the same palace, and Charles sometimes came to see him work.

In Germany, medals became popular among the prosperous "burgers" of the wealthy cities of Augsburg and Nuremberg. Italian medals were modeled in wax or clay; but German artists cut them mostly in boxwood, pearwood, or soft stone. Artists like Hans Schwarz, Friedrich Hagenauer, Matthes Gebel, and Heinrich Aldegrever were among the leading masters of the German Renaissance, while Germain Pilon and Guillaume Dupré added luster to French Renaissance medals. An outstanding 16th-century German artist, the

292. John VIII Palaeologus, Emperor of Constantinople. Medal by Antonio di Puccio Pisano, called Pisanello (c. 1395-1455), made at Ferrara, 1438-1439. 103 mm.

293. *Portrait, by Sandro Botticelli, of a young man, interpreted by some as the famous painter and engraver Niccolo Fiorentino (1430-1514), holding a cast of his medal of Cosimo de' Medici.*

294. *Cosimo de' Medici, Pater patriae "Father of his Country" (1389-1464). Medal of the Florentine School (1464-1470), probably the work of Niccolo Fiorentino. 75 mm.*

295. *This portrait of Charles V, a masterwork of the German Renaissance, was cut into box-wood by Heinrich Aldegrever (?1502–?1555), one of the leading Westphalian silversmiths. 60 mm.*

goldsmith Hans Reinhart of Leipzig, produced a special kind of medallion: the religious medal. The art form enjoyed instant popularity, and religious medals, copied and recopied, were soon widely worn as amulets and good-luck pieces.

Alchemists' medals were an interesting product of the 1600's. For example, a German medal refers to the art of healing, showing a man wielding a cutlass surrounded by a circle of alchemistic signs symbolizing the seven planets and indicating the seven different metals from which this piece was supposedly struck. Intended as a talisman, it also functioned as an advertisement for Dr.

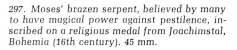

296. The Calvary, one among the many religious medals produced in Joachimstal, Bohemia, during the 16th century. 47 mm.

297. Moses' brazen serpent, believed by many to have magical power against pestilence, inscribed on a religious medal from Joachimstal, Bohemia (16th century). 45 mm.

298. Coin-sized medals, depicting St. George killing the dragon, issued by the Kremnitz mint in Hungary during the 17th and 18th centuries. Often worn as amulets. 37 & 45 mm.

232

299. *This superb medal of the Italian Baroque by Giovanni Hamerani for Pope Innocent XII commemorating the Curia Innocenziana on Monte Citorio in Rome, a building erected by the famous G. Bernini and D. Fontana. 35 mm.*

Leonhard Thurneisser of Basel, who claimed healing powers. In France under Louis XIV (1643-1715), hundreds of medals were created by such artists as Jean Mauger and Joseph Roettier; their allegorical scenes commemorated events in Louis's life. Some medals Louis presented to favorite subjects as gifts. Others were available for purchase and in this way entered the homes of commoners. The medals lack artistic merit and suffer from a uniformity of style, but they enjoyed great popularity in their day.

In England, three 17th-century artists, Thomas Rawlins, Thomas Simon, and John Roettier, breathed life into the products of the London mint. Rawlins, a goldsmith and engraver, served both Charles I and Charles II and designed many medals celebrating their reigns. In those days, when the king's supporters identified themselves by wearing a royal medal or badge, these objects possessed a special importance. It was Rawlins's contemporary, Simon, who was generally deemed the finest medalist of the time. The last years of Charles I's rule, the period under Cromwell, and the restoration of Charles II were all recorded in a series of beautiful medals that Simon produced, before the plague in 1665 put an end to his work. The third medalist, John Roettier, was invited to England by Charles II in 1661 with his brother Joseph (who later moved to France). The two Roettiers, with John's sons, represented a dynasty of gifted artists, and John Roettier's serene figures, in particular, forecast the classicist period that lay ahead.

233

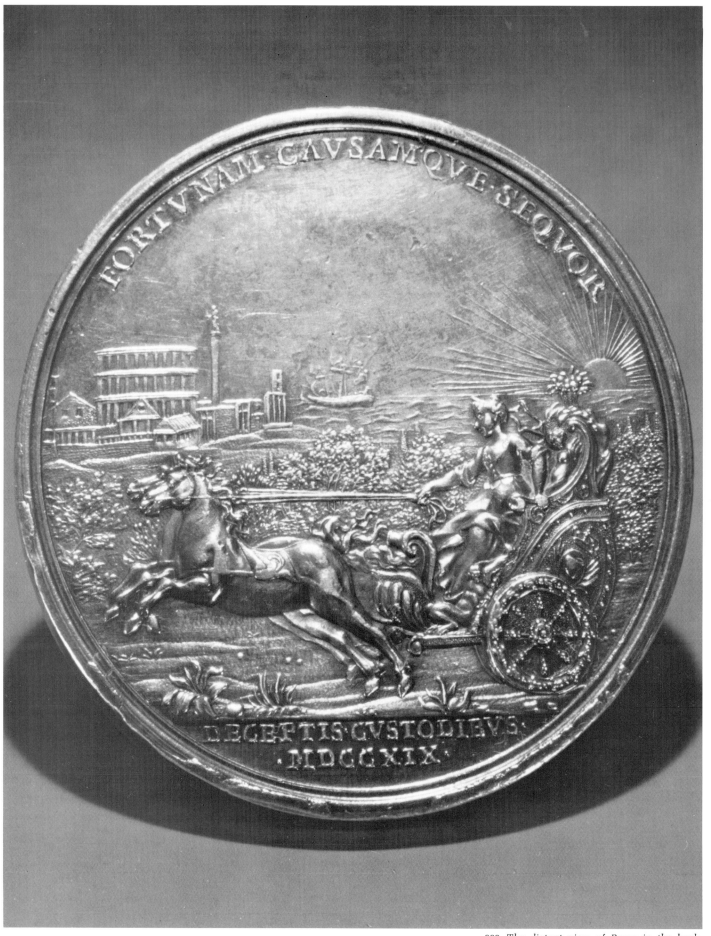

300. The distant view of Rome in the background of a typically Rococo scene on a medal by the Roman medalist Ottone Hamerani (1719) depicting the English Princess Clementina in a chariot. 48 mm.

301. A highly expressive portrait medal of the Duke of Espernon (1555-1642) by the French artist Guillaume Dupre. 56 mm.

It was in Germany that medalists of the 17th and 18th centuries reached their apogee. Almost every princely court had a resident medal engraver, and a number of artists were able to establish their own private engraving and minting firms and execute orders for a wide range of clients. The private enterprises did a flourishing business as medals, gaining in popularity, soon came to be struck for almost any occasion. There were various kinds of religious medals; some commemorating major calamities, and others marking the discovery of new riches or the sad and happy moments in the lives of individuals and, especially, the lives of princes. Kings demonstrated their appreciation for services performed by giving medals, medalettes, and jetons;

302. "The metallic history of the king of France" — the eventful rule of Louis XIV commemorated in a long series of medals engraved by Jean Mauger (c. 1648-1722). 41 mm.

they were struck in gold or silver and were distributed among the prince's friends and subjects.

Although medals of the Baroque era were generally smaller than Renaissance medals, many large showpieces were struck. One of the best examples of a German Baroque showpiece is one struck in Erfurt in 1634 to commemorate the death on the battlefield of King Gustavus II Adolphus of Sweden two years earlier. It is a work of the foremost German Baroque artist Sebastian Dadler who worked not only at Augsburg but also at Nuremberg and at the courts of the Saxon princes at Dresden. Living as he did during the Thirty Years' War, Dadler devoted many of his designs to the memorable events of the period, but what may be his masterpiece is a medal portrait of the famous Reformation leader John Calvin. In terms of productivity, however, the greatest of the German Baroque medalists was Christian Wermuth. Within a 20-year period he singlehandedly engraved, or was otherwise directly involved in the production of more than 1,300 medals; this is a rate of more than one medal a week. While working for the princes of Saxony, he established his own firm in Dresden and issued several catalogues listing his available medals. For silver medals his price was twice the value of the silver; for gold pieces he charged one-third more than the gold value. Few historical events in the 18th century went unrecorded by Wermuth. His series of popes and Roman emperors numbered in the hundreds of pieces, and he specialized in a new *genre*: the satirical medal. Wermuth produced close to 100 different satirical pieces, representing various scandals of his day: dishonesty, bribery, financial corruption, and the loose morals of the court of Saxony.

303. A forceful portrait of King Charles II of England by his favorite engraver, John Roettiers (1631-1703). 63 mm.

236

304. The dazzling richness of the German Baroque is expressed in this 1632 medal by Sebastian Dadler commemorating the apotheosis of Gustavus II Adolph of Sweden after his death on the battlefield. 80 mm.

305. Alchemistic signs referring to the seven planets and the seven basic metals indicating that Dr. L. Thurneisser could heal people through "transmutation" or chemical changes of metals, (early 17th century). 48 mm.

306. The years of deadly famine in Saxony – 1771 and 1772 – commemorated by the German engraver Johann Christian Reich (1740-1814). 34 mm.

308. Views of cities and battlefields were often pressed into wooden checkerboard pieces by the use of medallic dies. 53 & 62 mm.

◁ 307. A medal noting a princely visit to a mine in the German principality of Anhalt in 1694 and another contemporary medal from Osnabruck depicting the mining process. First left: 65 mm.

The momentous events in France at the close of the 18th century, the Revolution and the rise of Napoleon, were reflected in contemporary medals. In particular, Napoleon selected the medal as a major means of creating and sustaining his image as hero and ruler. Following the example of the Bourbon kings who preceded him, Napoleon assembled a group of skilled engravers. Under the direction of Dominique Denon, these men produced nearly 2,000 different medals, commemorating virtually every event in the emperor's life.

The medals designed by Denon's group exhibited the main elements of the classicist period; their solemn and in some cases stern images imitated Roman grandeur. Nonetheless, the portraits that appeared on them impress us with their simple, pure outlines. The features are unadorned, and the most minute details are worked into broad planes that reflect the light evenly and quietly.

From Italy came Benedetto Pistrucci (1784-1855), one of the most representative artists of the classicist period. He worked in England and there, after 30 years of labor, created the masterpiece of his time: a gigantic, superbly modelled show piece commemorating Wellington's victory at Waterloo.

After Napoleon's downfall, the demand for medals decreased considerably, even though the tradition was continued by other 19th-century rulers. Two

239 members of a family of outstanding engravers, William and Leonard Wyon,

309. Libertas Americana, 1783, the inspired symbol of newly gained liberty, represented by Augustin Dupre as a young maiden "sprung from the prairies with unruly hair and dauntless spirit." 48 mm.

311. Napoleon Bonaparte, Consul, on a medal of 1803 by Romain V. Jeuffroy. 40 mm.

310. "Honor to the Ladies," by the medallist Daniel F. Loos from Berlin, is an expression of the German romantic movement around 1800. 36 mm.

produced most of the medals struck in England during Queen Victoria's long reign. The royal families of Italy, Belgium, Prussia, France, and Russia, too, employed well-trained and imaginative engravers who busily commemorated events in the rulers' lives. Yet, through repetition, many originally fine images, such as the figure of Victory, were turned into mere clichés, cold and dispirited. Occasionally, fine medallic work was still produced, reflecting the thorough professional training the various engravers had received in the schools of Paris, Munich, or Rome, but outstanding creative talent was rare.

France chanced to produce one such artist, Pierre Jean David d'Angers, who had spent his formative years under Italian influence. An indefatigable worker of the Romantic school, David d'Angers often produced in a single year more medals than others could prepare in a lifetime. He created a seemingly endless series of portrait medallions, a "gallery of contemporaries," as he called it. In his hands the bronze medallion, cast rather than struck (an art neglected since Renaissance times), recaptured an honored position in the medallic craft. David d'Angers's portrait series, conceived in the Romantic spirit and modeled with a sculptor's touch in high, bold relief, seem even today vibrant and full of humanity.

240

During the second half of the 19th century the art of the medal was completely revolutionized by the French artists Hubert Ponscarme, Jules C. Chaplain, and Oscar Roty, considered by some the greatest among modern medallists. They loosened the severity of the classicistic style, permitting the medal to develop as a bas-relief in miniature. Roty's compositions exhibit an especially strong lyrical character.

The serenity of the decades that preceded World War I was reflected not only in the art of France but also across the Atlantic. Victor D. Brenner, an American who studied in France, brought with him on his return not only

312. Pistrucci's finished model for the reverse of the Waterloo medal. 140 mm.

313. "Death" selling tickets at the Cunard Lines office, May 1915. Three versions of the famous Lusitania medal by Karl Goetz, the German original issues and the English copy with the wrong English spelling of "May." 56 mm.

the basic French approach to the medallic art but also French techniques. Brenner's portrait medals and plaquettes were sensitive, his allegories simple and of classic beauty. The play of high and low relief in his modeling is particularly noteworthy.

The giant of American sculptors, Augustus Saint-Gaudens was another who found the plaquette an excellent medium for portraiture. His many portraits not only comprise a valuable record of the important personalities of his day but also constitute fine works of art in themselves. His compositions for the 1892 Columbian Exposition in Chicago, showing Columbus setting foot in the New World, are particularly notable for their freedom of movement.

PROSPECTVS · INTERIOR · BASILICAE · VATICANAE · DEO · SACRAE · IN · HONOREM · BEATI · PETRI · PR · AP ·

I · EQ · BIANCHI · DELIN · ET · SCVL
AN · MDCCCLXIX

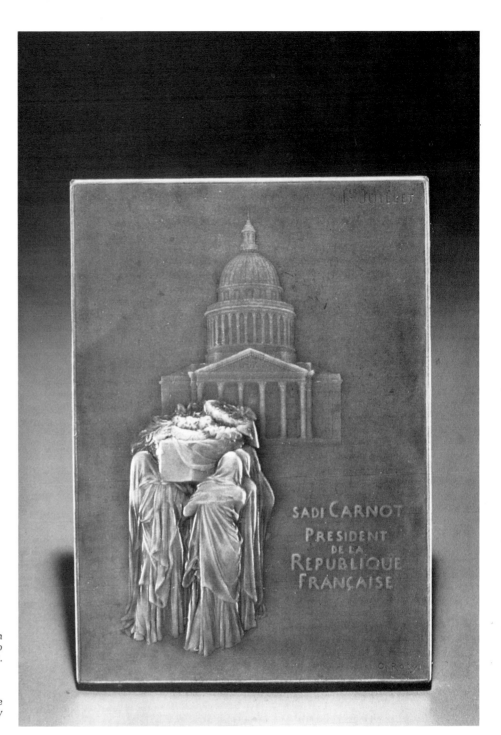

314. *The interior of the Vatican Basilica on an 1869 medal by the papal mint-engraver Ignazio Bianchi. It is a masterpiece of die-sinking art. 82 mm.*

315. *A masterpiece of French medallic art: the funeral medal of President Sadi Carnot by Oscar Roty, 1894. 57 x 79 mm.*

But it is in France that new forms of medallic expression have found public support and have combined a wide variety of talent with a wealth of novel concepts. Although many French medallists continue to use the traditional method of first modeling the composition in clay, others, like Raymond Joly, prefer such direct methods as *repousse* work or engraving the design directly in the steel die. These techniques, in addition to producing certain aesthetic effects, have the advantage of allowing the artist to transmit his ideas directly, without intermediary, mechanical reduction. The result is to preserve unaltered the spontaneity of the creative personality.

In the quest for an increased power of expression, more than one medallic artist of today has broken old barriers and reached a freedom never thought possible before in the design of a medal. To cite a single example, two recent

316. The fine artistic traditions of Japan seen in this medal struck in Tokyo in 1881 as an industrial exhibition award. 67 mm.

317. This plaquette, by Victor D. Brenner (1905), is a tribute to the famous American painter James McNeill Whistler. 75 x 50 mm.

JAMES MᶜNEILL WHISTLER
PAINTER ETCHER
AVTHOR

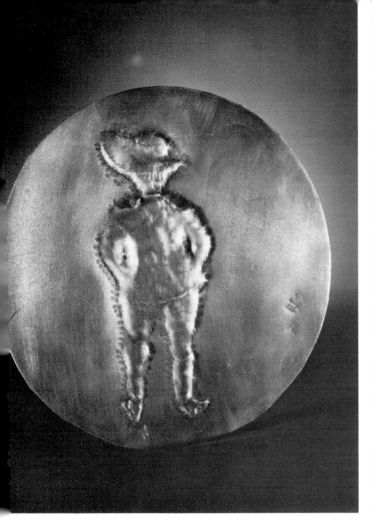

318. "Aristide Bruant", a repousse medal by Raymond Joly, 1971. 155 mm.

319. "The Last Supper", cast plaquette (1967), from Greece, by Dimitri Ferentinos. 155 x 180 mm.

320. The medalist Paul Vincze of London at work on a large relief in clay for a medal. Before striking, the model will be reduced mechanically.

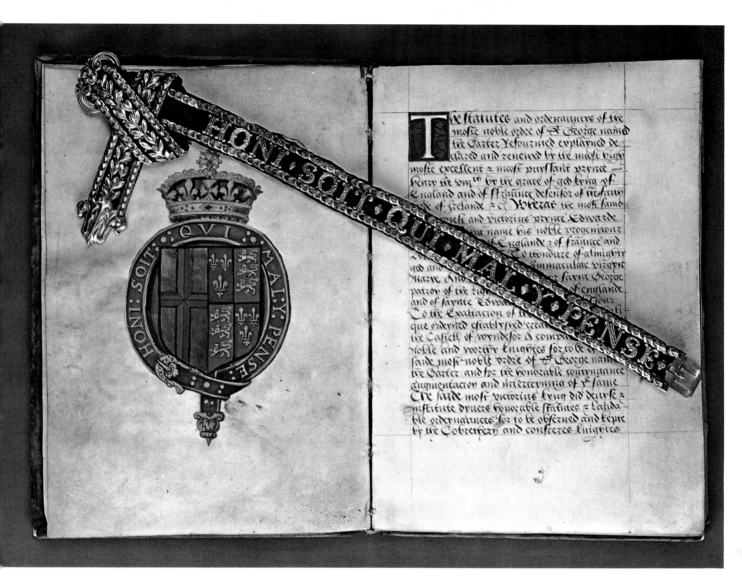

works — "Open Heart" and "The Medal of Medals," produced by Roger Bezombes in 1970 and 1972 respectively — have fairly earned these words of Pierre Dehaye, the director of the mint in Paris: "The medal, without any doubt, has fever. This is a favorable sign. Who would have believed it 25 years ago? From now on any surprise is possible."

Historically, Orders, Decorations and Medals of Merit have been sought by many, awarded to few and acclaimed by all. They are the tangible, often artistic symbols of extraordinary achievements commanding extraordinary respect. Like some forms of money, scarcity enhances their worth. But, unlike money, valor is the means of exchange needed to obtain these "riches". Modern Orders and Decorations emerged in the Middle Ages. For example, religious orders of knighthood were founded in the Holy Land during the Crusades. Secular Orders, created by princely Houses, imitated these chivalric organizations. Included among the most famous are: the Order of the Garter established by King Edward III of England in 1348; the Order of the Annunziata initiated by Amadeus VII of Savoy in 1355; and the Most Illustrious Order of the Golden Fleece organized in Flanders in 1430. By the 18th century, Orders of Merit were given for civil as well as military or religious achievements. Gold and diamonds sometimes adorn these symbols but no amount of money can legitimately buy the performance of the deeds so recognized. ☐ 248

321. Honi soit qui mal y pense — "Evil to him who evil thinks it" — from England's oldest distinction, the Most Noble Order of the Garter, shown here with a copy of the Statutes of the Order 1563, belonging to the Seventh Earl of Northumberland, leader of the rebellion against Queen Elizabeth I. 290 x 18 mm.

322. This jewelled badge of the Order of the Golden Fleece was made for Prince Lobkowitz in Vienna in 1848 for the planned coronation of Francis Joseph of Austria. 75 x 175 mm.

323. The Austrian "Slaves of Virtue" (1662) the oldest women's order instituted for charitable work.

324. Deutscher Ring, highest distinction of the German Foreign Institute conferred on non-Germans in recognition of services rendered to the Weimar Republic (c. 1930). Face of ring: 20 x 20 mm.

325. The clasped hands of an Indian chief and an officer seal the pact of "peace and friendship" on a medal (1801) given by President Thomas Jefferson to Indians. 90 mm.

326. The Salutation of the Virgin was depicted ▷ on the badge of the Order of the Annunziata, Italy's oldest and most outstanding distinction. Center medallion: 70 mm.

BIBLIOGRAPHY

The vastness of the numismatic field is reflected in an exceptionally extensive bibliography. It would be impossible therefore to attempt a comprehensive reading list. Only books of a general character are listed below. Catalogues and specialized studies have been omitted. For other titles see: Elvira Clain-Stefanelli, *Select Numismatic Bibliography*, New York, 1965 and Philip Grierson, *Bibliographie numismatique*, 2nd ed., Brussels, 1966.

Introduction

Carson, Robert A. G. *Coins, Ancient, Mediaeval and Modern*. London, 1962. — Sutherland, Carol H. V. *Art in Coinage; the Aesthetics of Money From Greece to the Present Day*. London, 1955. — Sutherland, Carol H. V. *Gold, Its Beauty, Power and Allure*. 2nd edition, New York, 1969. — Babelon, Jean. *Les monnaies racontent l'histoire*. Paris, 1963. — Porteous, John. *Coins in History*. New York, 1969. — Del Mar, Alexander. *A History of Money in Ancient Countries, From the Earliest Times to the Present*. London, 1885; Reprint, 1968. — Suhle, Arthur. *Kulturgeschichte der Munzen*. Munich, 1969.

Chapter I   Primitive Money

Quiggin, Alison H. *A Survey of Primitive Money: the Beginnings of Currency*. London, 1949; Reprint, 1964. — Einzig, Paul. *Primitive Money in its Ethnological, Historical and Economic Aspect*. 2nd edition, London, 1966. — Herskovits, Melville J. *Economic Anthropology*. New York, 1952.

Chapter II   Greek Coins

Kraay, Colin M. and Hirmer, Max. *Greek Coins*, New York, 1966. — Jenkins, Kenneth G. *Ancient Greek Coins*. London, 1972. — Seltman, Charles T. *Greek Coins: A History of Metallic Currency and Coinage Down to the Fall of the Hellenistic Kingdoms*. 3rd edition, London, 1960. Reprint, 1965. — Seltman, Charles T. *Masterpieces of Greek Coinage*. Oxford, 1949. — Head, Barclay. *Historia numorum. A Manual of Greek Numismatics*. 2nd edition, Oxford, 1911. Reprints: London, 1965 and Chicago, 1967. — Regling, Kurt. *Ancient Numismatics: the Coinage of Ancient Greece and Rome*. Transl. from Germ. Chicago, 1969. — Christ, Karl. *Antike Numismatik. Einfuhrung und Bibliographie*. Darmstadt, 1967.

Chapter III   Roman Coins

Mattingly, Harold. *Roman Coins, From the Earliest Time to the Fall of the Western Empire*. 2nd edition, London, 1960; Reprint, 1967. — Grant, Michael. *Roman History From Coins*. London, 1958; Reprint, 1968. — Grant, Michael. *Imperial Money*. London, 1954; Reprint, 1972. — Franke, Peter R. *Romische Kaiserportrats im Munzbild*. 3rd edition, Munich, 1972. — Franke, Peter R. *Kleinasien zur Romerzeit. Griechisches Leben im Spiegel der Munze*. Munich, 1968.

Chapter IV   Medieval Coins

Grierson, Philip. *Byzantine Coinage as Source Material. Proceedings of the XIII International Congress of Byzantine Studies*. Oxford, 1967. — Whitting, P. D. *Byzantine Coins*. London, 1973. — Engel, Arthur and Serrure, Raymond. *Traite de numismatique du moyen age*. 3 vols., Paris, 1891-1905; Reprint, 1964. — Lange, Kurt. *Munzkunst des Mittelalters*. Leipzig, 1942. — Steinhilber, Dirk. *Munzen des Mittelalters und der Neuzeit*. Pp. 163-193 in vol. 2 of *Keysers Kunst- und Antiquitatenbuch*. Heidelberg, 1959.

Chapter V   Renaissance to Modern Times

Engel, Arthur and Serrure, Raymond. *Traite de numismatique moderne et contemporaine*. 2 vols., Paris, 1897-99; Reprint, 1971. — Friedensburg, Ferdinand. *Munzkunde und Geldgeschichte der Einzelstaaten des Mittelalters und der neueren Zeit*. Munich, 1926. — Samhaber, Ernst. *Das Geld, eine Kulturgeschichte*. Munich, 1964. — Kochs, Hermann. *Gepragtes Gold. Geschichte und Geschichten um Munzen und Medaillen*. Stuttgart, 1967.

Chapter VI   The New World

A. LATIN AMERICA: Burzio, Humberto F. *Diccionario de la moneda hispano-americana*. 3 vols. Santiago de Chile, 1956-58. — Medina, Jose Toribio. *Las monedas coloniales hispano-americanas*. Santiago de Chile, 1919. — Pradeau, Alberto F. *Numismatic History of Mexico From the Pre-Columbian Epoch to 1823*. Los Angeles, 1938.

B. UNITED STATES: Crosby, Sylvester S. *The Early Coins of America*. Boston, 1875; Reprint, 1970. — Vermeule, Cornelius. *Numismatic Art in America, Aesthetics of the United States Coinage*. Cambridge, Mass., 1971. — Nussbaum, Arthur. *A History of the Dollar*. 2nd edition, New York, 1958.

Chapter VII   Near and Far East

Codrington, Oliver. *A Manual of Musulman Numismatics*. London, 1904; Reprint, 1969. — Sircar, D. C. *Studies in Indian Coins*. Delhi, 1968. — Gupta, P. L. *Coins*. New Delhi, 1969. — Coole, Arthur Braddan. *Coins in China's History*. 4th edition, Denver, 1965. — Wang Yu-Ch'uan. *Early Chinese Coinage*. New York, 1951. — The Bank of Japan. *A Brief History of Money in Japan*. Tokyo, 1964.

Chapter VIII   Paper Money

Pick, Albert. *Papiergeld, ein Handbuch fur Sammler und Liebhaber*. Braunschweig, 1967. — Narbeth, Colin. *Collecting Paper Money: a Beginner's Guide*. London, 1968. — Loehr, August O. von. *Entwicklung von Wertpapieren und Geldzeichen*. Vienna, 1952.

Chapter IX   Counterfeiters and Collectors

A. COLLECTORS: Clain-Stefanelli, Elvira E. *Numismatics an Ancient Science*. Washington, D.C., 1965.

B. COUNTERFEITERS: Scott, Kenneth. *Counterfeiting in Colonial America*. New York, 1957. — Bloom, Murray Teigh. *Money of Their Own; The Great Counterfeiters*. New York, 1957. — Ruland, Bernd. *Vorsicht: Falschgeld*. Zurich, 1967.

Chapter X   Medals

A. MEDALS: Bernhart, Max. *Medaillen und Plaketten*. 3rd edition by Tyll Kroha. Braunschweig, 1966. — Babelon, Jean. *La medaille et les medailleurs*. Paris, 1927. — Forrer, Leonard. *Biographical Dictionary of Medallists, Coin, Gem and Seal-Engravers, 500 B.C.-A.D. 1900*. 8 vols. London, 1902-30; Reprint, 1965. — Hill, Sir George F. *Medals of the Renaissance*. Oxford, 1920.

B. DECORATIONS: Purves, Alec A. *Collecting Medals and Decorations*. London, 1968. — Méricka, Václav. *Orders and Decorations*. London, 1967.

ACKNOWLEDGMENTS

The authors would like to express their appreciation to Professor Philip Grierson for his kind help in reading the chapter on the Middle Ages; to Silvio Bedini, Deputy-Director, National Museum of History and Technology, Harvey G. Stack, Norman C. Stack, Benjamin Stack from New York; Louis Zara; Mr. Sherwood Harris, for their invaluable advice; to Hannelore H. Aceto, Richard K. Hofmeister, Alfred F. Harrell, Jr. and Henry A. Alexander, Photographic Services, Smithsonian Institution, for their photographic work; to Frank A. Pietropaoli, Charles G. Berger and Robert G. Billingsley, Library of the Museum of History and Technology, for their assistance; to Dr. Lajos Kupa, Budapest, Hungary; Mr. Robert E. Hecht, Jr., Paris, France; and Dr. Leo Mildenberg, Zurich, Switzerland for obtaining important information; and to Alexander Clain-Stefanelli for his perceptive reading of the manuscript.

Special thanks go to Gerald Stearn for his skilful arrangement and editing of the text.

PHOTOGRAPHIC CREDITS

The majority of coins, medals and currencies photographed in this book come from the National Numismatic Collections of the Smithsonian Institution. Others include: the United States Secret Service, Washington, D.C. *fig. 285;* Stack's, New York, *fig. 196* (book); and various other private collections: *figs. 11* (wampum and blue beads), *23 (a, b), 24 (c), 26, 27, 28, 29, 30, 31, 32, 33, 34, 35, 36, 37, 38, 39 (a, b), 40, 41, 43, 44, 46, 48 (a), 49 (a, b, c), 50, 51, 52, 53, 54, 55, 56, 57, 59 (a), 60 (d, e), 61 (c), 62 (a, b), 63, 65, 66, 68 (10, 23), 69, 70, 71, 72, 73, 74, 75, 76, 77, 78, 79, 80, 81, 82, 84, 85, 86 (coins), 89 (2, 3, 6, 8, 10, 11), 91, 92, 93 (d, f, h, i, j), 94, 97, 98 (coins), 99 (b), 100 (c), 101, 106 (a, b, d, e, f), 107, 111 (d), 112 (a, b, d, e), 119 (a, c, e, f), 120, 121, 122, 126, 128 (a), 129 (a, b), 131 (b), 133 (a, b), 135 (a, b), 136 (a, b), 138 (2, 12), 139 (a, b, c, d, f, g, j, k), 140, 144 (a), 152 (d, g, h, i), 154, 155, 158, 170, 193, 194, 215 (f, g, h, i, k, m, r), 216 (a), 219 (a, b), 221 (c), 223 (b), 225 (a), 227 (b), 229 (b), 230, 232 (a, b), 233 (a, c, d), 235 (b), 240, 265, 280, 286, 289, 291 (a, i, j), 299, 302 (a).*

All photography is by Lee Boltin except for the following black and white illustrations reproduced by courtesy of: Smithsonian Institution Photographic Services Division, figures *33, 34, 35, 37, 38, 39 (coins), 40, 41, 46, 51, 52, 53, 54, 102, 114, 123, 124, 127, 143, 150, 163, 169, 173, 197, 202, 205, 246, 248, 251, 256, 272, 278, 284, 317, 323, 325;* National Gallery of Art, Washington, D.C., *fig. 292, 294;* Freer Gallery of Art, Washington, D.C., *fig. 216;* Antikenmuseum, Basel, *fig. 39 (background);* Archives Photographiques, Paris, figures *98 (background), 244, 247,* Biblioteca Vaticana, Museo Profano, Rome, *fig. 81;* British Museum, *fig. 127;* Bibliothèque Nationale, Paris, figures *276, 278;* Bodleian Library, Oxford, England, *fig. 229;* Estate of J. K. Lilly, Jr., *fig. 279;* Istituto Archeologico Germanico, Rome, *fig. 78;* Museo Capitolino, Rome, *fig. 93;* Museo Nazionale, Naples, *fig. 59;* Musée de la Légion d'honneur, Paris, *fig. 175;* Musée Royal, Antwerp, figures *274, 275;* Museum of Fine Arts, Boston, Mass., *fig. 42;* Dr. Leo Mildenberg, *fig. 31;* Oeffentliche Kunstsammlung, Basel, *fig. 168;* Rheinisches Landesmuseum, Trier, *fig. 96;* Staatliche Antikensammlungen, Munich, *fig. 47;* Larry Stevens, *fig. 214;* Topkapi Palace Museum, Portrait Gallery, Istanbul, *fig. 222;* Uffizi, Florence, *fig. 293;* Paul Vincze, London, *fig. 320;* Wadsworth Atheneum, Hartford, Connecticut, *fig. 4;* La Zecca, Rome, *fig. 312;* Dr. Vladimir Clain-Stefanelli, figures *17 (background), 36, 49 (a), 50, 55, 56, 80, 84, 86 (background), 92, 99 (background), 125, 133 (background).* Ferdinandeum Austria: *Schwaz Bergbuch, fig. 142; Dai Nihon Kahei Shi* (History of Japanese Currency), Vol. III (1926), *fig. 236;* Harper's Weekly, 27.I.1866, *fig. 205;* Franz Unterkircher; *A Treasury of Illuminations.* Putnam, 1967, p. 23, *fig. 100;* Adrian Eeles, *Canaletto.* London, 1969, *fig. 154.*

INDEX

Roettier, John, 130, 132, 233
Roettier, Joseph, 233
Roger II, King of Naples and Sicily, 104
Roma, 59, 60
Romano, Giulio, 115
Romanoff dynasty, 142
Romanus IV Diogenes, Emperor, 88, 180
Rome, 15, 22, 52, 229; Empire, 72-73, 75-78, 215;
   Imperial frontier, 79-81; minting, 65-67;
   provinces, 81; Republic, 59-65; Triumvirate
   to Principate, 67-70
Romulus Augustus, 91
Romulus and Remus, 59, 62
Roosevelt, Franklin D., 170
Roosevelt, Theodore, 169-70
Roty, Oscar, 242
Rudolph II, Emperor, 137
Rum, Sultanate of, 180
Russia, 16, 23, 141-42, 203-04, 209

Saint-Gaudens, Augustus, 170, 242
Saint-Urbain, Ferdinand, 127
Saladin, Sultan of Egypt and Syria, 180
San Francisco mint, 167
San Martin, Jose, 152
Sarto, Andrea del, 119
Sasanian Empire, 175-76
Scandinavia, 23
Scantilla, Manlia, 77
Schliemann, Heinrich, 22
Schlumberger, G. L., 222
Schwab, Max, 119, 120
Schwartz, Hans, 229
Scipio, Lucius Cornelius, 64
Scipio Africanus, 64
Scot, Robert, 165
Seelander, Nicolaus, 222
Seljuk Turks, 88, 89, 180, 181
Seleucos, 46, 48
Serbia, 109
Seymour, Jane, 121
Sforza, Francesco, 114
Sforza, Galeazzo Maria, 114
Sforza, Ludovico Maria (il Moro), 114
Shapur I, King of Persia, 175
Sher Shah Suri, 183
Shih Huang-ti, Emperor, 185
Sicily, 31, 34, 35
Sigismund, Archduke, 115-16, 117
Simon, Thomas, 130, 132, 233
Sinnock, John R., 170
Sixtus IV, Pope, 115
Smithsonian Institution, 220
Solomon Islands, 16, 18
Somers, Sir George, 154
South America, 148-56
South Carolina, 195, 196
Spain, 31, 79, 107-8, 179; and Mexico, 147;
   and South America, 148-56
Spinelli, Niccolo, 229
Stickney, Matthew A., 220
Strada, Jacobus, 218
Suetonius, 72
Sully, Thomas, 167
Sung dynasty, 186
Sun Yat-sen, 187
Sweden, 23, 139, 194, 215
Syracuse, 33-34, 35

Tamerlane, 89
T'ang dynasty, 186, 187, 193

Taras, 40, 41
Tarentum, 40-41, 59
Tarpea, 62
Thebes, 42
Theodora, Empress, 85
Theodoric, 92
Thirty Years' War, 135, 137, 139
Thrace, 46, 80
Thurneisser, Leonhard, 233
Tiberius, Emperor, 79, 81
Tiberius II Constantine, Emperor, 86
Toyotomi, Hideyoshi, 188
Trajan, Emperor, 76
Trebizond, 89
Tron, Nicolo, Doge of Venice, 113
Tudor dynasty, 120-22
Turkey, 175, 176, 180, 181

Umayyad dynasty, 176, 179
United States, 158-70, 195-99, 215-16, 242;
   Civil War period, 169, 198-99; Colonial
   period, 15-16, 158-64, 195-96, 215, 220;
   Revolutionary period, 161
United States Congress, 164-65
United States Mint, 165, 169
United States Treasury, 198
Urban VIII, Pope, 126

Vandals, 91, 92
Varin, Jean, 127, 128
Venice, 104, 113, 124
Vercingetorix, 64, 80
Vermont, 162
Vespasianus, Flavius, 75
Victoria, Queen, 133-34, 240
Victory, 34, 44, 46, 48, 60, 63, 69, 78,
   92, 94, 151
Villa, Pancho, 151, 152
Vinci, Leonardo da, 114, 119
Virgil, 104
Virginia, 161, 195
Visigoths, 91, 92
Voigt, Henry, 165
Voigt, Karl, 137

Wallenstein, Eusebius, 137
War of 1812, 166
Wars of the Roses, 102
Washington, George, 164, 165, 170
Watkinson, M. R., 169
Weinman, Adolph, 170
Wenceslaus II, King of Bohemia, 108
Wermuth, Christian, 236
West Indies, 154
Wilhelm II, Emperor, 138
William, Duke of Normandy, 102
William I of Orange, 122
Wolsey, Thomas Cardinal, 121
World War I, 199, 201, 203-4, 208
World War II, 208, 216-17
Wood, William, 160
Wyon, Leonard, 239-40
Wyon, William, 133, 239-40

Yap, 18
Yazdegerd III, King of Persia, 175
Young, Brigham, 168
Yuan dynasty, 186, 193

Zapata, Emiliano, 151
Zeus, 37, 42, 44, 46
Zoroastrianism, 175